Six Women's
Slave Narratives

THE SCHOMBURG LIBRARY OF
NINETEENTH-CENTURY BLACK WOMEN WRITERS

General Editor, Henry Louis Gates, Jr.

Titles are listed chronologically; collections that include works published over a span of years are listed according to the publication date of their initial work.

Six Women's Slave Narratives

With an Introduction by
WILLIAM L. ANDREWS

❧ ❧ ❧

❧ ❧ ❧

New York   Oxford
OXFORD UNIVERSITY PRESS

Oxford University Press

Oxford   New York   Toronto
Delhi   Bombay   Calcutta   Madras   Karachi
Petaling Jaya   Singapore   Hong Kong   Tokyo
Nairobi   Dar es Salaam   Cape Town
Melbourne   Auckland

and associated companies in
Berlin   Ibadan

Library of Congress Cataloging-in-Publication Data

Six women's slave narratives.
(The Schomburg library of nineteenth-century black women writers)
Contents: The history of Mary Prince, a West Indian
slave/originally edited by Thomas Pringle—Memoir
of old Elizabeth, a coloured woman—The story of
Mattie J. Jackson/written and arranged by L. S.
Thompson—[etc.]
1. Slaves—United States—Biography.   2. Women
slaves—United States—Biography.   I. Series.
E444.S59   1988   973′.0880625 [B]   87-28107
ISBN 0-19-505262-5
ISBN 0-19-505267-6 (set)
ISBN 0-19-506083-0 (pbk)

Memoir of Old Elizabeth, a Coloured Woman is reprinted by courtesy of the William R.
Perkins Library at Duke University.
Lucy A. Delaney's *From the Darkness Cometh the Light or Struggles for Freedom* is reprinted
by courtesy of The Western Reserve Historical Society Library.
Annie L. Burton's *Memories of Childhood's Slavery Days* is reprinted by courtesy of the
Boston Public Library.

2 4 6 8 10 9 7 5 3 1

Printed in the United States of America

The
Schomburg Library
of
Nineteenth-Century
Black Women Writers
is
Dedicated
in Memory
of
PAULINE AUGUSTA COLEMAN GATES

1916–1987

PUBLISHER'S NOTE

FOREWORD
In Her Own Write

Henry Louis Gates, Jr.

One muffled strain in the Silent South, a jarring chord and a vague and uncomprehended cadenza has been and still is the Negro. And of that muffled chord, the one mute and voiceless note has been the sadly expectant Black Woman, ...

The "other side" has not been represented by one who "lives there." And not many can more sensibly realize and more accurately tell the weight and the fret of the "long dull pain" than the open-eyed but hitherto voiceless Black Woman of America.

. . . as our Caucasian barristers are not to blame if they cannot *quite* put themselves in the dark man's place, neither should the dark man be wholly expected fully and adequately to reproduce the exact Voice of the Black Woman.

— ANNA JULIA COOPER, *A Voice From the South* (1892)

The birth of the Afro-American literary tradition occurred in 1773, when Phillis Wheatley published a book of poetry. Despite the fact that her book garnered for her a remarkable amount of attention, Wheatley's journey to the printer had been a most arduous one. Sometime in 1772, a young African girl walked demurely into a room in Boston to undergo an oral examination, the results of which would determine the direction of her life and work. Perhaps she was shocked upon entering the appointed room. For there, perhaps gath-

ered in a semicircle, sat eighteen of Boston's most notable
citizens. Among them were John Erving, a prominent Boston merchant; the Reverend Charles Chauncy, pastor of the
Tenth Congregational Church; and John Hancock, who would
later gain fame for his signature on the Declaration of Independence. At the center of this group was His Excellency,
Thomas Hutchinson, governor of Massachusetts, with Andrew Oliver, his lieutenant governor, close by his side.

Why had this august group been assembled? Why had it
seen fit to summon this young African girl, scarcely eighteen
years old, before it? This group of "the most respectable
Characters in *Boston*," as it would later define itself, had assembled to question closely the African adolescent on the
slender sheaf of poems that she claimed to have "written by
herself." We can only speculate on the nature of the questions
posed to the fledgling poet. Perhaps they asked her to identify and explain—for all to hear—exactly who were the Greek
and Latin gods and poets alluded to so frequently in her
work. Perhaps they asked her to conjugate a verb in Latin
or even to translate randomly selected passages from the Latin,
which she and her master, John Wheatley, claimed that she
"had made some Progress in." Or perhaps they asked her to
recite from memory key passages from the texts of John Mil-
ton and Alexander Pope, the two poets by whom the African
claimed to be most directly influenced. We do not know.

We do know, however, that the African poet's responses
were more than sufficient to prompt the eighteen august
gentlemen to compose, sign, and publish a two-paragraph
"Attestation," an open letter "To the Publick" that prefaces
Phillis Wheatley's book and that reads in part:

> We whose Names are under-written, do assure the World,
> that the Poems specified in the following Page, were (as we

verily believe) written by Phillis, a young Negro Girl, who was but a few Years since, brought an uncultivated Barbarian from *Africa*, and has ever since been, and now is, under the Disadvantage of serving as a Slave in a Family in this Town. She has been examined by some of the best Judges, and is thought qualified to write them.

So important was this document in securing a publisher for Wheatley's poems that it forms the signal element in the prefatory matter preceding her *Poems on Various Subjects, Religious and Moral*, published in London in 1773.

Without the published "Attestation," Wheatley's publisher claimed, few would believe that an African could possibly have written poetry all by herself. As the eighteen put the matter clearly in their letter, "Numbers would be ready to suspect they were not really the Writings of Phillis." Wheatley and her master, John Wheatley, had attempted to publish a similar volume in 1772 in Boston, but Boston publishers had been incredulous. One year later, "Attestation" in hand, Phillis Wheatley and her master's son, Nathaniel Wheatley, sailed for England, where they completed arrangements for the publication of a volume of her poems with the aid of the Countess of Huntington and the Earl of Dartmouth.

This curious anecdote, surely one of the oddest oral examinations on record, is only a tiny part of a larger, and even more curious, episode in the Enlightenment. Since the beginning of the sixteenth century, Europeans had wondered aloud whether or not the African "species of men," as they were most commonly called, *could* ever create formal literature, could ever master "the arts and sciences." If they could, the argument ran, then the African variety of humanity was fundamentally related to the European variety. If not, then it seemed clear that the African was destined by nature

to be a slave. This was the burden shouldered by Phillis
Wheatley when she successfully defended herself and the au-
thorship of her book against counterclaims and doubts.

Indeed, with her successful defense, Wheatley launched
two traditions at once—the black American literary tradition
and the black woman's literary tradition. If it is extraordinary
that not just one but both of these traditions were founded
simultaneously by a black woman—certainly an event unique
in the history of literature—it is also ironic that this important fact of common, coterminous literary origins seems to
have escaped most scholars.

That the progenitor of the black literary tradition was a
woman means, in the most strictly literal sense, that all subsequent black writers have evolved in a matrilinear line of
descent, and that each, consciously or unconsciously, has extended and revised a canon whose foundation was the poetry
of a black woman. Early black writers seem to have been
keenly aware of Wheatley's founding role, even if most of
her white reviewers were more concerned with the implica-
tions of her race than her gender. Jupiter Hammon, for example, whose 1760 broadside "An Evening Thought. Salvation by Christ, With Penitential Cries" was the first
individual poem published by a black American, acknowledged Wheatley's influence by selecting her as the subject of
his second broadside, "An Address to Miss Phillis Wheatly
[*sic*], Ethiopian Poetess, in Boston," which was published at
Hartford in 1778. And George Moses Horton, the second
Afro-American to publish a book of poetry in English (1829),
brought out in 1838 an edition of his *Poems By A Slave*
bound together with Wheatley's work. Indeed, for fifty-six
years, between 1773 and 1829, when Horton published *The
Hope of Liberty*, Wheatley was the *only* black person to have
published a book of imaginative literature in English. So

central was this black woman's role in the shaping of the Afro-American literary tradition that, as one historian has maintained, the history of the reception of Phillis Wheatley's poetry *is* the history of Afro-American literary criticism. Well into the nineteenth century, Wheatley and the black literary tradition were the same entity.

But Wheatley is not the only black woman writer who stands as a pioneering figure in Afro-American literature. Just as Wheatley gave birth to the genre of black poetry, Ann Plato was the first Afro-American to publish a book of essays (1841) and Harriet E. Wilson was the first black person to publish a novel in the United States (1859).

Despite this pioneering role of black women in the tradition, however, many of their contributions before this century have been all but lost or unrecognized. As Hortense Spillers observed as recently as 1983,

> With the exception of a handful of autobiographical narratives from the nineteenth century, the black woman's realities are virtually suppressed until the period of the Harlem Renaissance and later. Essentially the black woman as artist, as intellectual spokesperson for her own cultural apprenticeship, has not existed before, for anyone. At the source of [their] own symbol-making task, [the community of black women writers] confronts, therefore, a tradition of work that is quite recent, its continuities, broken and sporadic.

Until now, it has been extraordinarily difficult to establish the formal connections between early black women's writing and that of the present, precisely because our knowledge of their work has been broken and sporadic. Phillis Wheatley, for example, while certainly the most reprinted and discussed poet in the tradition, is also one of the least understood. Ann Plato's seminal work, *Essays* (which includes biographies and poems), has not been reprinted since it was published a cen-

tury and a half ago. And Harriet Wilson's *Our Nig,* her
compelling novel of a black woman's expanding consciousness in a racist Northern antebellum environment, never received even *one* review or comment at a time when virtually
all works written by black people were heralded by abolitionists as salient arguments against the existence of human slavery. Many of the books reprinted in this set experienced a
similar fate, the most dreadful fate for an author: that of
being ignored then relegated to the obscurity of the rare book
section of a university library. We can only wonder how
many other texts in the black woman's tradition have been
lost to this generation of readers or remain unclassified or
uncatalogued and, hence, unread.

This was not always so, however. Black women writers
dominated the final decade of the nineteenth century, perhaps
spurred to publish by an 1886 essay entitled "The Coming
American Novelist," which was published in *Lippincott's
Monthly Magazine* and written by "A Lady From Philadelphia." This pseudonymous essay argued that the "Great
American Novel" would be written by a black person. Her
argument is so curious that it deserves to be repeated:

> When we come to formulate our demands of the Coming
> American Novelist, we will agree that he must be native-
> born. His ancestors may come from where they will, but we
> must give him a birthplace and have the raising of him. Still,
> the longer his family has been here the better he will represent
> us. Suppose he should have no country but ours, no traditions
> but those he has learned here, no longings apart from us, no
> future except in our future—the orphan of the world, he
> finds with us his home. And with all this, suppose he refuses
> to be fused into that grand conglomerate we call the "Amer-
> ican type." With us, he is not of us. He is original, he has
> humor, he is tender, he is passive and fiery, he has been

taught what we call justice, and he has his own opinion about it. He has suffered everything a poet, a dramatist, a novelist need suffer before he comes to have his lips anointed. And with it all he is in one sense a spectator, a little out of the race. How would these conditions go towards forming an original development? In a word, suppose the coming novelist is of African origin? When one comes to consider the subject, there is no improbability in it. One thing is certain,—our great novel will not be written by the typical American.

An atypical American, indeed. Not only would the great American novel be written by an African-American, it would be written by an African-American *woman:*

Yet farther: I have used the generic masculine pronoun because it is convenient; but Fate keeps revenge in store. It was a woman who, taking the wrongs of the African as her theme, wrote the novel that awakened the world to their reality, and why should not the coming novelist be a woman as well as an African? She—the woman of that race—has some claims on Fate which are not yet paid up.

It is these claims on fate that we seek to pay by publishing The Schomburg Library of Nineteenth-Century Black Women Writers.

This theme would be repeated by several black women authors, most notably by Anna Julia Cooper, a prototypical black feminist whose 1892 *A Voice From the South* can be considered to be one of the original texts of the black feminist movement. It was Cooper who first analyzed the fallacy of referring to "the Black man" when speaking of black people and who argued that just as white men cannot speak through the consciousness of black men, neither can black *men* "fully and adequately . . . reproduce the exact Voice of the Black Woman." Gender and race, she argues, cannot be conflated, except in the instance of a black woman's voice, and it is this voice which must be uttered and to which we must listen. As Cooper puts the matter so compellingly:

> It is not the intelligent woman vs. the ignorant woman; nor the white woman vs. the black, the brown, and the red,—it is not even the cause of woman vs. man. Nay, 'tis woman's strongest vindication for speaking that *the world needs to hear her voice.* It would be subversive of every human interest that the cry of one-half the human family be stifled. Woman in stepping from the pedestal of statue-like inactivity in the domestic shrine, and daring to think and move and speak,— to undertake to help shape, mold, and direct the thought of her age, is merely completing the circle of the world's vision. Hers is every interest that has lacked an interpreter and a defender. Her cause is linked with that of every agony that has been dumb—every wrong that needs a voice.
>
> It is no fault of man's that he has not been able to see truth from her standpoint. It does credit both to his head and heart that no greater mistakes have been committed or even wrongs perpetrated while she sat making tatting and snipping paper flowers. Man's own innate chivalry and the mutual interdependence of their interests have insured his treating her cause, in the main at least, as his own. And he is pardonably surprised and even a little chagrined, perhaps, to find his legislation not considered "perfectly lovely" in every respect. But in any case his work is only impoverished by her remaining dumb. The world has had to limp along with the wobbling gait and one-sided hesitancy of a man with one eye. Suddenly the bandage is removed from the other eye and the whole body is filled with light. It sees a circle where before it saw a segment. The darkened eye restored, every member rejoices with it.

The myopic sight of the darkened eye can only be restored when the full range of the black woman's voice, with its own special timbres and shadings, remains mute no longer.

Similarly, Victoria Earle Matthews, an author of short stories and essays, and a cofounder in 1896 of the National Association of Colored Women, wrote in her stunning essay, "The Value of Race Literature" (1895), that "when the literature of our race is developed, it will of necessity be different in all essential points of greatness, true heroism and real Christianity from what we may at the present time, for convenience, call American literature." Matthews argued that this great tradition of Afro-American literature would be the textual outlet "for the unnaturally suppressed inner lives which our people have been compelled to lead." Once these "unnaturally suppressed inner lives" of black people are unveiled, no "grander diffusion of mental light" will shine more brightly, she concludes, than that of the articulate Afro-American woman:

> And now comes the question, What part shall we women play in the Race Literature of the future? . . . within the compass of one small journal ["Woman's Era"] we have struck out a new line of departure—a journal, a record of Race interests gathered from all parts of the United States, carefully selected, moistened, winnowed and garnered by the ablest intellects of educated colored women, shrinking at no lofty theme, shirking no serious duty, aiming at every possible excellence, and determined to do their part in the future uplifting of the race.
>
> If twenty women, by their concentrated efforts in one literary movement, can meet with such success as has engendered, planned out, and so successfully consummated this convention, what much more glorious results, what wider spread success, what grander diffusion of mental light will not come forth at the bidding of the enlarged hosts of women writers, already called into being by the stimulus of your efforts?
>
> And here let me speak one word for my journalistic sisters

who have already entered the broad arena of journalism. Before the "Woman's Era" had come into existence, no one except themselves can appreciate the bitter experience and sore disappointments under which they have at all times been compelled to pursue their chosen vocations.

If their brothers of the press have had their difficulties to contend with, I am here as a sister journalist to state, from the fullness of knowledge, that their task has been an easy one compared with that of the colored woman in journalism.

Woman's part in Race Literature, as in Race building, is the most important part and has been so in all ages. . . . All through the most remote epochs she has done her share in literature. . . .

One of the most important aspects of this set is the republication of the salient texts from 1890 to 1910, which literary historians could well call "The Black Woman's Era." In addition to Mary Helen Washington's definitive edition of Cooper's *A Voice From the South,* we have reprinted two novels by Amelia Johnson, Frances Harper's *Iola Leroy,* two novels by Emma Dunham Kelley, Alice Dunbar-Nelson's two impressive collections of short stories, and Pauline Hopkins's three serialized novels as well as her monumental novel, *Contending Forces*—all published between 1890 and 1910. Indeed, black women published more works of fiction in these two decades than black men had published in the previous half century. Nevertheless, this great achievement has been ignored.

Moreover, the writings of nineteenth-century Afro-American women in general have remained buried in obscurity, accessible only in research libraries or in overpriced and poorly edited reprints. Many of these books have never been reprinted at all; in some instances only one or two copies are extant. In these works of fiction, poetry, autobiography, biography, essays, and journalism resides the mind of the nineteenth-century Afro-American woman. Until these works are made readily available to teachers and their students, a significant segment of the black tradition will remain silent.

Oxford University Press, in collaboration with the Schomburg Center for Research in Black Culture, is publishing thirty volumes of these compelling works, each of which contains an introduction by an expert in the field. The set includes such rare texts as Johnson's *The Hazeley Family* and *Clarence and Corinne*, Plato's *Essays*, the most complete edition of Phillis Wheatley's poems and letters, Emma Dunham Kelley's pioneering novel *Megda*, several previously unpublished stories and a novel by Alice Dunbar-Nelson, and the first collected volumes of Pauline Hopkins's three serialized novels and Frances Harper's poetry. We also present four volumes of poetry by such women as Mary Eliza Tucker Lambert, Adah Menken, Josephine Heard, and Maggie Johnson. Numerous slave and spiritual narratives, a newly discovered novel—*Four Girls at Cottage City*—by Emma Dunham Kelley (-Hawkins), and the first American edition of *Wonderful Adventures of Mrs. Seacole in Many Lands* are also among the texts included.

In addition to resurrecting the works of black women authors, it is our hope that this set will facilitate the resurrection of the Afro-American woman's literary tradition itself by unearthing its nineteenth-century roots. In the works of Nella Larsen and Jessie Fauset, Zora Neale Hurston and Ann Petry, Lorraine Hansberry and Gwendolyn Brooks, Paule Marshall and Toni Cade Bambara, Audre Lorde and Rita Dove, Toni Morrison and Alice Walker, Gloria Naylor and Jamaica Kincaid, these roots have branched luxuriantly. The eighteenth- and nineteenth-century authors whose works are presented in this set founded and nurtured the black women's literary tradition, which must be revived, explicated, analyzed, and debated before we can understand more completely the formal shaping of this tradition within a tradition, a coded literary universe through which, regrettably, we are only just beginning to navigate our way. As Anna Cooper said nearly one hundred years ago, we have been blinded by the loss of sight in one eye and have therefore been unable to detect the full *shape* of the Afro-American literary tradition.

Literary works configure into a tradition not because of some mystical collective unconscious determined by the biology of race or gender, but because writers read other writers and *ground* their representations of experience in models of language provided largely by other writers to whom they feel akin. It is through this mode of literary revision, amply evident in the *texts* themselves—in formal echoes, recast metaphors, even in parody—that a "tradition" emerges and defines itself.

This is formal bonding, and it is only through formal bonding that we can know a literary tradition. The collective publication of these works by black women now, for the first time, makes it possible for scholars and critics, male and female, black and white, to *demonstrate* that black women writers read, and revised, other black women writers. To demonstrate this set of formal literary relations is to demonstrate that sexuality, race, and gender are both the condition and the basis of *tradition*—but tradition as found in discrete acts of language use.

A word is in order about the history of this set. For the past decade, I have taught a course, first at Yale and then at Cornell, entitled "Black Women and Their Fictions," a course that I inherited from Toni Morrison, who developed it in the mid-1970s for Yale's Program in Afro-American Studies. Although the course was inspired by the remarkable accomplishments of black women novelists since 1970, I gradually extended its beginning date to the late nineteenth century, studying Frances Harper's *Iola Leroy* and Anna Julia Cooper's *A Voice From the South*, both published in 1892. With the discovery of Harriet E. Wilson's seminal novel, *Our Nig* (1859), and Jean Yellin's authentication of Harriet Jacobs's brilliant slave narrative, *Incidents in the Life of a Slave Girl* (1861), a survey course spanning over a century and a quarter emerged.

But the discovery of *Our Nig*, as well as the interest in nineteenth-century black women's writing that this discovery generated, convinced me that even the most curious and diligent scholars knew very little of the extensive history of the creative writings of Afro-American women before 1900. Indeed, most scholars of Afro-American literature had never even read most of the books published by black women, simply because these books—of poetry, novels, short stories, essays, and autobiography—were mostly accessible only in rare book sections of university libraries. For reasons unclear to me even today, few of these marvelous renderings of the Afro-American woman's consciousness were reprinted in the late 1960s and early 1970s, when so many other texts of the Afro-American literary tradition were resurrected from the dark and silent graveyard of the out-of-print and were reissued in facsimile editions aimed at the hungry readership for canonical texts in the nascent field of black studies.

So, with the help of several superb research assistants—including David Curtis, Nicola Shilliam, Wendy Jones, Sam Otter, Janadas Devan, Suvir Kaul, Cynthia Bond, Elizabeth Alexander, and Adele Alexander—and with the expert advice of scholars such as William Robinson, William Andrews, Mary Helen Washington, Maryemma Graham, Jean Yellin, Houston A. Baker, Jr., Richard Yarborough, Hazel Carby, Joan R. Sherman, Frances Foster, and William French, dozens of bibliographies were used to compile a list of books written or narrated by black women mostly before 1910. Without the assistance provided through this shared experience of scholarship, the scholar's true legacy, this project could not have been conceived. As the list grew, I was struck by how very many of these titles that I, for example, had never even heard of, let alone read, such as Ann Plato's *Essays,* Louisa Picquet's slave narrative, or Amelia Johnson's two novels, *Clarence and Corinne* and *The Hazeley Family.* Through our research with the Black Periodical Fiction and Poetry Project (funded by NEH and the Ford Foundation), I also realized that several novels by black women, including three works of fiction by Pauline Hopkins, had been serialized in black periodicals, but had never been collected and published as books. Nor had the several books of poetry published by black women, such as the prolific Frances E. W. Harper, been collected and edited. When I discovered still another "lost" novel by an Afro-American woman (*Four Girls at Cottage City,* published in 1898 by Emma Dunham Kelley-Hawkins), I decided to attempt to edit a collection of reprints of these works and to publish them as a "library" of black women's writings, in part so that I could read them myself.

Convincing university and trade publishers to undertake this project proved to be a difficult task. Despite the commercial success of *Our Nig* and of the several reprint series of women's works (such as Virago, the Beacon Black Women Writers Series, and Rutgers' American Women Writers Series), several presses rejected the project as "too large," "too limited," or as "commercially unviable." Only two publishers recognized the viability and the import of the project and, of these, Oxford's commitment to publish the titles simultaneously as a set made the press's offer irresistible.

While attempting to locate original copies of these exceedingly rare books, I discovered that most of the texts were housed at the Schomburg Center for Research in Black Culture, a branch of The New York Public Library, under the direction of Howard Dodson. Dodson's infectious enthusiasm for the project and his generous collaboration, as well as that of his stellar staff (especially Diana Lachatanere, Sharon Howard, Ellis Haizip, Richard Newman, and Betty Gubert), led to a joint publishing initiative that produced this set as part of the Schomburg's major fund-raising campaign. Without Dodson's foresight and generosity of spirit, the set would not have materialized. Without William P. Sisler's masterful editorship at Oxford and his staff's careful attention to detail, the set would have remained just another grand idea that tends to languish in a scholar's file cabinet.

I would also like to thank Dr. Michael Winston and Dr. Thomas C. Battle, Vice-President of Academic Affairs and the Director of the Moorland-Spingarn Research Center (respectively) at Howard University, for their unending encouragement, support, and collaboration in this project, and Esme E. Bhan at Howard for her meticulous research and bibliographical skills. In addition, I would like to acknowledge the aid of the staff at the libraries of Duke University, Cornell University (especially Tom Weissinger and Donald Eddy), the Boston Public Library, the Western Reserve Historical Society, the Library of Congress, and Yale University. Linda Robbins, Marion Osmun, Sarah Flanagan, and Gerard Case, all members of the staff at Oxford, were extraordinarily effective at coordinating, editing, and producing the various segments of each text in the set. Candy Ruck, Nina de Tar, and Phillis Molock expertly typed reams of correspondence and manuscripts connected to the project.

I would also like to express my gratitude to my colleagues who edited and introduced the individual titles in the set. Without their attention to detail, their willingness to meet strict deadlines, and their sheer enthusiasm for this project, the set could not have been published. But finally and ultimately, I would hope that the publication of the set would help to generate even more scholarly interest in the black women authors whose work is presented here. Struggling against the seemingly insurmountable barriers of racism *and* sexism, while often raising families and fulfilling full-time professional obligations, these women managed nevertheless to record their thoughts and feelings and to *testify* to all who dare read them that the will to harness the power of collective endurance and survival is the will to write.

The Schomburg Library of Nineteenth-Century Black Women Writers is dedicated in memory of Pauline Augusta Coleman Gates, who died in the spring of 1987. It was she who inspired in me the love of learning and the love of literature. I have encountered in the books of this set no will more determined, no courage more noble, no mind more sublime, no self more celebratory of the achievements of all Afro-American women, and indeed of life itself, than her own.

A NOTE FROM
THE SCHOMBURG CENTER

Howard Dodson

The Schomburg Center for Research in Black Culture, The New York Public Library, is pleased to join with Dr. Henry Louis Gates and Oxford University Press in presenting The Schomburg Library of Nineteenth-Century Black Women Writers. This thirty-volume set includes the work of a generation of black women whose writing has only been available previously in rare book collections. The materials reprinted in twenty-four of the thirty volumes are drawn from the unique holdings of the Schomburg Center.

A research unit of The New York Public Library, the Schomburg Center has been in the forefront of those institutions dedicated to collecting, preserving, and providing access to the records of the black past. In the course of its two generations of acquisition and conservation activity, the Center has amassed collections totaling more than 5 million items. They include over 100,000 bound volumes, 85,000 reels and sets of microforms, 300 manuscript collections containing some 3.5 million items, 300,000 photographs and extensive holdings of prints, sound recordings, film and videotape, newspapers, artworks, artifacts, and other book and nonbook materials. Together they vividly document the history and cultural heritages of people of African descent worldwide.

Though established some sixty-two years ago, the Center's book collections date from the sixteenth century. Its oldest item, an Ethiopian Coptic Tunic, dates from the eighth or ninth century. Rare materials, however, are most available for the nineteenth-century African-American experience. It is from these holdings that the majority of the titles selected for inclusion in this set are drawn.

The nineteenth century was a formative period in African-American literary and cultural history. Prior to the Civil War, the majority of black Americans living in the United States were held in bondage. Law and practice forbade teaching them to read or write. Even after the war, many of the impediments to learning and literary productivity remained. Nevertheless, black men and women of the nineteenth century persevered in both areas. Moreover, more African-Americans than we yet realize turned their observations, feelings, social viewpoints, and creative impulses into published works. In time, this nineteenth-century printed record included poetry, short stories, histories, novels, autobiographies, social criticism, and theology, as well as economic and philosophical treatises. Unfortunately, much of this body of literature remained, until very recently, relatively inaccessible to twentieth-century scholars, teachers, creative artists, and others interested in black life. Prior to the late 1960s, most Americans (black as well as white) had never heard of these nineteenth-century authors, much less read their works.

The civil rights and black power movements created unprecedented interest in the thought, behavior, and achievements of black people. Publishers responded by revising traditional texts, introducing the American public to a new generation of African-American writers, publishing a variety of thematic anthologies, and reprinting a plethora of "classic texts" in African-American history, literature, and art. The reprints usually appeared as individual titles or in a series of bound volumes or microform formats.

The Schomburg Center, which has a long history of supporting publishing that deals with the history and culture of Africans in diaspora, became an active participant in many of the reprint revivals of the 1960s. Since hard copies of original printed works are the preferred formats for producing facsimile reproductions, publishers frequently turned to the Schomburg Center for copies of these original titles. In addition to providing such material, Schomburg Center staff members offered advice and consultation, wrote introductions, and occasionally entered into formal copublishing arrangements in some projects.

Most of the nineteenth-century titles reprinted during the 1960s, however, were by and about black men. A few black women were included in the longer series, but works by lesser known black women were generally overlooked. The Schomburg Library of Nineteenth-Century Black Women Writers is both a corrective to these previous omissions and an important contribution to Afro-American literary history in its own right. Through this collection of volumes, the thoughts, perspectives, and creative abilities of nineteenth-century African-American women, as captured in books and pamphlets published in large part before 1910, are again being made available to the general public. The Schomburg Center is pleased to be a part of this historic endeavor.

I would like to thank Professor Gates for initiating this project. Thanks are due both to him and Mr. William P. Sisler of Oxford University Press for giving the Schomburg Center an opportunity to play such a prominent role in the set. Thanks are also due to my colleagues at The New York Public Library and the Schomburg Center, especially Dr. Vartan Gregorian, Richard De Gennaro, Paul Fasana, Betsy

Pinover, Richard Newman, Diana Lachatanere, Glenderlyn Johnson, and Harold Anderson for their assistance and support. I can think of no better way of demonstrating than in this set the role the Schomburg Center plays in assuring that the black heritage will be available for future generations.

CONTENTS

INTRODUCTION

William L. Andrews

The six black women's stories reprinted in this book represent
most of the major themes and narrative forms that appear in
Afro-American women's autobiographies from the nineteenth
and early twentieth centuries. In *The History of Mary Prince,
a West Indian Slave* (1831), we read the first female slave
narrative from the Americas, a story of a lone woman's
appalling suffering and admirable courage in the pursuit of
freedom. *The Story of Mattie J. Jackson* (1866), which, like
The History of Mary Prince, is a dictated slave narrative,
recalls Prince's record of struggle, but its conclusion is more
characteristic of nineteenth-century black women's autobiography; it records not only Jackson's achievement of personal
freedom but also her reunion with her mother, brother, and
stepfather in Massachusetts after the Civil War. The *Memoir
of Old Elizabeth, a Coloured Woman* (1863) blends the slave
narrative and the spiritual autobiography traditions in black
women's writing. Elizabeth's story shows how evangelical
Christianity became a crucial source of comfort and power
for nineteenth-century women who sought liberation from the
restrictions of caste and gender roles. Lucy A. Delaney's
From the Darkness Cometh the Light or Struggles for Freedom
(c. 1891)* illustrates the continuing vitality of the slave
narrative as the black female literary tradition approached the
twentieth century. But while reiterating many of the themes

---

*Publication date taken from Russell C. Brignano, *Black Americans in Au-
tobiography* (Durham, N.C.: Duke University Press, 1984), p. 21.

of her literary predecessors, Delaney extends her story beyond her family's reunion in freedom to record, in brief, the success she has made of her life in the quarter-century since the end of the Civil War. Recounting such successes in the postwar North, while eulogizing black motherhood in the antebellum South, are the basic concerns of both Kate Drumgoold's *A Slave Girl's Story* (1898) and Annie L. Burton's *Memories of Childhood's Slavery Days* (1909).

The fundamental theme that underlies all of these autobiographies is, in Delaney's words, the "true, steadfast heart and noble soul" of the Afro-American woman, especially instanced by the slave mother. Writing narratives of slavery offered women like Drumgoold and Burton, who themselves had had little direct experience of bondage, the opportunity to celebrate their mothers as examples of genuine female heroism. These women knew, as Delaney explicitly stated, that in the eyes of whites the best a black woman might signify was "the common place virtues of an honest woman." But as early as Prince's story, female slave narrators portrayed the enslaved black woman as a person of near-indomitable dedication to the highest principles of human dignity and individual freedom.

Mary Prince testifies simply yet eloquently to the tenacious integrity of her own selfhood despite overwhelming efforts to subvert it and brutalize her. Her patience with and endurance of the wrongs done to her seem almost astonishing. She had her breaking-point, however, and when she reached it her willingness to live by the stoic Christian's code gave out. In her verbal and physical resistance to her sadistic master and mistress, the black woman's determination not just to endure but to triumph over injustice is underlined. This was an important precedent for the black woman's autobiography in America. Mattie Jackson endorses this idea of the slave woman's allegiance to personal liberty, but her story adds a special chorus of praise for the enslaved mother. The altruism of Jackson's mother, who repeatedly sacrificed her own yearning for freedom to ensure the liberation of her children, is celebrated even more than Jackson's own intrepid escape from bondage. Perhaps the most dramatic scenes in the autobiographies of Jackson, Delaney, and Burton are those that depict the herculean (and usually successful) efforts of slave mothers to keep their families together in slavery or to reunite them after emancipation.

Thus the slave mother, or some comparable black maternal figure, more than the female narrator herself, plays the hero's role in most early black women's autobiographies. The mother inspires within her daughter the hope of freedom and provides an example of a woman who will not give in to despair. Sometimes the mother furnishes material as well as moral assistance to her daughter when she strikes for freedom. It is usually the mother who reunites the family after slavery and war have scattered them. And at least in one case, the black matron acts as midwife to the birth of her daughter's autobiography itself. Without the urging of her mother and the literary assistance of her stepmother, Jackson declares, her autobiography would never have been created.

Whether celebrating black female selfhood in general or the nurturing power of the slave mother in particular, women's slave narratives first came into existence under the aegis of the abolitionist movement in England and the Americas. In his preface to her life story, Prince's editor, Thomas Pringle, summarizes the purpose that many abolitionists believed a slave narrative could serve in their crusade. According to Pringle, personal statements like Prince's guaranteed that, instead of learning what antislavery agitators thought about slavery and the slave, "good people in England might hear from a slave what a slave had felt and suffered." The slave narrative evolved between 1830 and 1860 as a way of letting slaves themselves have a voice in their cause as both eyewitnesses to the horrors of bondage and I-witnesses to their own feelings as human beings caught up in such a monstrous system. By the mid-nineteenth century, a number of fugitive slaves, like Moses Roper, William Wells Brown, and the famed Frederick Douglass, had opened the minds and hearts of thousands of white people in the English-speaking world to the feelings and sufferings of the enslaved.

But what of the female slave? Did the great male slave narrators like Brown and Douglass speak for her? Did they know what she "had felt and suffered"? As we reconstruct the history of black autobiography in its formative century, from 1760 to 1865, we find that only rarely did escaped female slaves ask for or receive the kind of attention that encouraged them to dictate or write their life stories. Mary Prince was unusual in that she approached her editor, Thomas Pringle, with the specific suggestion of writing her history. Hers was among the earliest slave narratives designed to tell the ugly but necessary truth about a socioeconomic system in the British West Indies that few people in England understood apart from the propaganda of the slaveowners. The way Prince tells that truth, both in the detail with which she recounts atrocities and in the frankness with which she speaks of many West Indian whites, must have surprised, if not shocked, many of her readers. Women, especially those of Prince's caste and class, were not expected to speak out so bluntly in public, especially about their supposed betters.

Pringle's "Supplement to the History of Mary Prince"

pictures her as the personification of such traditional feminine
virtues as "decency," "propriety of conduct," and particularly
"delicacy" in all matters of behavior, qualities that endeared
her to the women in his family. But the white man also notes
that the former slave woman had "a somewhat violent and
hasty temper, and a considerable share of natural pride and
self-importance." He labels these traits as "defects" of her
character, though they do not keep him from judging her
"on the whole as respectable and well-behaved a person in
her station, as any domestic, white or black" that he had ever
seen. What even a well-intentioned Thomas Pringle could
not see was that without these "defects" of character, Mary
Prince probably would not have survived the assault on her
sense of selfhood and personal worth that her owners, the
Woods, kept up for more than five years. A male ex-slave
like Frederick Douglass might easily claim as a virtue "a
considerable share of natural pride and self-importance." Such
qualities were essential to that "sense of my own manhood"
that, according to his *Narrative* (1845), Douglass had to
preserve if he was ever to rise up against his master. But if
a woman, black or white, exhibited the same qualities, she
contradicted all that true *womanhood* meant in the nineteenth
century. A white woman risked the charge of "unsexing"
herself, of deserting her proper station in life and becoming
something unnatural and morally perverse. A black woman
who felt strongly enough about her "self-importance" to
defend it with a "violent temper" risked the worst sort of
physical reprisals from whites. The racist mythology of the
era did not treat black women as women but as breeding
animals who had no right to even the limited degree of self-
regard that white women were allowed in a male-dominated
culture.

Mary Prince argues implicitly against this mythology by showing how cruel whites pushed her to the limits of her endurance. Only by talking back, saying no, and finally refusing to live any longer with the abusive Woods couple could Prince hope to preserve her physical and mental health and someday return to her husband. Her story concludes with a notable assertion from a black woman: "I know what slaves feel—I can tell by myself what other slaves feel, and by what they have told me. The man that says slaves be quite happy in slavery—that they don't want to be free—that man is either ignorant or a lying person." In this remark Prince, a black female slave, declares herself to be a more reliable authority on slavery than any white man and to be fully capable of speaking for all her fellow slaves, both male and female, against any white man. The implication of this declaration should not be underestimated, since it constitutes the first claim in the Afro-American autobiographical tradition for the black woman's authority as a spokesperson for *all* black people, regardless of gender, on the subject of "what slaves feel" about the morality of slavery.

What slaves like Mattie Jackson and her mother felt about slavery differs little from the feelings expressed by Prince in her narrative. The fact that both the narratives of Prince and Jackson were ghostwritten by persons sympathetic to the abolitionist cause requires us to remember that the power to write their own stories as they saw fit did not come to female slaves as early as it did to male slaves. Little of the "somewhat violent and hasty temper" that Pringle attributes to Prince is actually expressed in her narrative. We may wonder whether she restrained her anger and bitterness toward her persecutors when she recounted her story to her unnamed female aman-uensis. Or might Pringle have softened Prince's tone or emotions when he edited her words, so that she would not lose that "delicacy" that he felt was so praiseworthy in her? In any case, Mattie Jackson's ghostwriter, a black woman herself, seems to have been happy to let the escaped slave woman speak more freely about her actions and feelings, though they might bother some readers. It is not by accident that Jackson's narrative concludes with her frank admission that she took twenty-five dollars from her master on the eve of her flight to freedom in order "to bear my expenses." Jackson did not care if some readers objected to this as stealing. She wanted her readers to understand all that freedom meant to her. If in democratic America "the laborer was worthy of his hire," then a black female laborer, especially a slave, was worthy of hers—regardless of whether the master (or her reader) agreed. Such a laborer need not ask for anyone's approval in demanding economic justice. She may seize it for herself. Jackson was determined to make her readers realize that the black woman owed nothing to slavery, though the slaveowner owed much to her.

Mattie Jackson's story illustrates an important fact about the female slave narrative tradition. It calls for justice, not mere sympathy or pity, as the great aim and need of black women in America. The heart-warming marriage of Jackson's mother and the reunion of her family in Massachusetts confirm this woman's faith in divine justice. Throughout her oppression, she remained "confident of gaining" her freedom, "whatever might betide." This is not the only confirmation of justice that Jackson's story records, however. The "Summary" of the text pictures Jackson back in St. Louis, her hometown, where she has the satisfaction of seeing her erstwhile master and mistress, the Lewises, compelled to accept their "equality with the black man." In some female slave narratives, like Elizabeth Keckley's *Behind the Scenes* (re-printed in another volume in this series), the return of the former slave to the scene of her bondage is couched in a tone of forgiveness, even fondness, for the former master or mistress now much reduced in circumstances. But for Jackson justice demanded more than just her forgiveness of the Lewises. It required the humbling of their racist pride, which we witness in the comic moment when a shocked and flustered Lewis unconsciously drops a bow to Jackson, the one woman he would never have wanted or expected to meet on the streets of St. Louis.

White male pride, more than the evils of slavery as an institution, provides the principal antagonist to Elizabeth—a ninety-seven-year-old ex-slave who became a preacher—on her quest for freedom and justice. Her *Memoir* says little about slavery, though Elizabeth spent her first thirty years in bondage in Maryland. Still, what she does recall about her childhood indicates that she was never one to accept unquestioningly the authority of white men, even her master. In her early teens, she began to have heavenly visions, which convinced her that her calling in life was not as a slave but as an evangelist. Gaining her physical freedom, which she notes almost anticlimactically early in her story, demanded less commitment to her sense of self and mission than her preaching career, which she did not feel free to undertake until she was forty-two years old. Men in the church expected women, especially almost illiterate former slaves like Elizabeth, to keep silent and not presume to speak for God to them. Not until she could overcome her own self-doubt and sense of female inadequacy, not until she was sure that God "does not work by man's authority," could she learn to "look upon man as a very selfish being, when placed in a religious office, to presume to resist the work of the Almighty." Once she became convinced that hers was "the work of the Almighty," Elizabeth displayed remarkable courage as a minister of the social gospel. In the early nineteenth century, she went to Virginia where she inveighed against both the slavery of sin and the sin of slavery. White religious authorities could not shake her belief in herself as divinely ordained, and white secular power failed to intimidate her with threats of imprisonment.

Black, elderly, female, unmarried, and childless, Elizabeth might seem at first glance to have been among the most disadvantaged and powerless people of the antebellum era. But through evangelical Christianity she found her own sense of "natural pride and self-importance"—and an empowering life's work as well. Spiritual autobiographies like Elizabeth's, Jarena Lee's (reprinted elsewhere in this series), and Zilpha Elaw's furnish some of the earliest accounts we have of successful black career women in nineteenth-century America. To such women success was not measured by their social or economic status but by their faithfulness to their personal sense of calling. By identifying with her divine mission, Elizabeth developed a profound self-respect that brooked no opposition and accepted no compromise.

The development of an empowering sense of self-respect for black women is one of Lucy A. Delaney's major concerns, though she does not attribute her own achievement of this quality to her religious experience. In *From the Darkness Cometh the Light*, she candidly admits that she hated her master and forcibly resisted her mistress's one attempt to whip her. When told that she should accept her enslavement with "submission and patience," Delaney rejected such saintly behavior. "I could not feel anything but rebellion against my lot," she recalls. And yet, the slave woman as rebel is not punished for these transgressions against the traditional code of Christian womanhood. She is rewarded with her freedom in 1844, in large part because of the shrewdness and faith of Polly Berry, Delaney's mother. Born free, Berry was kidnapped and sold into slavery as a child. The mother of two daughters, she dedicated herself to their freedom, encouraging one to make a successful escape to Canada, and promising the other, Lucy, that "by the help of God and a good lawyer," she could win her daughter's freedom in a St. Louis court. Polly Berry's story testifies to the black woman's power to move heaven and earth, to convert both divine favor and white male privilege, to her own ends. Alone in her conviction that the cause of her daughters was both divinely justified and legally winnable, Polly Berry's victory exemplifies the kind of female self-confidence that her daughter's narrative seeks to inspire in her black women readers. Lucy Delaney's leadership among a number of black women's religious and benevolent organizations after the Civil War shows some of the ways that Polly Berry's example could be followed. The important thing, Delaney urges her women readers at the end of her story, is to make use of one's inborn talents for the glory of God and the benefit of the community.

" 'Can the negro race succeed, proportionately, as well as the whites, if given the same chance and an equal start?' " Delaney asks. The autobiographies of Annie L. Burton and Kate Drumgoold are designed to answer such a question affirmatively. Both are stories of women who were born in slavery but who were liberated in their childhood by the Union army. Neither woman can recall much personal physical suffering under slavery, and each pays tribute to kind female slaveowners who showed genuine concern for their welfare. Nevertheless, Burton details a number of tragedies that befell adult slaves during her "happy, carefree childhood days on the plantation," including whippings for hungry slaves who stole hogs and chickens, violent conflicts between slaves and jealous masters, and the sale of slave women who failed to produce children within a year of their marriages. Both Burton and Drumgoold also knew what it was like to be separated from their mothers because of slavery. Burton's mother was so outraged when her mistress whipped her that she ran away from her home near Clayton, Alabama, and disappeared for three years. Drumgoold's mother, to whom "the master could not do anything to make her feel like a slave," was sold from Virginia to Georgia in 1861. The profit from the sale paid a poor white man to serve as her master's proxy in the Confederate army. Yet when the war ended, both women returned to their children, determined to reclaim them and see to their education in the new era of freedom. The resourcefulness and strength of will of these two mothers during the chaotic days immediately following the collapse of the slave system in the South are truly marvelous.

Burton and Drumgoold were among the earliest black emigrants from the South to the North during the postwar era. In 1865 Drumgoold went with her mother to Brooklyn, New York, where, through the agency of friendly whites, she was converted to Christianity. She worked as a domestic servant and dedicated herself to obtaining an education so that she could become a teacher for the advancement of her race. Despite sickness and poverty, she saved enough of her earnings to attend boarding schools; by age twenty, she had received almost four years of formal training at the Wayland Seminary in Washington, D.C. After further schooling at

Harper's Ferry, she began her teaching career, in which she
labored for eleven years until poor health forced her to stop.
Burton did not move North until 1879, and she did not enjoy
the advantages of education that Drumgoold had, but her
story, like Drumgoold's, stresses the industry and capability
of the black Southern woman in a free and competitive
economy. First as a laundress and later as a cook, chambermaid, and housekeeper, Burton successfully supported herself
in Boston and New York. When her sister died, leaving a
son to be raised, Burton readily took up this responsibility,
moved to Georgia, and eventually became a restauranteur in
Jacksonville, Florida, and later in Boston. She did well
enough as an independent businesswoman to see her nephew
through college at Hampton Institute.

Burton and Drumgoold wrote their autobiographies with
a strong sense of destiny, believing that God wanted them to
tell their stories as inspirational examples to others of their
race. Burton calls herself "something of the type of Moses,"
evidently referring to her progress from the land of bondage
in the South to success and fulfillment in the promised land
of freedom in the North. Drumgoold's individual successes
verify her optimistic assertion of the inexorable progress of
"the Negro Race" in America. More socially conscious than
Burton, the schoolteacher wastes few opportunities in her
story to urge her black readers to remember God's special
regard for and expectations of black people. "His searching
eye rests on all of the negro race," Drumgoold observes, "to
see what use they are going to make of their time and talent."
Undoubtedly Burton and Drumgoold both felt that they had
made the most of their talents and responsibilities, which is
one reason why both autobiographers could look back on the
past, even the slave past, and see in it not something to be

ashamed of, but something that prefigured, in Drumgoold's words, "the light of another day." This ability of black women to recover in the darkness of past oppression the light for a better day unites female slave narrators from Mary Prince to Annie Burton in a heroic literary sisterhood.

THE

HISTORY OF MARY PRINCE,

A WEST INDIAN SLAVE.

RELATED BY HERSELF.

WITH A SUPPLEMENT BY THE EDITOR.

To which is added,

THE NARRATIVE OF ASA-ASA,

A CAPTURED AFRICAN.

" By our sufferings, since ye brought us
To the man-degrading mart,—
All sustain'd by patience, taught us
Only by a broken heart,—
Deem our nation brutes no longer,
Till some reason ye shall find
Worthier of regard, and stronger
Than the colour of our kind."   COWPER.

LONDON:
PUBLISHED BY F. WESTLEY AND A. H. DAVIS,
STATIONERS' HALL COURT;
AND BY WAUGH & INNES, EDINBURGH.

1831.

PREFACE.

THE idea of writing Mary Prince's history was first suggested by herself. She wished it to be done, she said, that good people in England might hear from a slave what a slave had felt and suffered; and a letter of her late master's, which will be found in the Supplement, induced me to accede to her wish without farther delay. The more immediate object of the publication will afterwards appear.

The narrative was taken down from Mary's own lips by a lady who happened to be at the time residing in my family as a visitor. It was written out fully, with all the narrator's repetitions and prolixities, and afterwards pruned into its present shape; retaining, as far as was practicable, Mary's exact expressions and peculiar phraseology. No fact of importance has been omitted, and not a single circumstance or sentiment has been added. It is essentially her own, without any material alteration farther than was requisite to exclude redundances and gross grammatical errors, so as to render it clearly intelligible.

After it had been thus written out, I went over the whole, carefully examining her on every fact and circumstance detailed; and in all that relates to her residence in Antigua I had the advantage of being assisted in this scrutiny by Mr. Joseph Phillips, who was a resident in that colony during the same period, and had known her there.

The names of all the persons mentioned by the narrator have been printed in full, except those of Capt. I—— and his wife, and that of Mr. D——, to whom conduct of peculiar atrocity is ascribed. These three individuals are now gone to answer at a far more awful tribunal than that of public opinion, for the deeds of which their former bondwoman accuses them; and to hold them

up more openly to human reprobation could no longer affect
themselves, while it might deeply lacerate the feelings of their
surviving and perhaps innocent relatives, without any commen-
surate public advantage.

Without detaining the reader with remarks on other points
which will be adverted to more conveniently in the Supplement,
I shall here merely notice farther, that the Anti-Slavery Society
have no concern whatever with this publication, nor are they in
any degree responsible for the statements it contains. I have
published the tract, not as their Secretary, but in my private
capacity; and any profits that may arise from the sale will be
exclusively appropriated to the benefit of Mary Prince herself.

THO. PRINGLE.

7, *Solly Terrace, Claremont Square,*
       January 25, 1831.

P. S. Since writing the above, I have been furnished by my
friend Mr. George Stephen, with the interesting narrative of
Asa-Asa, a captured African, now under his protection; and
have printed it as a suitable appendix to this little history.

T. P.

THE

HISTORY OF MARY PRINCE,

A WEST INDIAN SLAVE.

(*Related by herself.*)

I was born at Brackish-Pond, in Bermuda, on a farm belonging to Mr. Charles Myners. My mother was a household slave; and my father, whose name was Prince, was a sawyer belonging to Mr. Trimmingham, a ship-builder at Crow-Lane. When I was an infant, old Mr. Myners died, and there was a division of the slaves and other property among the family. I was bought along with my mother by old Captain Darrel, and given to his grandchild, little Miss Betsey Williams. Captain Williams, Mr. Darrel's son-in-law, was master of a vessel which traded to several places in America and the West Indies, and he was seldom at home long together.

Mrs. Williams was a kind-hearted good woman, and she treated all her slaves well. She had only one daughter, Miss Betsey, for whom I was purchased, and who was about my own age. I was made quite a pet of by Miss Betsey, and loved her very much. She used to lead me about by the hand, and call me her little nigger. This was the happiest period of my life; for I was too young to understand rightly my condition as a slave, and too thoughtless and full of spirits to look forward to the days of toil and sorrow.

My mother was a household slave in the same family. I was under her own care, and my little brothers and sisters were my play-fellows and companions. My mother had several fine children after she came to Mrs. Williams,—three girls and two boys. The tasks given out to us children were light, and we used to play together with Miss Betsey, with as much freedom almost as if she had been our sister.

My master, however, was a very harsh, selfish man; and we always dreaded his return from sea. His wife was herself much afraid of him; and, during his stay at home, seldom dared to shew her usual kindness to the slaves. He often left her, in the most distressed circumstances, to reside in other female society, at some place in the West Indies of which I have forgot the name. My poor mistress bore his ill-treatment with great patience, and all her slaves loved and pitied her. I was truly attached to her, and, next to my own mother, loved her better than any creature in the world. My obedience to her commands was cheerfully given: it sprung solely from the affection I felt for her, and not from fear of the power which the white people's law had given her over me.

I had scarcely reached my twelfth year when my mistress became too poor to keep so many of us at home; and she hired me out to Mrs. Pruden, a lady who lived about five miles off, in the adjoining parish, in a large house near the sea. I cried bitterly at parting with my dear mistress and Miss Betsey, and when I kissed my mother and brothers and sisters, I thought my young heart would break, it pained me so. But there was no help; I was forced to go. Good Mrs. Williams comforted me by saying that I should still be near the home I was about to quit, and might come over and see her and my kindred when-ever I could obtain leave of absence from Mrs. Pruden. A few hours after this I was taken to a strange house, and found myself among strange people. This separation seemed a sore trial to me then; but oh! 'twas light, light to the trials I have since endured!—'twas nothing—nothing to be mentioned with them; but I was a child then, and it was according to my strength.

I knew that Mrs. Williams could no longer maintain me; that she was fain to part with me for my food and clothing; and I tried to submit myself to the change. My new mistress was a passionate woman; but yet she did not treat me very unkindly. I do not remember her striking me but once, and that was for going to see Mrs. Williams when I heard she was sick, and staying longer than she had given me leave to do. All my employment at this time was nursing a sweet baby, little Master Daniel; and I grew so fond of my nursling that it was my greatest delight to walk out with him by the sea-shore, accompanied by his brother and sister, Miss Fanny and Master James. —Dear Miss Fanny! She was a sweet, kind young lady, and so fond of me that she wished me to learn all that she knew herself; and her me-thod of teaching me was as follows:—Directly she had said her lessons to her grandmamma, she used to come running to me, and make me repeat them one by one after her; and in a few months I was able not only to say my letters but to spell many small words. But this happy state was not to last long. Those days were too pleasant to last. My heart always softens when I think of them.

At this time Mrs. Williams died. I was told suddenly of her death, and my grief was so great that, forgetting I had the baby in my arms, I ran away directly to my poor mistress's house; but reached it only in time to see the corpse carried out. Oh, that was a day of sorrow,—a heavy day! All the slaves cried. My mother cried and lamented her sore; and I (foolish creature!) vainly entreated them to bring my dear mistress back to life. I knew nothing rightly about death then, and it seemed a hard thing to bear. When I thought about my mistress I felt as if the world was all gone wrong; and for many days and weeks I could think of nothing else. I returned to Mrs. Pruden's; but my sorrow was too great to be comforted, for my own dear mistress was always in my mind. Whether in the house or abroad, my thoughts were always talking to me about her.

I staid at Mrs. Pruden's about three months after this; I was then sent back to Mr. Williams to be sold. Oh, that was a sad sad time! I recollect the day well. Mrs. Pruden came to me and said, " Mary, you will have to go home directly; your master is going to be married, and he means to sell you and two of your sisters to raise money for the wedding." Hearing this I burst out a crying,—though I was then far from being sensible of the full weight of my misfortune, or of the misery that waited for me. Besides, I did not like to leave Mrs. Pruden, and the dear baby, who had grown very fond of me. For some time I could scarcely believe that Mrs. Pruden was in earnest, till I received orders for my immediate return.—Dear Miss Fanny! how she cried at parting with me, whilst I kissed and hugged the baby, thinking I should never see him again. I left Mrs. Pruden's, and walked home with a heart full of sorrow. The idea of being sold away from my mother and Miss Betsey was so frightful, that I dared not trust myself to think about it. We had been bought of Mr. Myners, as I have mentioned, by Miss Betsey's grandfather, and given to her, so that we were by right *her* property, and I never thought we should be separated or sold away from her.

When I reached the house, I went in directly to Miss Betsey. I found her in great distress; and she cried out as soon as she saw me, " Oh, Mary! my father is going to sell you all to raise money to marry that wicked woman. You are *my* slaves, and he has no right to sell you; but it is all to please her." She then told me that my mother was living with her father's sister at a house close by, and I went there to see her. It was a sorrowful meeting; and we lamented with a great and sore crying our unfortunate situation. " Here comes one of my poor picaninnies!" she said, the moment I came in, " one of the poor slave-brood who are to be sold to-morrow."

Oh dear! I cannot bear to think of that day,—it is too much.—It recalls the great grief that filled my heart, and the woeful thoughts that passed to and fro through my mind, whilst listening to the pitiful words of my poor mother, weeping for the loss of her children. I wish I could find words to tell you all I then felt and suffered. The great God above alone knows the thoughts of the poor slave's heart, and the bitter pains which follow such separations as these. All that we love taken away from us—Oh, it is sad, sad! and sore to be borne!—I got no sleep that night for thinking of the morrow; and dear Miss Betsey was scarcely less distressed. She could not bear to part with her old playmates, and she cried sore and would not be pacified.

The black morning at length came; it came too soon for my poor mother and us. Whilst she was putting on us the new osnaburgs in which we were to be sold, she said, in a sorrowful voice, (I shall never forget it!) " See, I am *shrouding* my poor children; what a task for a mother!"—She then called Miss Betsey to take leave of us. " I am going to carry my little chickens to market," (these were her very words,) " take your last look of them; may be you will see them no more." " Oh, my poor slaves! my own slaves!" said dear Miss Betsey, " you belong to me; and it grieves my heart to part with you."—Miss Betsey kissed us all, and, when she left us, my mother called the rest of the slaves to bid us good bye. One of them, a woman named Moll, came with her infant in her arms. "Ay!" said my mother, seeing her turn away and look at her child with the tears in her eyes, "your turn will come next." The slaves could say nothing to comfort us; they could only weep and lament with us. When I left my dear little brothers and the house in which I had been brought up, I thought my heart would burst.

Our mother, weeping as she went, called me away with the children Hannah and Dinah, and we took the road that led to Hamble Town, which we reached about four o'clock in the afternoon. We followed my mother to the market-place, where she placed us in a row against a large house, with our backs to the wall and our arms folded across our breasts. I, as the eldest, stood first, Hannah next to me, then Dinah; and our mother stood beside, crying over us. My heart throbbed with grief and terror so violently, that I pressed my hands quite tightly across my breast, but I could not keep it still, and it continued to leap as though it would burst out of my body. But who cared for that? Did one of the many by-standers, who were looking at us so carelessly, think of the pain that wrung the hearts of the negro woman and her young ones? No, no! They were not all bad, I dare say, but slavery hardens white people's hearts towards the blacks; and many of them were not slow to make their remarks upon us aloud, without regard to our grief—though their light words fell like cayenne on the fresh wounds of our hearts. Oh those white people have small hearts who can only feel for themselves.

At length the vendue master, who was to offer us for sale like sheep or cattle, arrived, and asked my mother which was the eldest. She said nothing, but pointed to me. He took me by the hand, and led me out into the middle of the street, and, turning me slowly round, exposed me to the view of those who attended the vendue. I was soon surrounded by strange men, who examined and handled me in the same manner that a butcher would a calf or a lamb he was about to purchase, and who talked about my shape and size in like words—as if I could no more understand their meaning than the dumb beasts. I was then put up to sale. The bidding commenced at a few pounds, and gradually rose to fifty-seven,* when I was knocked down to the highest bidder; and the people who stood by said that I had fetched a great sum for so young a slave.

I then saw my sisters led forth, and sold to different owners; so that we had not the sad satisfaction of being partners in bondage. When the sale was over, my mother hugged and kissed us, and mourned over us, begging of us to keep up a good heart, and do our duty to our new masters. It was a sad parting; one went one way, one another, and our poor mammy went home with nothing.†

---

* Bermuda currency; about £38 sterling.

† Let the reader compare the above affecting account, taken down from the mouth of this negro woman, with the following description of a vendue of slaves at the Cape of Good Hope, published by me in 1826, from the letter of a friend, —and mark their similarity in several characteristic circumstances. The resemblance is easily accounted for: slavery wherever it prevails produces similar effects.—" Having heard that there was to be a sale of cattle, farm stock, &c. by

My new master was a Captain I——, who lived at Spanish Point. After parting with my mother and sisters, I followed him to his store, and he gave me into the charge of his son, a lad about my own age, Master Benjy, who took me to my new home. I did not know where I was going, or what my new master would do with me. My heart was quite broken with grief, and my thoughts went back continually to those from whom I had been so suddenly parted. " Oh, my mother! my mother!" I kept saying to myself, " Oh, my mammy and my sisters and my brothers, shall I never see you again!"

Oh, the trials! the trials! they make the salt water come into my eyes when I think of the days in which I was afflicted—the times that are gone; when I mourned and grieved with a young heart for those whom I loved.

It was night when I reached my new home. The house was large, and built at the bottom of a very high hill; but I could not see much of it that night. I saw too much of it afterwards. The stones and the timber were the best things in it; they were not so hard as the hearts of the owners.*

Before I entered the house, two slave women, hired from another owner, who were at work in the yard, spoke to me, and asked who I belonged to? I replied, " I am come to live here." " Poor child, poor child !" they both said; " you must keep a good heart, if you are to live here."—When I went in, I stood up crying in a corner. Mrs. I—— came and took off my hat, a little black silk hat Miss Pruden made for me, and said in a rough voice, " You are not come here to stand up in corners and cry, you are come here to work." She then put a child into my arms, and, tired as I was, I was forced instantly to

auction, at a Veld-Cornet's in the vicinity, we halted our waggon one day for the purpose of procuring a fresh spann of oxen. Among the stock of the farm sold, was a female slave and her three children. The two eldest children were girls, the one about thirteen years of age, and the other about eleven; the youngest was a boy. The whole family were exhibited together, but they were sold separately, and to different purchasers. The farmers examined them as if they had been so many head of cattle. While the sale was going on, the mother and her children were exhibited on a table, that they might be seen by the company, which was very large. There could not have been a finer subject for an able painter than this unhappy group. The tears, the anxiety, the anguish of the mother, while she met the gaze of the multitude, eyed the different countenances of the bidders, or cast a heart-rending look upon the children ; and the simplicity and touching sorrow of the young ones, while they clung to their distracted parent, wiping their eyes, and half concealing their faces,—contrasted with the marked insensibility and jocular countenances of the spectators and purchasers, —furnished a striking commentary on the miseries of slavery, and its debasing effects upon the hearts of its abettors. While the woman was in this distressed situation she was asked, ' Can you feed sheep?' Her reply was so indistinct that it escaped me ; but it was probably in the negative, for her purchaser rejoined, in a loud and harsh voice, ' Then I will teach you with the sjamboc,' (a whip made of the rhinoceros' hide.) The mother and her three children were sold to three separate purchasers ; and they were literally torn from each other." —Ed.

* These strong expressions, and all of a similar character in this little narrative, are given verbatim as uttered by Mary Prince.—Ed.

take up my old occupation of a nurse.—I could not bear to look at my mistress, her countenance was so stern. She was a stout tall woman with a very dark complexion, and her brows were always drawn together into a frown. I thought of the words of the two slave women when I saw Mrs. I——, and heard the harsh sound of her voice.

The person I took the most notice of that night was a French Black called Hetty, whom my master took in privateering from another vessel, and made his slave. She was the most active woman I ever saw, and she was tasked to her utmost. A few minutes after my arrival she came in from milking the cows, and put the sweet-potatoes on for supper. She then fetched home the sheep, and penned them in the fold ; drove home the cattle, and staked them about the pond side ;* fed and rubbed down my master's horse, and gave the hog and the fed cow † their suppers ; prepared the beds, and undressed the children, and laid them to sleep. I liked to look at her and watch all her doings, for her's was the only friendly face I had as yet seen, and I felt glad that she was there. She gave me my supper of potatoes and milk, and a blanket to sleep upon, which she spread for me in the passage before the door of Mrs. I——'s chamber.

I got a sad fright, that night. I was just going to sleep, when I heard a noise in my mistress's room ; and she presently called out to inquire if some work was finished that she had ordered Hetty to do. " No, Ma'am, not yet," was Hetty's answer from below. On hearing this, my master started up from his bed, and just as he was, in his shirt, ran down stairs with a long cow-skin ‡ in his hand. I heard immediately after, the cracking of the thong, and the house rang to the shrieks of poor Hetty, who kept crying out, " Oh, Massa ! Massa ! me dead. Massa ! have mercy upon me—don't kill me outright."—This was a sad beginning for me. I sat up upon my blanket, trembling with terror, like a frightened hound, and thinking that my turn would come next. At length the house became still, and I forgot for a little while all my sorrows by falling fast asleep.

The next morning my mistress set about instructing me in my tasks. She taught me to do all sorts of household work ; to wash and bake, pick cotton and wool, and wash floors, and cook. And she taught me (how can I ever forget it!) more things than these ; she caused me to know the exact difference between the smart of the rope, the cart-whip, and the cow-skin, when applied to my naked body by her own cruel hand. And there was scarcely any punishment more dreadful than the blows I received on my face and head from her hard heavy fist. She was a fearful woman, and a savage mistress to her slaves.

There were two little slave boys in the house, on whom she vented her bad temper in a special manner. One of these children was a mulatto, called Cyrus, who had been bought while an infant in his mother's arms ; the other, Jack, was an African from the coast of Guinea, whom a sailor had given or sold to my master. Seldom a day passed without

* The cattle on a small plantation in Bermuda are, it seems, often thus staked or tethered, both night and day, in situations where grass abounds.

† A cow fed for slaughter.

‡ A thong of hard twisted hide, known by this name in the West Indies.

these boys receiving the most severe treatment, and often for no fault at all. Both my master and mistress seemed to think that they had a right to ill-use them at their pleasure; and very often accompanied their commands with blows, whether the children were behaving well or ill. I have seen their flesh ragged and raw with licks.—Lick—lick —they were never secure one moment from a blow, and their lives were passed in continual fear. My mistress was not contented with using the whip, but often pinched their cheeks and arms in the most cruel manner. My pity for these poor boys was soon transferred to myself; for I was licked, and flogged, and pinched by her pitiless fingers in the neck and arms, exactly as they were. To strip me naked—to hang me up by the wrists and lay my flesh open with the cow-skin, was an ordinary punishment for even a slight offence. My mistress often robbed me too of the hours that belong to sleep. She used to sit up very late, frequently even until morning; and I had then to stand at a bench and wash during the greater part of the night, or pick wool and cotton; and often I have dropped down overcome by sleep and fatigue, till roused from a state of stupor by the whip, and forced to start up to my tasks.

Poor Hetty, my fellow slave, was very kind to me, and I used to call her my Aunt; but she led a most miserable life, and her death was hastened (at least the slaves all believed and said so,) by the dreadful chastisement she received from my master during her pregnancy. It happened as follows. One of the cows had dragged the rope away from the stake to which Hetty had fastened it, and got loose. My master flew into a terrible passion, and ordered the poor creature to be stripped quite naked, notwithstanding her pregnancy, and to be tied up to a tree in the yard. He then flogged her as hard as he could lick, both with the whip and cow-skin, till she was all over streaming with blood. He rested, and then beat her again and again. Her shrieks were terrible. The consequence was that poor Hetty was brought to bed before her time, and was delivered after severe labour of a dead child. She appeared to recover after her confinement, so far that she was repeatedly flogged by both master and mistress afterwards; but her former strength never returned to her. Ere long her body and limbs swelled to a great size; and she lay on a mat in the kitchen, till the water burst out of her body and she died. All the slaves said that death was a good thing for poor Hetty; but I cried very much for her death. The manner of it filled me with horror. I could not bear to think about it; yet it was always present to my mind for many a day.

After Hetty died all her labours fell upon me, in addition to my own. I had now to milk eleven cows every morning before sunrise, sitting among the damp weeds; to take care of the cattle as well as the children; and to do the work of the house. There was no end to my toils—no end to my blows. I lay down at night and rose up in the morning in fear and sorrow; and often wished that like poor Hetty I could escape from this cruel bondage and be at rest in the grave. But the hand of that God whom then I knew not, was stretched over me; and I was mercifully preserved for better things. It was then, however, my heavy lot to weep, weep, weep, and that for years; to pass from one misery to another, and from one cruel master to a worse. But I must go on with the thread of my story.

One day a heavy squall of wind and rain came on suddenly, and my mistress sent me round the corner of the house to empty a large earthen jar. The jar was already cracked with an old deep crack that divided it in the middle, and in turning it upside down to empty it, it parted in my hand. I could not help the accident, but I was dreadfully frightened, looking forward to a severe punishment. I ran crying to my mistress, " O mistress, the jar has come in two." " You have broken it, have you?" she replied; " come directly here to me." I came trembling: she stripped and flogged me long and severely with the cow-skin; as long as she had strength to use the lash, for she did not give over till she was quite tired.—When my master came home at night, she told him of my fault; and oh, frightful! how he fell a swearing. After abusing me with every ill name he could think of, (too, too bad to speak in England,) and giving me several heavy blows with his hand, he said, " I shall come home to-morrow morning at twelve, on purpose to give you a round hundred." He kept his word—Oh sad for me! I cannot easily forget it. He tied me up upon a ladder, and gave me a hundred lashes with his own hand, and master Benjy stood by to count them for him. When he had licked me for some time he sat down to take breath; then after resting, he beat me again and again, until he was quite wearied, and so hot (for the weather was very sultry), that he sank back in his chair, almost like to faint. While my mistress went to bring him drink, there was a dreadful earthquake. Part of the roof fell down, and every thing in the house went—clatter, clatter, clatter. Oh I thought the end of all things near at hand; and I was so sore with the flogging, that I scarcely cared whether I lived or died. The earth was groaning and shaking; every thing tumbling about; and my mistress and the slaves were shrieking and crying out, " The earthquake! the earthquake!" It was an awful day for us all.

During the confusion I crawled away on my hands and knees, and laid myself down under the steps of the piazza, in front of the house. I was in a dreadful state—my body all blood and bruises, and I could not help moaning piteously. The other slaves, when they saw me, shook their heads and said, " Poor child! poor child!"—I lay there till the morning, careless of what might happen, for life was very weak in me, and I wished more than ever to die. But when we are very young, death always seems a great way off, and it would not come that night to me. The next morning I was forced by my master to rise and go about my usual work, though my body and limbs were so stiff and sore, that I could not move without the greatest pain.—Nevertheless, even after all this severe punishment, I never heard the last of that jar; my mistress was always throwing it in my face.

Some little time after this, one of the cows got loose from the stake, and eat one of the sweet-potatoe slips. I was milking when my master found it out. He came to me, and without any more ado, stooped down, and taking off his heavy boot, he struck me such a severe blow in the small of my back, that I shrieked with agony, and thought I was killed; and I feel a weakness in that part to this day. The cow was frightened at his violence, and kicked down the pail and spilt the milk all about. My master knew that this accident was his own fault, but he was so enraged that he seemed glad of an excuse to go on with his ill usage. I cannot remember how many licks he gave me then, but he beat me till I was unable to stand, and till he himself was weary.

After this I ran away and went to my mother, who was living with Mr. Richard Darrel. My poor mother was both grieved and glad to see me; grieved because I had been so ill used, and glad because she had not seen me for a long, long while. She dared not receive me into the house, but she hid me up in a hole in the rocks near, and brought me food at night, after every body was asleep. My father, who lived at Crow-Lane, over the salt-water channel, at last heard of my being hid up in the cavern, and he came and took me back to my master. Oh I was loth, loth to go back; but as there was no remedy, I was obliged to submit.

When we got home, my poor father said to Capt. I——, " Sir, I am sorry that my child should be forced to run away from her owner; but the treatment she has received is enough to break her heart. The sight of her wounds has nearly broke mine.—I entreat you, for the love of God, to forgive her for running away, and that you will be a kind master to her in future." Capt. I—— said I was used as well as I deserved, and that I ought to be punished for running away. I then took courage and said that I could stand the floggings no longer; that I was weary of my life, and therefore I had run away to my mother; but mothers could only weep and mourn over their children, they could not save them from cruel masters—from the whip, the rope, and the cow-skin. He told me to hold my tongue and go about my work, or he would find a way to settle me. He did not, however, flog me that day.

For five years after this I remained in his house, and almost daily received the same harsh treatment. At length he put me on board a sloop, and to my great joy sent me away to Turk's Island. I was not permitted to see my mother or father, or poor sisters and brothers, to say good bye, though going away to a strange land, and might never see them again. Oh the Buckra people who keep slaves think that black people are like cattle, without natural affection. But my heart tells me it is far otherwise.

We were nearly four weeks on the voyage, which was unusually long. Sometimes we had a light breeze, sometimes a great calm, and the ship made no way; so that our provisions and water ran very low, and we were put upon short allowance. I should almost have been starved had it not been for the kindness of a black man called Anthony, and his wife, who had brought their own victuals, and shared them with me.

When we went ashore at the Grand Quay, the captain sent me to the house of my new master, Mr. D——, to whom Captain I—— had sold me. Grand Quay is a small town upon a sandbank; the houses low and built of wood. Such was my new master's. The first person I saw, on my arrival, was Mr. D——, a stout sulky looking man, who carried me through the hall to show me to his wife and children. Next day I was put up by the vendue master to know how much I was worth, and I was valued at one hundred pounds currency.

My new master was one of the owners or holders of the salt ponds, and he received a certain sum for every slave that worked upon his premises, whether they were young or old. This sum was allowed him out of the profits arising from the salt works. I was immediately sent to work in the salt water with the rest of the slaves. This work was perfectly new to me. I was given a half barrel and a shovel, and had to stand up to my knees in the water, from four o'clock in the morning till nine, when we were given some Indian corn boiled in water, which we were obliged to swallow as fast as we could for fear the rain should come on and melt the salt. We were then called again to our tasks, and worked through the heat of the day; the sun flaming upon our heads like fire, and raising salt blisters in those parts which were not completely covered. Our feet and legs, from standing in the salt water for so many hours, soon became full of dreadful boils, which eat down in some cases to the very bone, afflicting the sufferers with great torment. We came home at twelve; ate our corn soup, called *blawly*, as fast as we could, and went back to our employment till dark at night. We then shovelled up the salt in large heaps, and went down to the sea, where we washed the pickle from our limbs, and cleaned the barrows and shovels from the salt. When we returned to the house, our master gave us each our allowance of raw Indian corn, which we pounded in a mortar and boiled in water for our suppers.

We slept in a long shed, divided into narrow slips, like the stalls used for cattle. Boards fixed upon stakes driven into the ground, without mat or covering, were our only beds. On Sundays, after we had washed the salt bags, and done other work required of us, we went into the bush and cut the long soft grass, of which we made trusses for our legs and feet to rest upon, for they were so full of the salt boils that we could get no rest lying upon the bare boards.

Though we worked from morning till night, there was no satisfying Mr. D——. I hoped, when I left Capt. I——, that I should have been better off, but I found it was but going from one butcher to another. There was this difference between them: my former master used to beat me while raging and foaming with passion; Mr. D—— was usually quite calm. He would stand by and give orders for a slave to be cruelly whipped, and assist in the punishment, without moving a muscle of his face; walking about and taking snuff with the greatest composure. Nothing could touch his hard heart—neither sighs, nor tears, nor prayers, nor streaming blood; he was deaf to our cries, and careless of our sufferings.—Mr. D—— has often stripped me naked, hung me up by the wrists, and beat me with the cow-skin, with his own hand, till my body was raw with gashes. Yet there was nothing very remarkable in this; for it might serve as a sample of the common usage of the slaves on that horrible island.

Owing to the boils in my feet, I was unable to wheel the barrow fast through the sand, which got into the sores, and made me stumble at every step; and my master, having no pity for my sufferings from this cause, rendered them far more intolerable, by chastising me for not being able to move so fast as he wished me. Another of our employments was to row a little way off from the shore in a boat, and dive for large stones to build a wall round our master's house. This was very hard work; and the great waves breaking over us continually, made us often so giddy that we lost our footing, and were in danger of being drowned.

Ah, poor me!—my tasks were never ended. Sick or well, it was work—work—work!—After the diving season was over, we were sent to the South Creek, with large bills, to cut up mangoes to burn lime with. Whilst one party of slaves were thus employed, another were sent to the other side of the island to break up coral out of the sea.

When we were ill, let our complaint be what it might, the only medicine given to us was a great bowl of hot salt water, with salt mixed with it, which made us very sick. If we could not keep up with the rest of the gang of slaves, we were put in the stocks, and severely flogged the next morning. Yet, not the less, our master expected, after we had thus been kept from our rest, and our limbs rendered stiff and sore with ill usage, that we should still go through the ordinary tasks of the day all the same.—Sometimes we had to work all night, measuring salt to load a vessel; or turning a machine to draw water out of the sea for the salt-making. Then we had no sleep—no rest—but were forced to work as fast as we could, and go on again all next day the same as usual. Work—work—work—Oh that Turk's Island was a horrible place! The people in England, I am sure, have never found out what is carried on there. Cruel, horrible place!

Mr. D—— had a slave called old Daniel, whom he used to treat in the most cruel manner. Poor Daniel was lame in the hip, and could not keep up with the rest of the slaves; and our master would order him to be stripped and laid down on the ground, and have him beaten with a rod of rough briar till his skin was quite red and raw. He would then call for a bucket of salt, and fling upon the raw flesh till the man writhed on the ground like a worm, and screamed aloud with agony. This poor man's wounds were never healed, and I have often seen them full of maggots, which increased his torments to an intolerable degree. He was an object of pity and terror to the whole gang of slaves, and in his wretched case we saw, each of us, our own lot, if we should live to be as old.

Oh the horrors of slavery!—How the thought of it pains my heart! But the truth ought to be told of it; and what my eyes have seen I think it is my duty to relate; for few people in England know what slavery is. I have been a slave—I have felt what a slave feels, and I know what a slave knows; and I would have all the good people in England to know it too, that they may break our chains, and set us free.

Mr. D—— had another slave called Ben. He being very hungry, stole a little rice one night after he came in from work, and cooked it for his supper. But his master soon discovered the theft; locked him up all night; and kept him without food till one o'clock the next day. He then hung Ben up by his hands, and beat him from time to time till the slaves came in at night. We found the poor creature hung up when we came home; with a pool of blood beneath him, and our master still licking him. But this was not the worst. My master's son was in the habit of stealing the rice and rum. Ben had seen him do this, and thought he might do the same, and when master found out that Ben had stolen the rice and swore to punish him, he tried to excuse himself by saying that Master Dickey did the same thing every night. The lad denied it to his father, and was so angry with Ben for informing against him, that out of revenge he ran and got a bayonet, and whilst the poor wretch was suspended by his hands and writhing under his wounds, he run it quite through his foot. I was not by when he did it, but I saw the wound when I came home, and heard Ben tell the manner in which it was done.

I must say something more about this cruel son of a cruel father.— He had no heart—no fear of God; he had been brought up by a bad father in a bad path, and he delighted to follow in the same steps. There was a little old woman among the slaves called Sarah, who was nearly past work; and, Master Dickey being the overseer of the slaves just then, this poor creature, who was subject to several bodily infirmities, and was not quite right in her head, did not wheel the barrow fast enough to please him. He threw her down on the ground, and after beating her severely, he took her up in his arms and flung her among the prickly-pear bushes, which are all covered over with sharp venomous prickles. By this her naked flesh was so grievously wounded, that her body swelled and festered all over, and she died a few days after. In telling my own sorrows, I cannot pass by those of my fellow-slaves —for when I think of my own griefs, I remember theirs.

I think it was about ten years I had worked in the salt ponds at Turk's Island, when my master left off business, and retired to a house he had in Bermuda, leaving his son to succeed him in the island. He took me with him to wait upon his daughters; and I was joyful, for I was sick, sick of Turk's Island, and my heart yearned to see my native place again, my mother, and my kindred.

I had seen my poor mother during the time I was a slave in Turk's Island. One Sunday morning I was on the beach with some of the slaves, and we saw a sloop come in loaded with slaves to work in the salt water. We got a boat and went aboard. When I came upon the deck I asked the black people, "Is there any one here for me?" "Yes," they said, "your mother." I thought they said this in jest—I could scarcely believe them for joy; but when I saw my poor mammy my joy was turned to sorrow, for she had gone from her senses. "Mammy," I said, "is this you?" She did not know me. "Mammy," I said, "what's the matter?" She began to talk foolishly, and said that she had been under the vessel's bottom. They had been over-taken by a violent storm at sea. My poor mother had never been on the sea before, and she was so ill, that she lost her senses, and it was long before she came quite to herself again. She had a sweet child with her —a little sister I had never seen, about four years of age, called Rebecca. I took her on shore with me, for I felt I should love her directly; and I kept her with me a week. Poor little thing! her's has been a sad life, and continues so to this day. My mother worked for some years on the island, but was taken back to Bermuda some time before my master carried me again thither.*

* Of the subsequent lot of her relatives she can tell but little. She says, her father died while she and her mother were at Turk's Island; and that he had been long

After I left Turk's Island, I was told by some negroes that came over from it, that the poor slaves had built up a place with boughs and leaves, where they might meet for prayers, but the white people pulled it down twice, and would not allow them even a shed for prayers. A flood came down soon after and washed away many houses, filled the place with sand, and overflowed the ponds: and I do think that this was for their wickedness; for the Buckra men* there were very wicked. I saw and heard much that was very very bad at that place.

I was several years the slave of Mr. D—— after I returned to my native place. Here I worked in the grounds. My work was planting and hoeing sweet-potatoes, Indian corn, plaintains, bananas, cabbages, pumpkins, onions, &c. I did all the household work, and attended upon a horse and cow besides,—going also upon all errands. I had to curry the horse—to clean and feed him—and sometimes to ride him a little. I had more than enough to do—but still it was not so very bad as Turk's Island.

My old master often got drunk, and then he would get in a fury with his daughter, and beat her till she was not fit to be seen. I remember on one occasion, I had gone to fetch water, and when I was coming up the hill I heard a great screaming; I ran as fast as I could to the house, put down the water, and went into the chamber, where I found my master beating Miss D—— dreadfully. I strove with all my strength to get her away from him; for she was all black and blue with bruises. He had beat her with his fist, and almost killed her. The people gave me credit for getting her away. He turned round and began to lick me. Then I said, " Sir, this is not Turk's Island." I can't repeat his answer, the words were too wicked—too bad to say. He wanted to treat me the same in Bermuda as he had done in Turk's Island.

He had an ugly fashion of stripping himself quite naked, and ordering me then to wash him in a tub of water. This was worse to me than all the licks. Sometimes when he called me to wash him I would not come, my eyes were so full of shame. He would then come to beat me. One time I had plates and knives in my hand, and I dropped both plates and knives, and some of the plates were broken. He struck me so severely for this, that at last I defended myself, for I thought it was high time to do so. I then told him I would not live longer with him, for he was a very indecent man—very spiteful, and too indecent; with no shame for his servants, no shame for his own flesh. So I went away to a neighbouring house and sat down and cried till the next morning, when I went home again, not knowing what else to do.

After that I was hired to work at Cedar Hills, and every Saturday night I paid the money to my master. I had plenty of work to do there—

dead and buried before any of his children in Bermuda knew of it, they being slaves on other estates. Her mother died after Mary went to Antigua. Of the fate of the rest of her kindred, seven brothers and three sisters, she knows nothing further than this—that the eldest sister, who had several children to her master, was taken by him to Trinidad; and that the youngest, Rebecca, is still alive, and in slavery in Bermuda. Mary herself is now about forty-three years of age.—*Ed.*

* Negro term for white people.

plenty of washing; but yet I made myself pretty comfortable. I earned two dollars and a quarter a week, which is twenty pence a day.

During the time I worked there, I heard that Mr. John Wood was going to Antigua. I felt a great wish to go there, and I went to Mr. D——, and asked him to let me go in Mr. Wood's service. Mr. Wood did not then want to purchase me; it was my own fault that I came under him, I was so anxious to go. It was ordained to be, I suppose; God led me there. The truth is, I did not wish to be any longer the slave of my indecent master.

Mr. Wood took me with him to Antigua, to the town of St. John's, where he lived. This was about fifteen years ago. He did not then know whether I was to be sold; but Mrs. Wood found that I could work, and she wanted to buy me. Her husband then wrote to my master to inquire whether I was to be sold? Mr. D—— wrote in reply, " that I should not be sold to any one that would treat me ill." It was strange he should say this, when he had treated me so ill himself. So I was purchased by Mr. Wood for 300 dollars, (or £100 Bermuda currency.)*

My work there was to attend the chambers and nurse the child, and to go down to the pond and wash clothes. But I soon fell ill of the rheumatism, and grew so very lame that I was forced to walk with a stick. I got the Saint Anthony's fire, also, in my left leg, and became quite a cripple. No one cared much to come near me, and I was ill a long long time; for several months I could not lift the limb. I had to lie in a little old out-house, that was swarming with bugs and other vermin, which tormented me greatly; but I had no other place to lie in. I got the rheumatism by catching cold at the pond side, from washing in the fresh water; in the salt water I never got cold. The person who lived in next yard, (a Mrs. Greene,) could not bear to hear my cries and groans. She was kind, and used to send an old slave woman to help me, who sometimes brought me a little soup. When the doctor found I was so ill, he said I must be put into a bath of hot water. The old slave got the bark of some bush that was good for the pains, which she boiled in the hot water, and every night she came and put me into the bath, and did what she could for me: I don't know what I should have done, or what would have become of me, had it not been for her. —My mistress, it is true, did send me a little food; but no one from our family came near me but the cook, who used to shove my food in at the door, and say, " Molly, Molly, there's your dinner." My mistress did not care to take any trouble about me; and if the Lord had not put it into the hearts of the neighbours to be kind to me, I must, I really think, have lain and died.

It was a long time before I got well enough to work in the house. Mrs. Wood, in the meanwhile, hired a mulatto woman to nurse the child; but she was such a fine lady she wanted to be mistress over me. I thought it very hard for a coloured woman to have rule over me because I was a slave and she was free. Her name was Martha Wilcox; she was a saucy woman, very saucy; and she went and complained of

---

* About £67. 10s. sterling.

me, without cause, to my mistress, and made her angry with me. Mrs. Wood told me that if I did not mind what I was about, she would get my master to strip me and give me fifty lashes : "You have been used to the whip," she said, " and you shall have it here." This was the first time she threatened to have me flogged ; and she gave me the threatening so strong of what she would have done to me, that I thought I should have fallen down at her feet, I was so vexed and hurt by her words. The mulatto woman was rejoiced to have power to keep me down. She was constantly making mischief ; there was no living for the slaves—no peace after she came.

I was also sent by Mrs. Wood to be put in the Cage one night, and was next morning flogged, by the magistrate's order, at her desire ; and this all for a quarrel I had about a pig with another slave woman. I was flogged on my naked back on this occasion : although I was in no fault after all ; for old Justice Dyett, when we came before him, said that I was in the right, and ordered the pig to be given to me. This was about two or three years after I came to Antigua.

When we moved from the middle of the town to the Point, I used to be in the house and do all the work and mind the children, though still very ill with the rheumatism. Every week I had to wash two large bundles of clothes, as much as a boy could help me to lift ; but I could give no satisfaction. My mistress was always abusing and fretting after me. It is not possible to tell all her ill language.—One day she followed me foot after foot scolding and rating me. I bore in silence a great deal of ill words : at last my heart was quite full, and I told her that she ought not to use me so ;—that when I was ill I might have lain and died for what she cared ; and no one would then come near me to nurse me, because they were afraid of my mistress. This was a great affront. She called her husband and told him what I had said. He flew into a passion : but did not beat me then ; he only abused and swore at me ; and then gave me a note and bade me go and look for an owner. Not that he meant to sell me ; but he did this to please his wife and to frighten me. I went to Adam White, a cooper, a free black, who had money, and asked him to buy me. He went directly to Mr. Wood, but was informed that I was not to be sold. The next day my master whipped me.

Another time (about five years ago) my mistress got vexed with me, because I fell sick and I could not keep on with my work. She complained to her husband, and he sent me off again to look for an owner. I went to a Mr. Burchell, showed him the note, and asked him to buy me for my own benefit ; for I had saved about 100 dollars, and hoped, with a little help, to purchase my freedom. He accordingly went to my master :—" Mr. Wood," he said, " Molly has brought me a note that she wants an owner. If you intend to sell her, I may as well buy her as another." My master put him off and said that he did not mean to sell me. I was very sorry at this, for I had no comfort with Mrs. Wood, and I wished greatly to get my freedom.

The way in which I made my money was this.—When my master and mistress went from home, as they sometimes did, and left me to take care of the house and premises, I had a good deal of time to myself, and made the most of it. I took in washing, and sold coffee and yams and other provisions to the captains of ships. I did not sit still idling during the absence of my owners; for I wanted, by all honest means, to earn money to buy my freedom. Sometimes I bought a hog cheap on board ship, and sold it for double the money on shore; and I also earned a good deal by selling coffee. By this means I by degrees acquired a little cash. A gentleman also lent me some to help to buy my freedom—but when I could not get free he got it back again. His name was Captain Abbot.

My master and mistress went on one occasion into the country, to Date Hill, for change of air, and carried me with them to take charge of the children, and to do the work of the house. While I was in the country, I saw how the field negroes are worked in Antigua. They are worked very hard and fed but scantily. They are called out to work before daybreak, and come home after dark; and then each has to heave his bundle of grass for the cattle in the pen. Then, on Sunday morning, each slave has to go out and gather a large bundle of grass; and, when they bring it home, they have all to sit at the manager's door and wait till he come out: often have they to wait there till past eleven o'clock, without any breakfast. After that, those that have yams or potatoes, or fire-wood to sell, hasten to market to buy a dog's worth * of salt fish, or pork, which is a great treat for them. Some of them buy a little pickle out of the shad barrels, which they call sauce, to season their yams and Indian corn. It is very wrong, I know, to work on Sunday or go to market; but will not God call the Buckra men to answer for this on the great day of judgment—since they will give the slaves no other day?

While we were at Date Hill Christmas came; and the slave woman who had the care of the place (which then belonged to Mr. Roberts the marshal), asked me to go with her to her husband's house, to a Methodist meeting for prayer, at a plantation called Winthorps. I went; and they were the first prayers I ever understood. One woman prayed; and then they all sung a hymn; then there was another prayer and another hymn; and then they all spoke by turns of their own griefs as sinners. The husband of the woman I went with was a black driver. His name was Henry. He confessed that he had treated the slaves very cruelly; but said that he was compelled to obey the orders of his master. He prayed them all to forgive him, and he prayed that God would forgive him. He said it was a horrid thing for a ranger † to have sometimes to beat his own wife or sister; but he must do so if ordered by his master.

I felt sorry for my sins also. I cried the whole night, but I was too much ashamed to speak. I prayed God to forgive me. This meeting had a great impression on my mind, and led my spirit to the Moravian church; so that when I got back to town, I went and prayed to have my name put down in the Missionaries' book; and I followed the church earnestly every opportunity. I did not then tell my mistress about it; for I knew that she would not give me leave to go. But I felt I *must* go.

* A dog is the 72nd part of a dollar.

† The head negro of an estate—a person who has the chief superintendence under the manager.

Whenever I carried the children their lunch at school, I ran round and went to hear the teachers.

The Moravian ladies (Mrs. Richter, Mrs. Olufsen, and Mrs. Sauter) taught me to read in the class; and I got on very fast. In this class there were all sorts of people, old and young, grey headed folks and children; but most of them were free people. After we had done spelling, we tried to read in the Bible. After the reading was over, the missionary gave out a hymn for us to sing. I dearly loved to go to the church, it was so solemn. I never knew rightly that I had much sin till I went there. When I found out that I was a great sinner, I was very sorely grieved, and very much frightened. I used to pray God to pardon my sins for Christ's sake, and forgive me for every thing I had done amiss; and when I went home to my work, I always thought about what I had heard from the missionaries, and wished to be good that I might go to heaven. After a while I was admitted a candidate for the holy Communion.—I had been baptized long before this, in August 1817, by the Rev. Mr. Curtin, of the English Church, after I had been taught to repeat the Creed and the Lord's Prayer. I wished at that time to attend a Sunday School taught by Mr. Curtin, but he would not receive me without a written note from my master, granting his permission. I did not ask my owner's permission, from the belief that it would be refused; so that I got no farther instruction at that time from the English Church.*

Some time after I began to attend the Moravian Church, I met with Daniel James, afterwards my dear husband. He was a carpenter and cooper to his trade; an honest, hard-working, decent black man, and a widower. He had purchased his freedom of his mistress, old Mrs. Baker, with money he had earned whilst a slave. When he asked me to marry him, I took time to consider the matter over with myself, and would not say yes till he went to church with me and joined the Moravians. He was very industrious after he bought his freedom; and he had hired a comfortable house, and had convenient things about him. We were joined in marriage, about Christmas 1826, in the Moravian Chapel at Spring Gardens, by the Rev. Mr. Olufsen. We could not be married in the English Church. English marriage is not allowed to slaves; and no free man can marry a slave woman.

When Mr. Wood heard of my marriage, he flew into a great rage, and sent for Daniel, who was helping to build a house for his old mistress. Mr. Wood asked him who gave him a right to marry a slave of his? My husband said, " Sir, I am a free man, and thought I had a right to choose a wife; but if I had known Molly was not allowed to have a husband, I should not have asked her to marry me." Mrs. Wood was more vexed about my marriage than her husband. She could not for-

* She possesses a copy of Mrs. Trimmer's " Charity School Spelling Book," presented to her by the Rev. Mr. Curtin, and dated August 30, 1817. In this book her name is written " Mary, Princess of Wales"—an appellation which, she says, was given her by her owners. It is a common practice with the colonists to give ridiculous names of this description to their slaves; being, in fact, one of the numberless modes of expressing the habitual contempt with which they regard the negro race.—In printing this narrative we have retained Mary's paternal name of Prince.—*Ed.*

D

give me for getting married, but stirred up Mr. Wood to flog me dreadfully with the horsewhip. I thought it very hard to be whipped at my time of life for getting a husband—I told her so. She said that she would not have nigger men about the yards and premises, or allow a nigger man's clothes to be washed in the same tub where hers were washed. She was fearful, I think, that I should lose her time, in order to wash and do things for my husband: but I had then no time to wash for myself; I was obliged to put out my own clothes, though I was always at the wash-tub.

I had not much happiness in my marriage, owing to my being a slave. It made my husband sad to see me so ill-treated. Mrs. Wood was always abusing me about him. She did not lick me herself, but she got her husband to do it for her, whilst she fretted the flesh off my bones. Yet for all this she would not sell me. She sold five slaves whilst I was with her; but though she was always finding fault with me, she would not part with me. However, Mr. Wood afterwards allowed Daniel to have a place to live in our yard, which we were very thankful for.

After this, I fell ill again with the rheumatism, and was sick a long time; but whether sick or well, I had my work to do. About this time I asked my master and mistress to let me buy my own freedom. With the help of Mr. Burchell, I could have found the means to pay Mr. Wood; for it was agreed that I should afterwards serve Mr. Burchell a while, for the cash he was to advance for me. I was earnest in the request to my owners; but their hearts were hard—too hard to consent. Mrs. Wood was very angry—she grew quite outrageous—she called me a black devil, and asked me who had put freedom into my head. "To be free is very sweet," I said: but she took good care to keep me a slave. I saw her change colour, and I left the room.

About this time my master and mistress were going to England to put their son to school, and bring their daughters home; and they took me with them to take care of the child. I was willing to come to England: I thought that by going there I should probably get cured of my rheumatism, and should return with my master and mistress, quite well, to my husband. My husband was willing for me to come away, for he had heard that my master would free me,—and I also hoped this might prove true; but it was all a false report.

The steward of the ship was very kind to me. He and my husband were in the same class in the Moravian Church. I was thankful that he was so friendly, for my mistress was not kind to me on the passage; and she told me, when she was angry, that she did not intend to treat me any better in England than in the West Indies—that I need not expect it. And she was as good as her word.

When we drew near to England, the rheumatism seized all my limbs worse than ever, and my body was dreadfully swelled. When we landed at the Tower, I shewed my flesh to my mistress, but she took no great notice of it. We were obliged to stop at the tavern till my master got a house; and a day or two after, my mistress sent me down into the wash-house to learn to wash in the English way. In the West Indies we wash with cold water—in England with hot. I told my mistress I was afraid that putting my hands first into the hot water and then into the cold, would increase the pain in my limbs. The doctor had told my mistress long before I came from the West Indies, that I was a sickly body and the washing did not agree with me. But Mrs. Wood would not release me from the tub, so I was forced to do as I could. I grew worse, and could not stand to wash. I was then forced to sit down with the tub before me, and often through pain and weakness was reduced to kneel or to sit down on the floor, to finish my task. When I complained to my mistress of this, she only got into a passion as usual, and said washing in hot water could not hurt any one;—that I was lazy and insolent, and wanted to be free of my work; but that she would make me do it. I thought her very hard on me, and my heart rose up within me. However I kept still at that time, and went down again to wash the child's things; but the English washerwomen who were at work there, when they saw that I was so ill, had pity upon me and washed them for me.

After that, when we came up to live in Leigh Street, Mrs. Wood sorted out five bags of clothes which we had used at sea, and also such as had been worn since we came on shore, for me and the cook to wash. Elizabeth the cook told her, that she did not think that I was able to stand to the tub, and that she had better hire a woman. I also said myself, that I had come over to nurse the child, and that I was sorry I had come from Antigua, since mistress would work me so hard, without compassion for my rheumatism. Mr. and Mrs. Wood, when they heard this, rose up in a passion against me. They opened the door and bade me get out. But I was a stranger, and did not know one door in the street from another, and was unwilling to go away. They made a dreadful uproar, and from that day they constantly kept cursing and abusing me. I was obliged to wash, though I was very ill. Mrs. Wood, indeed once hired a washerwoman, but she was not well treated, and would come no more.

My master quarrelled with me another time, about one of our great washings, his wife having stirred him up to do so. He said he would compel me to do the whole of the washing given out to me, or if I again refused, he would take a short course with me : he would either send me down to the brig in the river, to carry me back to Antigua, or he would turn me at once out of doors, and let me provide for myself. I said I would willingly go back, if he would let me purchase my own freedom. But this enraged him more than all the rest : he cursed and swore at me dreadfully, and said he would never sell my freedom—if I wished to be free, I was free in England, and I might go and try what freedom would do for me, and be d——d. My heart was very sore with this treatment, but I had to go on. I continued to do my work, and did all I could to give satisfaction, but all would not do.

Shortly after, the cook left them, and then matters went on ten times worse. I always washed the child's clothes without being commanded to do it, and any thing else that was wanted in the family; though still I was very sick—very sick indeed. When the great washing came round, which was every two months, my mistress got together again a great many heavy things, such as bed-ticks, bed-coverlets, &c. for me to wash. I told her I was too ill to wash such heavy things that day.

She said, she supposed I thought myself a free woman, but I was not; and if I did not do it directly I should be instantly turned out of doors. I stood a long time before I could answer, for I did not know well what to do. I knew that I was free in England, but I did not know where to go, or how to get my living; and therefore, I did not like to leave the house. But Mr. Wood said he would send for a constable to thrust me out; and at last I took courage and resolved that I would not be longer thus treated, but would go and trust to Providence. This was the fourth time they had threatened t turn me out, and, go where I might, I was determined now to take them at their word; though I thought it very hard, after I had lived with them for thirteen years, and worked for them like a horse, to be driven out in this way, like a beggar. My only fault was being sick, and therefore unable to please my mistress, who thought she never could get work enough out of her slaves; and I told them so: but they only abused me and drove me out. This took place from two to three months, I think, after we came to England.

When I came away, I went to the man (one Mash) who used to black the shoes of the family, and asked his wife to get somebody to go with me to Hatton Garden to the Moravian Missionaries: these were the only persons I knew in England. The woman sent a young girl with me to the mission house, and I saw there a gentleman called Mr. Moore. I told him my whole story, and how my owners had treated me, and asked him to take in my trunk with what few clothes I had. The missionaries were very kind to me—they were sorry for my destitute situation, and gave me leave to bring my things to be placed under their care. They were very good people, and they told me to come to the church.

When I went back to Mr. Wood's to get my trunk, I saw a lady, Mrs. Pell, who was on a visit to my mistress. When Mr. and Mrs. Wood heard me come in, they set this lady to stop me, finding that they had gone too far with me. Mrs. Pell came out to me, and said, " Are you really going to leave, Molly? Don't leave, but come into the country with me." I believe she said this because she thought Mrs. Wood would easily get me back again. I replied to her, " Ma'am, this is the fourth time my master and mistress have driven me out, or threatened to drive me—and I will give them no more occasion to bid me go. I was not willing to leave them, for I am a stranger in this country, but now I must go—I can stay no longer to be so used." Mrs. Pell then went up stairs to my mistress, and told that I would go, and that she could not stop me. Mrs. Wood was very much hurt and frightened when she found I was determined to go out that day. She said, " If she goes the people will rob her, and then turn her adrift." She did not say this to me, but she spoke it loud enough for me to hear; that it might induce me not to go, I suppose. Mr. Wood also asked me where I was going to. I told him where I had been, and that I should never have gone away had I not been driven out by my owners. He had given me a written paper some time before, which said that I had come with them to England by my own desire; and that was true. It said also that I left them of my own free will, because I was a free woman in England; and that

I was idle and would not do my work—which was not true. I gave this paper afterwards to a gentleman who inquired into my case.*

I went into the kitchen and got my clothes out. The nurse and the servant girl were there, and I said to the man who was going to take out my trunk, " Stop, before you take up this trunk, and hear what I have to say before these people. I am going out of this house, as I was ordered ; but I have done no wrong at all to my owners, neither here nor in the West Indies. I always worked very hard to please them, both by night and day ; but there was no giving satisfaction, for my mistress could never be satisfied with reasonable service. I told my mistress I was sick, and yet she has ordered me out of doors. This is the fourth time ; and now I am going out."

And so I came out, and went and carried my trunk to the Moravians. I then returned back to Mash the shoe-black's house, and begged his wife to take me in. I had a little West Indian money in my trunk ; and they got it changed for me. This helped to support me for a little while. The man's wife was very kind to me. I was very sick, and she boiled nourishing things up for me. She also sent for a doctor to see me, and he sent me medicine, which did me good, though I was ill for a long time with the rheumatic pains. I lived a good many months with these poor people, and they nursed me, and did all that lay in their power to serve me. The man was well acquainted with my situation, as he used to go to and fro to Mr. Wood's house to clean shoes and knives ; and he and his wife were sorry for me.

About this time, a woman of the name of Hill told me of the Anti-Slavery Society, and went with me to their office, to inquire if they could do any thing to get me my freedom, and send me back to the West Indies. The gentlemen of the Society took me to a lawyer, who examined very strictly into my case ; but told me that the laws of England could do nothing to make me free in Antigua.† However they did all they could for me : they gave me a little money from time to time to keep me from want ; and some of them went to Mr. Wood to try to persuade him to let me return a free woman to my husband ; but though they offered him, as I have heard, a large sum for my freedom, he was sulky and obstinate, and would not consent to let me go free.

This was the first winter I spent in England, and I suffered much from the severe cold, and from the rheumatic pains, which still at times torment me. However, Providence was very good to me, and I got many friends—especially some Quaker ladies, who hearing of my case, came and sought me out, and gave me good warm clothing and money. Thus I had great cause to bless God in my affliction.

When I got better I was anxious to get some work to do, as I was unwilling to eat the bread of idleness. Mrs. Mash, who was a laundress, recommended me to a lady for a charwoman. She paid me very handsomely for what work I did, and I divided the money with Mrs.

* See page 24.

† She came first to the Anti-Slavery Office in Aldermanbury, about the latter end of November 1828 ; and her case was referred to Mr. George Stephen to be investigated. More of this hereafter.—ED.

Mash; for though very poor, they gave me food when my own money was done, and never suffered me to want.

In the spring, I got into service with a lady, who saw me at the house where I sometimes worked as a charwoman. This lady's name was Mrs. Forsyth. She had been in the West Indies, and was accustomed to Blacks, and liked them. I was with her six months, and went with her to Margate. She treated me well, and gave me a good character when she left London.*

After Mrs. Forsyth went away, I was again out of place, and went to lodgings, for which I paid two shillings a week, and found coals and candle. After eleven weeks, the money I had saved in service was all gone, and I was forced to go back to the Anti-Slavery office to ask a supply, till I could get another situation. I did not like to go back— I did not like to be idle. I would rather work for my living than get it for nothing. They were very good to give me a supply, but I felt shame at being obliged to apply for relief whilst I had strength to work.

At last I went into the service of Mr. and Mrs. Pringle, where I have been ever since, and am as comfortable as I can be while separated from my dear husband, and away from my own country and all old friends and connections. My dear mistress teaches me daily to read the word of God, and takes great pains to make me understand it. I enjoy the great privilege of being enabled to attend church three times on the Sunday; and I have met with many kind friends since I have been here, both clergymen and others. The Rev. Mr. Young, who lives in the next house, has shown me much kindness, and taken much pains to instruct me, particularly while my master and mistress were absent in Scotland. Nor must I forget, among my friends, the Rev. Mr. Mortimer, the good clergyman of the parish, under whose ministry I have now sat for upwards of twelve months. I trust in God I have profited by what I have heard from him. He never keeps back the truth, and I think he has been the means of opening my eyes and ears much better to understand the word of God. Mr. Mortimer tells me that he cannot open the eyes of my heart, but that I must pray to God to change my heart, and make me to know the truth, and the truth will make me free.

I still live in the hope that God will find a way to give me my liberty, and give me back to my husband. I endeavour to keep down my fretting, and to leave all to Him, for he knows what is good for me better than I know myself. Yet, I must confess, I find it a hard and heavy task to do so.

I am often much vexed, and I feel great sorrow when I hear some people in this country say, that the slaves do not need better usage, and do not want to be free.† They believe the foreign people,‡ who deceive them, and say slaves are happy. I say, Not so. How can slaves be happy when they have the halter round their neck and the

* She refers to a written certificate which will be inserted afterwards.

† The whole of this paragraph especially, is given as nearly as was possible in Mary's precise words.

‡ She means West Indians.

whip upon their back? and are disgraced and thought no more of than beasts?—and are separated from their mothers, and husbands, and children, and sisters, just as cattle are sold and separated? Is it happiness for a driver in the field to take down his wife or sister or child, and strip them, and whip them in such a disgraceful manner? —women that have had children exposed in the open field to shame! There is no modesty or decency shown by the owner to his slaves; men, women, and children are exposed alike. Since I have been here I have often wondered how English people can go out into the West Indies and act in such a beastly manner. But when they go to the West Indies, they forget God and all feeling of shame, I think, since they can see and do such things. They tie up slaves like hogs—moor* them up like cattle, and they lick them, so as hogs, or cattle, or horses never were flogged;—and yet they come home and say, and make some good people believe, that slaves don't want to get out of slavery. But they put a cloak about the truth. It is not so. All slaves want to be free—to be free is very sweet. I will say the truth to English people who may read this history that my good friend, Miss S——, is now writing down for me. I have been a slave myself—I know what slaves feel—I can tell by myself what other slaves feel, and by what they have told me. The man that says slaves be quite happy in slavery—that they don't want to be free—that man is either ignorant or a lying person. I never heard a slave say so. I never heard a Buckra man say so, till I heard tell of it in England. Such people ought to be ashamed of themselves. They can't do without slaves, they say. What's the reason they can't do without slaves as well as in England? No slaves here— no whips—no stocks—no punishment, except for wicked people. They hire servants in England; and if they don't like them, they send them away: they can't lick them. Let them work ever so hard in England, they are far better off than slaves. If they get a bad master, they give warning and go hire to another. They have their liberty. That's just what *we* want. We don't mind hard work, if we had proper treatment, and proper wages like English servants, and proper time given in the week to keep us from breaking the Sabbath. But they won't give it: they will have work—work—work, night and day, sick or well, till we are quite done up; and we must not speak up nor look amiss, however much we be abused. And then when we are quite done up, who cares for us, more than for a lame horse? This is slavery. I tell it, to let English people know the truth; and I hope they will never leave off to pray God, and call loud to the great King of England, till all the poor blacks be given free, and slavery done up for evermore.

* A West Indian phrase: to fasten or tie up.

SUPPLEMENT

TO THE

HISTORY OF MARY PRINCE.

———

BY THE EDITOR.

———

Leaving Mary's narrative, for the present, without comment to the reader's reflections, I proceed to state some circumstances connected with her case which have fallen more particularly under my own notice, and which I consider it incumbent now to lay fully before the public.

About the latter end of November, 1828, this poor woman found her way to the office of the Anti-Slavery Society in Aldermanbury, by the aid of a person who had become acquainted with her situation, and had advised her to apply there for advice and assistance. After some preliminary examination into the accuracy of the circumstances related by her, I went along with her to Mr. George Stephen, solicitor, and requested him to investigate and draw up a statement of her case, and have it submitted to counsel, in order to ascertain whether or not, under the circumstances, her freedom could be legally established on her return to Antigua. On this occasion, in Mr. Stephen's presence and mine, she expressed, in very strong terms, her anxiety to return thither if she could go as a free person, and, at the same time, her extreme apprehensions of the fate that would probably await her if she returned as a slave. Her words were, " I would rather go into my grave than go back a slave to Antigua, though I wish to go back to my husband very much—very much—very much ! I am much afraid my owners would separate me from my husband, and use me very hard, or perhaps sell me for a field negro;—and slavery is too too bad. I would rather go into my grave !"

The paper which Mr. Wood had given her before she left his house, was placed by her in Mr. Stephen's hands. It was expressed in the following terms :—

" I have already told Molly, and now give it her in writing, in order that there may be no misunderstanding on her part, that as I brought her from Antigua at her own request and entreaty, and that she is consequently now free, she is of course at liberty to take her baggage and go where she pleases. And, in consequence of her late conduct, she must do one of two things—either quit the house, or return to Antigua by the earliest opportunity, as she does not evince a disposition to make herself useful. As she is a stranger in London, I do not wish to turn her out, or would do so, as two female servants are sufficient for my establishment. If after this she does remain, it will be only during her good behaviour : but on no consideration will I allow her wages or any other remuneration for her services.   " JOHN A. WOOD."

" London, August 18, 1828."

This paper, though not devoid of inconsistencies, which will be apparent to any attentive reader, is craftily expressed ; and was well devised to serve the purpose which the writer had obviously in view, namely, to frustrate any appeal which the friendless black woman might make to the sympathy of strangers, and thus prevent her from obtaining an asylum, if she left his house, from any respectable family. As she had no one to refer to for a character in this country except himself, he doubtless calculated securely on her being speedily driven back, as soon as the slender fund she had in her possession was expended, to throw herself unconditionally upon his tender mercies ; and his disappointment in this expectation appears to have exasperated his feelings of resentment towards the poor woman, to a degree which few persons alive to the claims of common justice, not to speak of christianity or common humanity, could easily have anticipated. Such, at least, seems the only intelligible inference that can be drawn from his subsequent conduct.

The case having been submitted, by desire of the Anti-Slavery Committee, to the consideration of Dr. Lushington and Mr. Sergeant Stephen, it was found that there existed no legal means of compelling Mary's master to grant her manumission ; and that if she returned to Antigua, she would inevitably fall again under his power, or that of his attorneys, as a slave. It was, however, resolved to try what could be effected for her by amicable negotiation ; and with this view Mr. Ravenscroft, a solicitor, (Mr. Stephen's relative,) called upon Mr. Wood, in order to ascertain whether he would consent to Mary's manumission on any reasonable terms, and to refer, if required, the amount of compensation for her value to arbitration. Mr. Ravenscroft with some difficulty obtained one or two interviews, but found Mr. Wood so full of animosity against the woman, and so firmly bent against any arrangement having her freedom for its object, that the negotiation was soon broken off as hopeless. The angry slave-owner declared " that he would not move a finger about her in this country, or grant her manumission on any terms whatever ; and that if she went back to the West Indies, she must take the consequences."

This unreasonable conduct of Mr. Wood, induced the Anti-Slavery Committee, after several other abortive attempts to effect a compromise, to think of bringing the case under the notice of Parliament. The heads of Mary's statement were accordingly engrossed in a Petition, which Dr. Lushington offered to present, and to give notice at the same time of his intention to bring in a Bill to provide for the entire emancipation of all slaves brought to England with the owner's consent. But before this step was taken, Dr. Lushington again had recourse to negociation with the master ; and, partly through the friendly intervention of Mr. Manning, partly by personal conference, used every persuasion in his power to induce Mr. Wood to relent ánd let the bondwoman go free.

E

Seeing the matter thus seriously taken up, Mr. Wood became at length alarmed,—not relishing, it appears, the idea of having the case publicly discussed in the House of Commons; and to avert this result he submitted to temporize—assumed a demeanour of unwonted civility, and even hinted to Mr. Manning (as I was given to understand) that if he was not driven to utter hostility by the threatened exposure, he would probably meet our wishes " in his own time and way." Having gained time by these manœuvres, he adroitly endeavoured to cool the ardour of Mary's new friends, in her cause, by representing her as an abandoned and worthless woman, ungrateful towards him, and undeserving of sympathy from others; allegations which he supported by the ready affirmation of some of his West India friends, and by one or two plausible letters procured from Antigua. By these and like artifices he appears completely to have imposed on Mr. Manning, the respectable West India merchant whom Dr. Lushington had asked to negotiate with him; and he prevailed so far as to induce Dr. Lushington himself (actuated by the benevolent view of thereby best serving Mary's cause,) to abstain from any remarks upon his conduct when the petition was at last presented in Parliament. In this way he dextrously contrived to neutralize all our efforts, until the close of the Session of 1829; soon after which he embarked with his family for the West Indies.

Every exertion for Mary's relief having thus failed; and being fully convinced from a twelvemonth's observation of her conduct, that she was really a well-disposed and respectable woman; I engaged her, in December 1829, as a domestic servant in my own family. In this capacity she has remained ever since; and I am thus enabled to speak of her conduct and character with a degree of confidence I could not have otherwise done. The importance of this circumstance will appear in the sequel.

From the time of Mr. Wood's departure to Antigua, in 1829, till June or July last, no farther effort was attempted for Mary's relief. Some faint hope was still cherished that this unconscionable man would at length relent, and " in his own time and way," grant the prayer of the exiled negro woman. After waiting, however, nearly twelvemonths longer, and seeing the poor woman's spirits daily sinking under the sickening influence of hope deferred, I resolved on a final attempt in her behalf, through the intervention of the Moravian Missionaries, and of the Governor of Antigua. At my request, Mr. Edward Moore, agent of the Moravian Brethren in London, wrote to the Rev. Joseph Newby, their Missionary in that island, empowering him to negotiate in his own name with Mr. Wood for Mary's manumission, and to procure his consent, if possible, upon terms of ample pecuniary compensation. At the same time the excellent and benevolent William Allen, of the Society of Friends, wrote to Sir Patrick Ross, the Governor of the Colony, with whom he was on terms of friendship, soliciting him to use his influence in persuading Mr. Wood to consent: and I confess I was sanguine enough to flatter myself that we should thus at length prevail. The result proved, however, that I had not yet fully appreciated the character of the man we had to deal with.

Mr. Newby's answer arrived early in November last, mentioning that he had done all in his power to accomplish our purpose, but in vain; and that if Mary's manumission could not be obtained without Mr. Wood's consent, he believed there was no prospect of its ever being effected.

A few weeks afterwards I was informed by Mr. Allen, that he had received a letter from Sir Patrick Ross, stating that he also had used his best endeavours in the affair, but equally without effect. Sir Patrick at the same time inclosed a letter, addressed by Mr. Wood to his Secretary, Mr. Taylor, assigning his reasons for persisting in this extraordinary course. This letter requires our special attention. Its tenor is as follows:—

" My dear Sir,

" In reply to your note relative to the woman Molly, I beg you will have the kindness to oblige me by assuring his Excellency that I regret exceedingly my inability to comply with his request, which under other circumstances would afford me very great pleasure.

" There are many and powerful reasons for inducing me to refuse my sanction to her returning here in the way she seems to wish. It would be to reward the worst species of ingratitude, and subject myself to insult whenever she came in my way. Her moral character is very bad, as the police records will shew; and she would be a very troublesome character should she come here without any restraint. She is not a native of this country, and I know of no relation she has here. I induced her to take a husband, a short time before she left this, by providing a comfortable house in my yard for them, and prohibiting her going out after 10 to 12 o'clock (our bed-time) without special leave. This she considered the greatest, and indeed the only, grievance she ever complained of, and all my efforts could not prevent it. In hopes of inducing her to be steady to her husband, who was a free man, I gave him the house to occupy during our absence; but it appears the attachment was too loose to bind her, and he has taken another wife: so on that score I do her no injury.—In England she made her election, and quitted my family. This I had no right to object to; and I should have thought no more of it, but not satisfied to leave quietly, she gave every trouble and annoyance in her power, and endeavoured to injure the character of my family by the most vile and infamous falsehoods, which was embodied in a petition to the House of Commons, and would have been presented, had not my friends from this island, particularly the Hon. Mr. Byam and Dr. Coull, come forward, and disproved what she had asserted.

" It would be beyond the limits of an ordinary letter to detail her baseness, though I will do so should his Excellency wish it; but you may judge of her depravity by one circumstance, which came out before Mr. Justice Dyett, in a quarrel with another female.

* * * * * , * * * * *

" Such a thing I could not have believed possible. *

" Losing her value as a slave in a pecuniary point of view I consider of no consequence; for it was our intention, had she conducted herself properly and returned with us, to have given her freedom. She has taken her freedom; and all I wish is, that she would enjoy it without meddling with me.

" Let me again repeat, if his Excellency wishes it, it will afford me great plea-

---

* I omit the circumstance here mentioned, because it is too indecent to appear in a publication likely to be perused by females. It is, in all probability, a vile calumny; but even if it were perfectly true, it would not serve Mr. Wood's case one straw.—Any reader who wishes it, may see the passage referred to, in the autograph letter in my possession. T. P.

sure to state such particulars of her, and which will be incontestably proved by numbers here, that I am sure will acquit me in his opinion of acting unkind or ungenerous towards her. I'll say nothing of the liability I should incur, under the Consolidated Slave Law, of dealing with a free person as a slave.

" My only excuse for entering so much into detail must be that of my anxious wish to stand justified in his Excellency's opinion.

" I am, my dear Sir,

Yours very truly,

JOHN A. WOOD.

" 20th Oct. 1830."

" *Charles Taylor, Esq.*

&c. &c. &c.

" I forgot to mention that it was at her own special request that she accompanied me to England—and also that she had a considerable sum of money with her, which she had saved in my service. I knew of £36 to £40, at least, for I had some trouble to recover it from a white man, to whom she had lent it.

" J. A. W."

Such is Mr. Wood's justification of his conduct in thus obstinately refusing manumission to the Negro-woman who had escaped from his " house of bondage."

Let us now endeavour to estimate the validity of the excuses assigned, and the allegations advanced by him, for the information of Governor Sir Patrick Ross, in this deliberate statement of his case.

1. To allow the woman to return home free, would, he affirms " be to reward the worst species of ingratitude."

He assumes, it seems, the sovereign power of pronouncing a virtual sentence of banishment, for the alleged crime of ingratitude. Is this then a power which any man ought to possess over his fellow-mortal? or which any good man would ever wish to exercise? And, besides, there is no evidence whatever, beyond Mr. Wood's mere assertion, that Mary Prince owed him or his family the slightest mark of gratitude. Her account of the treatment she received in his service, *may* be incorrect; but her simple statement is at least supported by minute and feasible details, and, unless rebutted by positive facts, will certainly command credence from impartial minds more readily than his angry accusation, which has something absurd and improbable in its very front. Moreover, is it not absurd to term the assertion of her *natural rights* by a slave,—even supposing her to have been kindly dealt with by her " owners," and treated in every respect the reverse of what Mary affirms to have been her treatment by Mr. Wood and his wife,—" the *worst* species of ingratitude?" This may be West Indian ethics, but it will scarcely be received as sound doctrine in Europe.

2. To permit her return would be " to subject himself to insult whenever she came in his way."

This is a most extraordinary assertion. Are the laws of Antigua then so favourable to the free blacks, or the colonial police so feebly administered, that there are no sufficient restraints to protect a rich colonist like Mr. Wood,—a man who counts among his familiar friends the Honourable Mr. Byam, and Mr. Taylor the Government Secretary,—from being insulted by a poor Negro-woman? It is preposterous.

3. Her moral character is so bad, that she would prove very troublesome should she come to the colony " without any restraint."

"Any restraint?" Are there no restraints (supposing them necessary) short of absolute slavery to keep "troublesome characters" in order? But this, I suppose, is the *argumentum ad gubernatorem*—to frighten the governor. She is such a termagant, it seems, that if she once gets back to the colony *free*, she will not only make it too hot for poor Mr. Wood, but the police and courts of justice will scarce be a match for her! Sir Patrick Ross, no doubt, will take care how he intercedes farther for so formidable a virago! How can one treat such arguments seriously?

4. She is not a native of the colony, and he knows of no relation she has there.

True: But was it not her home (so far as a slave can have a home) for thirteen or fourteen years? Were not the connexions, friendships, and associations of her mature life formed there? Was it not there she hoped to spend her latter years in domestic tranquillity with her husband, free from the lash of the taskmaster? These considerations may appear light to Mr. Wood, but they are every thing to this poor woman.

5. He induced her, he says, to take a husband, a short time before she left Antigua, and gave them a comfortable house in his yard, &c. &c.

This paragraph merits attention. He "*induced her to take a husband?*" If the fact were true, what brutality of mind and manners does it not indicate among these slave-holders? They refuse to legalize the marriages of their slaves, but *induce* them to form such temporary connexions as may suit the owner's conveniency, just as they would pair the lower animals; and this man has the effrontery to tell us so! Mary, however, tells a very different story, (see page 17;) and her assertion, independently of other proof, is at least as credible as Mr. Wood's. The reader will judge for himself as to the preponderance of internal evidence in the conflicting statements.

6. He alleges that she was, before marriage, licentious, and even depraved in her conduct, and unfaithful to her husband afterwards.

These are serious charges. But if true, or even partially true, how comes it that a person so correct in his family hours and arrangements as Mr. Wood professes to be, and who expresses so edifying a horror of licentiousness, could reconcile it to his conscience to keep in the bosom of his family so *depraved*, as well as so *troublesome* a character for at least thirteen years, and confide to her for long periods too the charge of his house and the care of his children—for such I shall shew to have been the facts? How can he account for not having rid himself with all speed, of so disreputable an inmate—he who values her loss so little "in a pecuniary point of view?" How can he account for having sold *five other slaves* in that period, and yet have retained this shocking woman—nay, even have refused to sell her, on more than one occasion, when offered her full value? It could not be from ignorance of her character, for the circumstance which he adduces as a proof of her shameless depravity, and which I have omitted on account of its indecency, occurred, it would appear, not less than *ten years ago*. Yet, notwithstanding her alleged ill qualities and habits of gross immorality, he has not only constantly refused to part with her; but after thirteen long years, brings her to England as an attendant on his wife and children, with the avowed intention of carrying her back along with his maiden daughter, a young lady returning from school! Such are the extraordinary facts; and until Mr. Wood shall reconcile these singular inconsistencies between his actions and his allegations, he must not be surprised if we in England prefer giving credit to the former rather than the latter; although at present it appears somewhat difficult to say which side of the alternative is the more creditable to his own character.

7. Her husband, he says, has taken another wife; " so that on that score," he adds, " he does her no injury."

Supposing this fact be true, (which I doubt, as I doubt every mere assertion from so questionable a quarter,) I shall take leave to put a question or two to Mr. Wood's conscience. Did he not write from England to his friend Mr. Darrel, soon after Mary left his house, directing him to turn her husband, Daniel James, off his premises, on account of her offence; telling him to inform James at the same time that his wife had *taken up* with another man, who had robbed her of all she had—a calumny as groundless as it was cruel? I further ask if the person who invented this story (whoever he may be,) was not likely enough to impose similar fabrications on the poor negro man's credulity, until he may have been induced to prove false to his marriage vows, and to " take another wife," as Mr. Wood coolly expresses it? But withal, I strongly doubt the fact of Daniel James' infidelity; for there is now before me a letter from himself to Mary, dated in April 1830, couched in strong terms of conjugal affection; expressing his anxiety for her speedy return, and stating that he had lately " received a grace" (a token of religious advancement) in the Moravian church, a circumstance altogether incredible if the man were living in open adultery, as Mr. Wood's assertion implies.

8. Mary, he says, endeavoured to injure the character of his family by infamous falsehoods, which were embodied in a petition to the House of Commons, and would have been presented, had not his friends from Antigua, the Hon. Mr. Byam, and Dr. Coull, disproved her assertions.

I can say something on this point from my own knowledge. Mary's petition contained simply a brief statement of her case, and, among other things, mentioned the treatment she had received from Mr. and Mrs. Wood. Now the principal facts are corroborated by other evidence, and Mr. Wood must bring forward very different testimony from that of Dr. Coull before well-informed persons will give credit to his contradiction. The value of that person's evidence in such cases will be noticed presently. Of the Hon. Mr. Byam I know nothing, and shall only at present remark that it is not likely to redound greatly to his credit to appear in such company. Furthermore, Mary's petition *was* presented, as Mr. Wood ought to know; though it was not discussed, nor his conduct exposed as it ought to have been.

9. He speaks of the liability he should incur, under the Consolidated Slave Law, of dealing with a free person as a slave.

Is not this pretext hypocritical in the extreme? What liabiltiy could he possibly incur by voluntarily resigning the power, conferred on him by an iniquitous colonial law, of re-imposing the shackles of slavery on the bondwoman from whose limbs they had fallen when she touched the free soil of England ?—There exists no liability from which he might not have been easily secured, or for which he would not have been fully compensated.

He adds in a postscript that Mary had a considerable sum of money with her,—from £36 to £40 at least, which she had saved in his service. The fact is, that she had at one time 113 dollars in cash; but only a very small portion of that sum appears to have been brought by her to England, the rest having been partly advanced, as she states, to assist her husband, and partly lost by being lodged in unfaithful custody.

Finally, Mr. Wood repeats twice that it will afford him great pleasure to state for the governor's satisfaction, if required, such particulars of " the woman Molly," upon incontestable evidence, as he is sure will acquit him in his Excellency's opinion " of acting unkind or ungenerous towards her."

This is well: and I now call upon Mr. Wood to redeem his pledge; —to bring forward facts and proofs fully to elucidate the subject; —to reconcile, if he can, the extraordinary discrepancies which I have pointed out between his assertions and the actual facts, and especially between his account of Mary Prince's character and his own conduct in regard to her. He has now to produce such a statement as will acquit him not only in the opinion of Sir Patrick Ross, but of the British public. And in this position he has spontaneously placed himself, in attempting to destroy, by his deliberate criminatory letter, the poor woman's fair fame and reputation,—an attempt but for which the present publication would probably never have appeared.

Here perhaps we might safely leave the case to the judgment of the public; but as this negro woman's character, not the less valuable to her because her condition is so humble, has been so unscrupulously blackened by her late master, a party so much interested and inclined to place her in the worst point of view,—it is incumbent on me, as her advocate with the public, to state such additional testimony in her behalf as I can fairly and conscientiously adduce.

My first evidence is Mr. Joseph Phillips, of Antigua. Having submitted to his inspection Mr. Wood's letter and Mary Prince's narrative, and requested his candid and deliberate sentiments in regard to the actual facts of the case, I have been favoured with the following letter from him on the subject:—

" London, January 18, 1831.

" Dear Sir,

" In giving you my opinion of Mary Prince's narrative, and of Mr. Wood's letter respecting her, addressed to Mr. Taylor, I shall first mention my opportunities of forming a proper estimate of the conduct and character of both parties

" I have known Mr. Wood since his first arrival in Antigua in 1803. He was then a poor young man, who had been brought up as a ship carpenter in Bermuda. He was afterwards raised to be a clerk in the Commissariat department, and realised sufficient capital to commence business as a merchant. This last profession he has followed successfully for a good many years, and is understood to have accumulated very considerable wealth. After he entered into trade, I had constant intercourse with him in the way of business; and in 1824 and 1825, I was regularly employed on his premises as his clerk; consequently, I had opportunities of seeing a good deal of his character both as a merchant and as a master of slaves. The former topic I pass over as irrelevant to the present subject: in reference to the latter, I shall merely observe that he was not, in regard to ordinary matters, more severe than the ordinary run of slave owners ; but, if seriously offended, he was not of a disposition to be easily appeased, and would spare no cost or sacrifice to gratify his vindictive feelings. As regards the exaction of work from domestic slaves, his wife was probably more severe than himself—it was almost impossible for the slaves ever to give her entire satisfaction.

" Of their slave Molly (or Mary) I know less than of Mr. and Mrs. Wood ; but I saw and heard enough of her, both while I was constantly employed on Mr. Wood's premises, and while I was there occasionally on business, to be quite certain that she was viewed by her owners as their most respectable and trustworthy female slave. It is within my personal knowledge that she had usually the charge of the house in their absence, was entrusted with the keys, &c. ; and was always considered by the neighbours and visitors as their confidential household servant, and as a person in whose integrity they placed unlimited confidence,—although when Mrs.Wood was at home, she was no doubt kept pretty closely at washing and other hard work. A decided proof of the estimation in which she was held by her owners exists in the fact that Mr. Wood uniformly refused to part with her, whereas he sold five other slaves while she was with them. Indeed, she always appeared to me to be a slave of superior intelligence and respectability ; and I always understood such to be her general character in the place.

" As to what Mr. Wood alleges about her being frequently before the police, &c. I can only say I never heard of the circumstance before ; and as I lived for twenty years in the same small town, and in the vicinity of their residence, I think I could scarcely have failed to become acquainted with it, had such been the fact. She might, however, have been occasionally before the magistrate in consequence of little disputes among the slaves, without any serious imputation on her general respectability. She says she was twice summoned to appear as a witness on such occasions ; and that she was once sent by her mistress to be confined in the Cage, and was afterwards flogged by her desire. This cruel practice is very common in Antigua ; and, in my opinion, is but little creditable to the slave owners and magistrates by whom such arbitrary punishments are inflicted, frequently for very trifling faults. Mr. James Scotland is the only magistrate in the colony who invariably refuses to sanction this reprehensible practice.

" Of the immoral conduct ascribed to Molly by Mr. Wood, I can say nothing further than this—that I have heard she had at a former period (previous to her marriage) a connexion with a white person, a Capt. ———, which I have no doubt was broken off when she became seriously impressed with religion. But, at any rate, such connexions are so common, I might almost say universal, in our slave colonies, that except by the missionaries and a few serious persons, they are considered, if faults at all, so very venial as scarcely to deserve the name of immorality. Mr. Wood knows this colonial estimate of such connexions as well as I do ; and, however false such an estimate must be allowed to be, especially when applied to their own conduct by persons of education, pretending to adhere to the pure Christian rule of morals,—yet when he ascribes to a negro slave, to whom legal marriage was denied, such great criminality for laxity of this sort, and professes to be so exceedingly shocked and amazed at the tale he himself relates, he must, I am confident, have had a farther object in view than the information of Mr. Taylor or Sir Patrick Ross. He must, it is evident, have been aware that his letter would be sent to Mr. Allen, and accordingly adapted it, as more important documents from the colonies are often adapted, *for effect in England.* The tale of the slave Molly's immoralities, be assured, was not intended for Antigua so much as for Stoke Newington, and Peckham, and Aldermanbury.

" In regard to Mary's narrative generally, although I cannot speak to the accuracy of the details, except in a few recent particulars, I can with safety declare that I see no reason to question the truth of a single fact stated by her, or even to suspect her in any instance of intentional exaggeration. It bears in my judgment the genuine stamp of truth and nature. Such is my unhesitating opinion, after a residence of twenty-seven years in the West Indies.

To T. Pringle, Esq.   "I remain, &c.   "JOSEPH PHILLIPS."

"P. S. As Mr. Wood refers to the evidence of Dr. T. Coull in opposition to Mary's assertions, it may be proper to enable you justly to estimate the worth of that person's evidence in cases connected with the condition and treatment of slaves. You are aware that in 1829, Mr. M'Queen of Glasgow, in noticing a Report of the "Ladies' Society of Birmingham for the relief of British Negro Slaves," asserted with his characteristic audacity, that the statement which it contained respecting distressed and deserted slaves in Antigua was "an abominable falsehood." Not contented with this, and with insinuating that I, as agent of the society in the distribution of their charity in Antigua, had fraudulently duped them out of their money by a fabricated tale of distress, Mr. M'Queen proceeded to libel me in the most opprobrious terms, as "a man of the most worthless and abandoned character."* Now I know from good authority that

---

* In elucidation of the circumstances above referred to, I subjoin the following extracts from the Report of the Birmingham Ladies' Society for 1830 :—

"As a portion of the funds of this association has been appropriated to assist the benevolent efforts of a society which has for fifteen years afforded relief to distressed and deserted slaves in Antigua, it may not be uninteresting to our friends to learn the manner in which the agent of this society has been treated for simply obeying the command of our Saviour, by ministering, like the good Samaritan, to the distresses of the helpless and the desolate. The society's proceedings being adverted to by a friend of Africa, at one of the public meetings held in this country, a West Indian planter, who was present, wrote over to his friends in Antigua, and represented the conduct of the distributors of this charity in such a light, that it was deemed worthy of the cognizance of the House of Assembly. Mr. Joseph Phillips, a resident of the island, who had most kindly and disinterestedly exerted himself in the distribution of the money from England among the poor deserted slaves, was brought before the Assembly, and most severely interrogated : on his refusing to deliver up his private correspondence with his friends in England, he was thrown into a loathsome jail, where he was kept for nearly five months; while his loss of business, and the oppressive proceedings instituted against him, were involving him in poverty and ruin. On his discharge by the House of Assembly, he was seized in their lobby for debt, and again imprisoned."

"In our report for the year 1826, we quoted a passage from the 13th Report of the Society for the relief of deserted Slaves in the island of Antigua, in reference to a case of great distress. This statement fell into the hands of Mr. M'Queen, the Editor of the Glasgow Courier. Of the consequences resulting from this circumstance we only gained information through the Leicester Chronicle, which had copied an article from the Weekly Register of Antigua, dated St. John's, September 22, 1829. We find from this that Mr. M'Queen affirms, that 'with the exception of the fact that the society is, as it deserves to be, duped out of its money, the whole tale' (of the distress above referred to) 'is an abominable falsehood.' This statement, which we are informed has appeared in many of the public papers, is COMPLETELY REFUTED in our Appendix, No. 4, to which we refer our readers. Mr. M'Queen's statements, we regret to say, would lead many to believe that there are no deserted Negroes to assist; and that the case mentioned was a perfect fabrication. He also distinctly avers, that the disinterested and humane agent of the society, Mr. Joseph Phillips, is 'a man of the most worthless and abandoned character.' In opposition to this statement, we learn the good character of Mr. Phillips from those who have long been acquainted with his laudable exertions in the cause of humanity, and from the Editor of the Weekly Register of Antigua, who speaks, on his own knowledge,

it was *upon Dr. Coull's information* that Mr. M'Queen founded this impudent contradiction of notorious facts, and this audacious libel of my personal character. From this single circumstance you may judge of the value of his evidence in the case of Mary Prince. I can furnish further information respecting Dr. Coull's colonial proceedings, both private and judicial, should circumstances require it." "J. P."

I leave the preceding letter to be candidly weighed by the reader in opposition to the inculpatory allegations of Mr. Wood—merely remarking that Mr. Wood will find it somewhat difficult to impugn the evidence of Mr. Phillips, whose " upright," " unimpeached," and " unexceptionable" character, he has himself vouched for in unqualified terms, by affixing his signature to the testimonial published in the Weekly Register of Antigua in 1825. (See Note below.)

The next testimony in Mary's behalf is that of Mrs. Forsyth, a lady in whose service she spent the summer of 1829.—(See page 21.) This lady, on leaving London to join her husband, voluntarily presented Mary with a certificate, which, though it relates only to a recent and short period of her history, is a strong corroboration of the habitual respectability of her character. It is in the following terms :—

" Mrs. Forsyth states, that the bearer of this paper (Mary James,) has been with her for the last six months ; that she has found her an excellent character, being honest, industrious, and sober ; and that she parts with her on no other account than this—that being obliged to travel with her husband, who has lately come from abroad in bad health, she has no farther need of a servant. Any person wishing to engage her, can have her character in full from Miss Robson, 4, Keppel Street, Russel Square, whom Mrs. Forsyth has requested to furnish particulars to any one desiring them.

" 4, Keppel Street, 28th Sept. 1829."

In the last place, I add my own testimony in behalf of this negro woman. Independently of the scrutiny, which, as Secretary of the Anti-Slavery Society, I made into her case when she first applied for assistance, at 18, Aldermanbury, and the watchful eye I kept upon her conduct for the ensuing twelvemonths, while she was the occasional pensioner of the Society, I have now had the opportunity of closely observing her conduct for fourteen months, in the situation of a domes-

---

of more than twenty years back ; confidently appealing at the same time to the inhabitants of the colony in which he resides for the truth of his averments, and producing a testimonial to Mr. Phillips's good character signed by two members of the Antigua House of Assembly, and by Mr. Wyke, the collector of his Majesty's customs, and by Antigua merchants, as follows—' that they have been acquainted with him the last four years and upwards, and he has always conducted himself in an upright becoming manner—his character we know to be unimpeached, and his morals unexceptionable.'

    (Signed)   " Thomas Saunderson   John D. Taylor
               John A. Wood   George Wyke
               Samuel L. Darrel   Giles S. Musson
                     Robert Grant."

" St. John's, Antigua, June 28, 1825."

In addition to the above testimonies, Mr. Phillips has brought over to England with him others of a more recent date, from some of the most respectable persons in Antigua—sufficient to cover with confusion all his unprincipled calumniators. See also his account of his own case in the Anti-Slavery Reporter, No. 74, p. 69.

tic servant in my own family; and the following is the deliberate opinion of Mary's character, formed not only by myself, but also by my wife and sister-in-law, after this ample period of observation. We have found her perfectly honest and trustworthy in all respects; so that we have no hesitation in leaving every thing in the house at her disposal. She had the entire charge of the house during our absence in Scotland for three months last autumn, and conducted herself in that charge with the utmost discretion and fidelity. She is not, it is true, a very expert housemaid, nor capable of much hard work, (for her constitution appears to be a good deal broken,) but she is careful, industrious, and anxious to do her duty and to give satisfaction. She is capable of strong attachments, and feels deep, though unobtrusive, gratitude for real kindness shown her. She possesses considerable natural sense, and has much quickness of observation and discrimination of character. She is remarkable for *decency* and *propriety* of conduct—and her *delicacy*, even in trifling minutiæ, has been a trait of special remark by the females of my family. This trait, which is obviously quite unaffected, would be a most inexplicable anomaly, if her former habits had been so indecent and depraved as Mr. Wood alleges. Her chief faults, so far as we have discovered them, are, a somewhat violent and hasty temper, and a considerable share of natural pride and self-importance; but these defects have been but rarely and transiently manifested, and have scarcely occasioned an hour's uneasiness at any time in our household. Her religious knowledge, notwithstanding the pious care of her Moravian instructors in Antigua, is still but very limited, and her views of christianity indistinct; but her profession, whatever it may have of imperfection, I am convinced, has nothing of insincerity. In short, we consider her on the whole as respectable and well-behaved a person in her station, as any domestic, white or black, (and we have had ample experience of both colours,) that we have ever had in our service.

But after all, Mary's character, important though its exculpation be to her, is not really the point of chief practical interest in this case. Suppose all Mr. Wood's defamatory allegations to be true—suppose him to be able to rake up against her out of the records of the Antigua police, or from the veracious testimony of his brother colonists, twenty stories as bad or worse than what he insinuates—suppose the whole of her own statement to be false, and even the whole of her conduct since she came under our observation here to be a tissue of hypocrisy;—suppose all this—and leave the negro woman as black in character as in complexion,*—yet it would affect not the main facts—which are these. —1. Mr. Wood, not daring in England to punish this woman arbitrarily, as he would have done in the West Indies, drove her out of his house, or

* If it even were so, how strong a plea of palliation might not the poor negro bring, by adducing the neglect of her various owners to afford religious instruction or moral discipline, and the habitual influence of their evil *example* (to say the very least,) before her eyes? What moral good could she possibly learn— what moral evil could she easily escape, while under the uncontrolled power of such masters as she describes Captain I—— and Mr. D—— of Turk's Island? All things considered, it is indeed wonderful to find her such as she now is. But as she has herself piously expressed it, "that God whom then she knew not mercifully preserved her for better things."

left her, at least, only the alternative of returning instantly to Antigua, with the certainty of severe treatment there, or submitting in silence to what she considered intolerable usage in his household. 2. He has since obstinately persisted in refusing her manumission, to enable her to return home in security, though repeatedly offered more than ample compensation for her value as a slave; and this on various frivolous pretexts, but really, and indeed not unavowedly, in order to *punish* her for leaving his service in England, though he himself had professed to give her that option. These unquestionable facts speak volumes.*

---

* Since the preceding pages were printed off, I have been favoured with a communication from the Rev. J. Curtin, to whom among other acquaintances of Mr. Wood is in this country, the entire proof sheets of this pamphlet had been sent for inspection. Mr. Curtin corrects some omissions and inaccuracies in Mary Prince's narrative (see page 17,) by stating, 1. That she was baptized, not in August, but on the 6th of April, 1817; 2. That sometime before her baptism, on her being admitted a catechumen, preparatory to that holy ordinance, she brought a note from her owner, Mr. Wood, recommending her for religious instruction, &c.; 3. That it was his usual practice, when any adult slaves came on *week days* to school, to require their owners' permission for their attendance; but that on *Sundays* the chapel was open indiscriminately to all.—Mary, after a personal interview with Mr. Curtin, and after hearing his letter read by me, still maintains that Mr. Wood's note recommended her for baptism merely, and that she never received any religious instruction whatever from Mr. and Mrs. Wood, or from any one else at that period beyond what she has stated in her narrative. In regard to her non-admission to the Sunday school without permission from her owners, she admits that she may possibly have mistaken the clergyman's meaning on that point, but says that such was certainly her impression at the time, and the actual cause of her non-attendance.

Mr. Curtin finds in his books some reference to Mary's connection with a Captain ————, (the individual, I believe, alluded to by Mr. Phillips at page 32); but he states that when she attended his chapel she was always decently and becomingly dressed, and appeared to him to be in a situation of trust in her mistress's family.

Mr. Curtin offers no comment on any other part of Mary's statement; but he speaks in very favourable, though general terms of the respectability of Mr. Wood, whom he had known for many years in Antigua; and of Mrs. Wood, though she was not personally known to him, he says, that he had "heard her spoken of by those of her acquaintance, as a lady of very mild and amiable manners."

Another friend of Mr. and Mrs. Wood, a lady who had been their guest both in Antigua and England, alleges that Mary has grossly misrepresented them in her narrative; and says that she "can vouch for their being the most benevolent, kind-hearted people that can possibly live." She has declined, however, to furnish me with any written correction of the misrepresentations she complains of, although I offered to insert her testimony in behalf of her friends, if sent to me in time. And having already kept back the publication a fortnight waiting for communications of this sort, I will not delay it longer. Those who have withheld their strictures have only themselves to blame.

Of the general character of Mr. and Mrs. Wood, I would not designedly give any *unfair* impression. Without implicitly adopting either the *ex parte* view of Mary Prince, or the unmeasured encomiums of their friends, I am willing to believe them to be, on the whole, fair, perhaps favourable, specimens of colonial character. Let them even be rated, if you will, in the very highest and most benevolent class of slaveholders; and, laying every thing else entirely out of view, let Mr. Wood's conduct in this affair be tried exclusively by the facts established beyond dispute, and by his own statement of the case in his letter to Mr. Taylor. But then, I ask, if the very *best* and *mildest* of your slave-owners can act as Mr. Wood is proved to have acted, what is to be expected of persons whose mildness, or equity, or common humanity no one will dare to vouch for? If such things are done in the green tree, what will be done in the dry?—And what else then can Colonial Slavery possibly be, even in its best estate, but a system incurably evil and iniquitous?—I require no other data—I need add no further comment.

The case affords a most instructive illustration of the true spirit of the slave system, and of the pretensions of the slaveholders to assert, not merely their claims to a " vested right" in the *labour* of their bondmen, but to an indefeasible property in them as their " absolute chattels." It furnishes a striking practical comment on the assertions of the West Indians that self-interest is a sufficient check to the indulgence of vindictive feelings in the master; for here is a case where a man (a *respectable* and *benevolent* man as his friends aver,) prefers losing entirely the full price of the slave, for the mere satisfaction of preventing a poor black woman from returning home to her husband! If the pleasure of thwarting the benevolent wishes of the Anti-Slavery Society in behalf of the deserted negro, be an additional motive with Mr. Wood, it will not much mend his wretched plea.

I may here add a few words respecting the earlier portion of Mary Prince's narrative. The facts there stated must necessarily rest entirely, —since we have no collateral evidence,—upon their intrinsic claims to probability, and upon the reliance the reader may feel disposed, after perusing the foregoing pages, to place on her veracity. To my judgment, the internal evidence of the truth of her narrative appears remarkably strong. The circumstances are related in a tone of natural sincerity, and are accompanied in almost every case with characteristic and minute details, which must, I conceive, carry with them full conviction to every candid mind that this negro woman has actually seen, felt, and suffered all that she so impressively describes; and that the picture she has given of West Indian slavery is not less true than it is revolting.

But there may be some persons into whose hands this tract may fall, so imperfectly acquainted with the real character of Negro Slavery, as to be shocked into partial, if not absolute incredulity, by the acts of inhuman oppression and brutality related of Capt. I—— and his wife, and of Mr. D——, the salt manufacturer of Turk's Island. Here, at least, such persons may be disposed to think, there surely must be *some* exaggeration; the facts are too shocking to be credible. The facts are indeed shocking, but unhappily not the less credible on that account. Slavery is a curse to the oppressor scarcely less than to the oppressed : its natural tendency is to brutalize both. After a residence myself of six years in a slave colony, I am inclined to doubt whether, as regards its *demoralizing* influence, the master is not even a greater object of compassion than his bondman. Let those who are disposed to doubt the atrocities related in this narrative, on the testimony of a sufferer, examine the details of many cases of similar barbarity that have lately come before the public, on unquestionable evidence. Passing over the reports of the Fiscal of Berbice,* and the Mauritius horrors recently unveiled,† let them consider the case of Mr. and Mrs. Moss, of the Bahamas, and their slave Kate, so justly denounced by the Secretary for the Colonies ; ‡—the cases of Eleanor Mead,§—of Henry Williams,‖—and

* See Anti-Slavery Reporter, Nos. 5 and 16.   † Ibid, No. 44.
   ‡ Ibid, No. 47.   § Ibid, No. 64, p. 345 ; No. 71, p. 481.
      ‖ Ibid, No. 65, p. 356 ; No. 69, p. 431.

of the Rev. Mr. Bridges and Kitty Hylton,* in Jamaica. These cases alone might suffice to demonstrate the inevitable tendency of slavery as it exists in our colonies, to brutalize the master to a truly frightful degree —a degree which would often cast into the shade even the atrocities related in the narrative of Mary Prince; and which are sufficient to prove, independently of all other evidence, that there is nothing in the revolting character of the facts to affect their credibility; but that on the contrary, similar deeds are at this very time of frequent occurrence in almost every one of our slave colonies. The system of coercive labour may vary in different places; it may be more destructive to human life in the cane culture of Mauritius and Jamaica, than in the predial and domestic bondage of Bermuda or the Bahamas,—but the spirit and character of slavery are every where the same, and cannot fail to produce similar effects. Wherever slavery prevails, there will inevitably be found cruelty and oppression. Individuals who have preserved humane, and amiable, and tolerant dispositions towards their black dependents, may doubtless be found among slave-holders; but even where a happy instance of this sort occurs, such as Mary's first mistress, the kind-hearted Mrs. Williams, the favoured condition of the slave is still as precarious as it is rare: it is every moment at the mercy of events; and must always be held by a tenure so proverbially uncertain as that of human prosperity, or human life. Such examples, like a feeble and flickering streak of light in a gloomy picture, only serve by contrast to exhibit the depth of the prevailing shades. Like other exceptions, they only prove the general rule: the unquestionable tendency of the system is to vitiate the best tempers, and to harden the most feeling hearts. " Never be kind, nor speak kindly to a slave," said an accomplished English lady in South Africa to my wife: " I have now," she added, " been for some time a slave-owner, and have found, from vexatious experience in my own household, that nothing but harshness and hauteur will do with slaves."

I might perhaps not inappropriately illustrate this point more fully by stating many cases which fell under my own personal observation, or became known to me through authentic sources, at the Cape of Good Hope—a colony where slavery assumes, as it is averred, a milder aspect than in any other dependency of the empire where it exists; and I could shew, from the judicial records of that colony, received by me within these few weeks, cases scarcely inferior in barbarity to the worst of those to which I have just specially referred; but to do so would lead me too far from the immediate purpose of this pamphlet, and extend it to an inconvenient length. I shall therefore content myself with quoting a single short passage from the excellent work of my friend Dr. Walsh, entitled " Notices of Brazil,"—a work which, besides its other merits, has vividly illustrated the true spirit of Negro Slavery, as it displays itself not merely in that country, but wherever it has been permitted to open its Pandora's box of misery and crime.

Let the reader ponder on the following just remarks, and compare the facts stated by the Author in illustration of them, with the circumstances related at pages 6 and 7 of Mary's narrative:—

* Anti-Slavery Reporter, Nos. 66, 69, and 76.

" If then we put out of the question the injury inflicted on others, and merely consider the deterioration of feeling and principle with which it operates on ourselves, ought it not to be a sufficient, and, indeed, unanswerable argument, against the permission of Slavery ?

" The exemplary manner in which the paternal duties are performed at home, may mark people as the most fond and affectionate parents ; but let them once go abroad, and come within the contagion of slavery, and it seems to alter the very nature of a man ; and the father has sold, and still sells, the mother and his children, with as little compunction as he would a sow and her litter of pigs ; and he often disposes of them together.

" This deterioration of feeling is conspicuous in many ways among the Brazilians. They are naturally a people of a humane and good-natured disposition, and much indisposed to cruelty or severity of any kind. Indeed, the manner in which many of them treat their slaves is a proof of this, as it is really gentle and considerate ; but the natural tendency to cruelty and oppression in the human heart, is continually evolved by the impunity and uncontrolled licence in which they are exercised. I never walked through the streets of Rio, that some house did not present to me the semblance of a bridewell, where the moans and the cries of the sufferers, and the sounds of whips and scourges within, announced to me that corporal punishment was being inflicted. Whenever I remarked this to a friend, I was always answered that the refractory nature of the slave rendered it necessary, and no house could properly be conducted unless it was practised. But this is certainly not the case ; and the chastisement is constantly applied in the very wantonness of barbarity, and would not, and dared not, be inflicted on the humblest wretch in society, if he was not a slave, and so put out of the pale of pity.

" Immediately joining our house was one occupied by a mechanic, from which the most dismal cries and moans constantly proceeded. I entered the shop one day, and found it was occupied by a saddler, who had two negro boys working at his business. He was a tawny, cadaverous-looking man, with a dark aspect ; and he had cut from his leather a scourge like a Russian knout, which he held in his hand, and was in the act of exercising on one of the naked children in an inner room : and this was the cause of the moans and cries we heard every day, and almost all day long.

" In the rear of our house was another, occupied by some women of bad character, who kept, as usual, several negro slaves. I was awoke early one morning by dismal cries, and looking out of the window, I saw in the back yard of the house, a black girl of about fourteen years old ; before her stood her mistress, a white woman, with a large stick in her hand. She was undressed except her petticoat and chemise, which had fallen down and left her shoulders and bosom bare. Her hair was streaming behind, and every fierce and malevolent passion was depicted in her face. She too, like my hostess at Governo [another striking illustration of the *dehumanizing* effects of Slavery,] was the very representation of a fury. She was striking the poor girl, whom she had driven up into a corner, where she was on her knees appealing for mercy. She shewed her none, but continued to strike her on the head and thrust the stick into her face, till she was herself exhausted, and her poor victim covered with blood. This scene was renewed every morning, and the cries and moans of the poor suffering blacks, announced that they were enduring the penalty of slavery, in being the objects on which the irritable and malevolent passions of the whites are allowed to vent themselves with impunity ; nor could I help deeply deploring that state of society in which the vilest characters in the community are allowed an almost uncontrolled power of life and death, over their innocent, and far more estimable fellow-creatures."—(Notices of Brazil, vol. ii. p. 354-356.)

In conclusion, I may observe that the history of Mary Prince furnishes a corollary to Lord Stowell's decision in the case of the slave Grace, and that it is most valuable on this account. Whatever opinions may be held by some readers on the grave question of immediately abolishing Colonial Slavery, nothing assuredly can be more repugnant to the feelings of Englishmen than that the system should be permitted to extend its baneful influence to this country. Yet such is the case, when the slave landed in England still only possesses that qualified degree of freedom, that a change of domicile will determine it. Though born a British subject, and resident within the shores of England, he is cut off from his dearest natural rights by the sad alternative of regaining them at the expence of liberty, and the certainty of severe treatment. It is true that he has the option of returning; but it is a cruel mockery to call it a voluntary choice, when upon his return depend his means of subsistence and his re-union with all that makes life valuable. Here he has tasted "the sweets of freedom," to quote the words of the unfortunate Mary Prince; but if he desires to restore himself to his family, or to escape from suffering and destitution, and the other evils of a climate uncongenial to his constitution and habits, he must abandon the enjoyment of his late-acquired liberty, and again subject himself to the arbitrary power of a vindictive master.

The case of Mary Prince is by no means a singular one ; many of the same kind are daily occurring : and even if the case were singular, it would still loudly call for the interference of the legislature. In instances of this kind no injury can possibly be done to the owner by confirming to the slave his resumption of his natural rights. It is the master's spontaneous act to bring him to this country; he knows when he brings him that he divests himself of his property; and it is, in fact, a minor species of slave trading, when he has thus enfranchised his slave, to re-capture that slave by the necessities of his condition, or by working upon the better feelings of his heart. Abstractedly from all legal technicalities, there is no real difference between thus compelling the return of the enfranchised negro, and trepanning a free native of England by delusive hopes into perpetual slavery. The most ingenious casuist could not point out any essential distinction between the two cases. Our boasted liberty is the dream of imagination, and no longer the characteristic of our country, if its bulwarks can thus be thrown down by colonial special pleading. It would well become the character of the present Government to introduce a Bill into the Legislature making perpetual that freedom which the slave has acquired by his passage here, and thus to declare, in the most ample sense of the words, (what indeed we had long fondly believed to be the fact, though it now appears that we have been mistaken,) THAT NO SLAVE CAN EXIST WITHIN THE SHORES OF GREAT BRITAIN.

NARRATIVE OF LOUIS ASA-ASA,

A CAPTURED AFRICAN.

THE following interesting narrative is a convenient supplement to the history of Mary Prince. It is given, like hers, as nearly as possible in the narrator's words, with only so much correction as was necessary to connect the story, and render it grammatical. The concluding passage in inverted commas, is entirely his own.

While Mary's narrative shews the disgusting character of colonial slavery, this little tale explains with equal force the horrors in which it originates.

It is necessary to explain that Louis came to this country about five years ago, in a French vessel called the Pearl. She had lost her reckoning, and was driven by stress of weather into the port of St. Ives, in Cornwall. Louis and his four companions were brought to London upon a writ of Habeas Corpus at the instance of Mr. George Stephen; and, after some trifling opposition on the part of the master of the vessel, were discharged by Lord Wynford. Two of his unfortunate fellow-sufferers died of the measles at Hampstead; the other two returned to Sierra Leone; but poor Louis, when offered the choice of going back to Africa, replied, " Me no father, no mother now; me stay with you." And here he has ever since remained; conducting himself in a way to gain the good will and respect of all who know him. He is remarkably intelligent, understands our language perfectly, and can read and write well. The last sentences of the following narrative will seem almost too peculiar to be his own; but it is not the first time that in conversation with Mr. George Stephen, he has made similar remarks. On one occasion in particular, he was heard saying to himself in the kitchen, while sitting by the fire apparently in deep thought, " Me think,—me think——" A fellow-servant inquired what he meant; and he added, " Me think what a good thing I came to England! Here, I know what " God is, and read my Bible; in my country they have no God, no " Bible."

How severe and just a reproof to the guilty wretches who visit his country only with fire and sword! How deserved a censure upon the not less guilty men, who dare to vindicate the state of slavery, on the lying pretext, that its victims are of an inferior nature! And scarcely less deserving of reprobation are those who have it in their power to prevent these crimes, but who remain inactive from indifference, or are dissuaded from throwing the shield of British power over the victim of oppression, by the sophistry, and the clamour, and the avarice of the oppressor. It is the reproach and the sin of England. May God avert from our country the ruin which this national guilt deserves!

We lament to add, that the Pearl which brought these negroes to our shore, was restored to its owners at the instance of the French Government, instead of being condemned as a prize to Lieut. Rye, who, on his own responsibility, detained her, with all her manacles and chains and other detestable proofs of her piratical occupation on board. We trust it is not yet too late to demand investigation into the reasons for restoring her.

The Negro Boy's Narrative.

My father's name was Clashoquin; mine is Asa-Asa. He lived in a country called Bycla, near Egie, a large town. Egie is as large as Brighton; it was some way from the sea. I had five brothers and sisters. We all lived together with my father and mother; he kept a horse, and was respectable, but not one of the great men. My uncle was one of the great men at Egie: he could make men come and work for him: his name was Otou. He had a great deal of land and cattle. My father sometimes worked on his own land, and used to make charcoal. I was too little to work; my eldest brother used to work on the land; and we were all very happy.

A great many people, whom we called Adinyes, set fire to Egie in the morning before daybreak; there were some thousands of them. They killed a great many, and burnt all their houses. They staid two days, and then carried away all the people whom they did not kill.

They came again every now and then for a month, as long as they could find people to carry away. They used to tie them by the feet, except when they were taking them off, and then they let them loose; but if they offered to run away, they would shoot them. I lost a great many friends and relations at Egie; about a dozen. They sold all they carried away, to be slaves. I know this because I afterwards saw them as slaves on the other side of the sea. They took away brothers, and sisters, and husbands, and wives; they did not care about this. They were sold for cloth or gunpowder, sometimes for salt or guns; sometimes they got four or five guns for a man: they were English guns, made like my master's that I clean for his shooting. The Adinyés burnt a great many places besides Egie. They burnt all the country wherever they found villages; they used to shoot men, women, and children, if they ran away.

They came to us about eleven o'clock one day, and directly they came they set our house on fire. All of us had run away. We kept together, and went into the woods, and stopped there two days. The Adinyés then went away, and we returned home and found every thing burnt. We tried to build a little shed, and were beginning to get comfortable again. We found several of our neighbours lying about wounded; they had been shot. I saw the bodies of four or five little children whom they had killed with blows on the head. They had carried away their fathers and mothers, but the children were too small for slaves, so they killed them. They had killed several others, but these were all that I saw. I saw them lying in the street like dead dogs.

In about a week after we got back, the Adinyés returned, and burnt all the sheds and houses they had left standing. We all ran away again; we went to the woods as we had done before.—They followed us the next day. We went farther into the woods, and staid there about four days and nights; we were half starved; we only got a few potatoes. My uncle Otou was with us. At the end of this time, the Adinyés found us. We ran away. They called my uncle to go to them; but he refused, and they shot him immediately: they killed him. The rest of us ran on, and they did not get at us till the next day. I ran up into a tree: they followed me and brought me down. They tied my feet. I do not know if they found my father and mother, and brothers and sisters: they had run faster than me, and were half a mile farther when I got up into the tree: I have never seen them since.— There was a man who ran up into the tree with me: I believe they shot him, for I never saw him again.

They carried away about twenty besides me. They carried us to the sea. They did not beat us: they only killed one man, who was very ill and too weak to carry his load: they made all of us carry chickens and meat for our food; but this poor man could not carry his load, and they ran him through the body with a sword.—He was a neighbour of ours. When we got to the sea they sold all of us, but not to the same person. They sold us for money; and I was sold six times over, sometimes for money, sometimes for cloth, and sometimes for a gun. I was about thirteen years old. It was about half a year from the time I was taken, before I saw the white people.

We were taken in a boat from place to place, and sold at every place we stopped at. In about six months we got to a ship, in which we first saw white people: they were French. They bought us. We found here a great many other slaves; there were about eighty, including women and children. The Frenchmen sent away all but five of us into another very large ship. We five staid on board till we got to England, which was about five or six months. The slaves we saw on board the ship were chained together by the legs below deck, so close they could not move. They were flogged very cruelly: I saw one of them flogged till he died; we could not tell what for. They gave them enough to eat. The place they were confined in below deck was so hot and nasty I could not bear to be in it. A great many of the slaves were ill, but they were not attended to. They used to flog me very bad on board the ship: the captain cut my head very bad one time.

"I am very happy to be in England, as far as I am very well;—but
" I have no friend belonging to me, but God, who will take care of me
" as he has done already. I am very glad I have come to England, to
" know who God is. I should like much to see my friends again, but
" I do not now wish to go back to them: for if I go back to my own

" country, I might be taken as a slave again. I would rather stay here,
" where I am free, than go back to my country to be sold. I shall stay
" in England as long as (please God) I shall live. I wish the King of
" England could know all I have told you. I wish it that he may see
" how cruelly we are used. We had no king in our country, or he
" would have stopt it. I think the king of England might stop it, and
" this is why I wish him to know it all. I have heard say he is good ;
" and if he is, he will stop it if he can. I am well off myself, for I am
" well taken care of, and have good bed and good clothes ; but I wish
" my own people to be as comfortable."

" LOUIS ASA-ASA."

" *London, January* 31, 1831."

London :—S. Bagster, Jun., Printer, Bartholomew Close.

MEMOIR

OF

OLD ELIZABETH,

A

COLOURED WOMAN.

---◆---

"There is neither Jew nor Greek, there is neither bond nor free, there is neither male nor female, for ye are all one in Christ Jesus."

GAL. iii. 25.

---◆---

PHILADELPHIA:

COLLINS, PRINTER, 705 JAYNE STREET.

1863.

MEMOIR

OF

OLD ELIZABETH,

A

COLOURED WOMAN.

---◆---

"There is neither Jew nor Greek, there is neither bond nor free, there is neither male nor female, for ye are all one in Christ Jesus."

GAL. iii. 25.

---◆---

PHILADELPHIA:

COLLINS, PRINTER, 705 JAYNE STREET,

1863.

MEMOIR, &C.

In the following Narrative of "OLD ELIZABETH," which was taken mainly from her own lips in her 97th year, her simple language has been adhered to as strictly as was consistent with perspicuity and propriety.

I was born in Maryland in the year 1766. My parents were slaves. Both my father and mother were religious people, and belonged to the Methodist Society. It was my father's practice to read in the Bible aloud to his children every sabbath morning. At these seasons, when I was but five years old, I often felt the overshadowing of the Lord's Spirit, without at all understanding what it meant; and these incomes and influences continued to attend me until I was eleven years old, particularly when I was alone, by which I was preserved from doing anything that I thought was wrong.

In the eleventh year of my age, my master sent me to another farm, several miles from my parents, brothers, and sisters, which was a great trouble to me. At last I grew so lonely and sad I thought I should die, if I did not see my mother. I asked the overseer if I might go, but being positively denied, l concluded to go without his knowledge. When I reached home my mother was away. I set off and walked twenty miles before I found her. I staid with her for several days, and we returned together. Next day I was sent back to my new place, which renewed my sorrow. At parting, my mother told me that I had "nobody in the wide world to look to but God." These words fell upon my heart with pondrous weight, and seemed to add to my grief. I went back repeating as I went, "none but God in the wide world." On reaching the farm, I found the overseer was displeased at me for going without his liberty. He tied me with a rope, and gave me some stripes of which I carried the marks for weeks.

After this time, finding as my mother said, I had none in the world to look to but God, I betook myself to prayer, and in every lonely place I found an altar. I mourned sore like a dove and chattered forth my sorrow, moaning in the corners of the field, and under the fences.

I continued in this state for about six months, feeling as though my head were waters, and I could do nothing but weep. I lost my appetite, and not being able to take enough food to sustain nature, I became so weak I had but little strength to work; still I was required to do all my duty. One evening, after the duties of the day were ended, I thought I could not live over the night, so threw myself on a bench, expecting to die, and without being prepared to meet my Maker; and my spirit cried within me, must I die in this state, and be banished from Thy presence forever? I own I am a sinner in Thy sight, and not fit to live where thou art. Still it was my fervent desire that the Lord would pardon me. Just at this season, I saw with my spiritual eye, an awful gulf of misery. As I thought I was about to plunge into it, I heard a voice saying, "rise up and pray," which strengthened me. I fell on my knees and prayed the best I could the Lord's prayer. Knowing no more to say, I halted, but continued on my knees. My spirit was then *taught* to pray, "Lord, have mercy on me—Christ save me." Immediately there appeared a director, clothed in white raiment. I thought he took me by the hand and said, "come with me." He led me down a long journey to a fiery gulf, and left me standing upon the brink of this awful pit. I began to scream for mercy, thinking I was about to be plunged to the belly of hell, and believed I should sink to endless ruin. Although I prayed and wrestled with all my might, it seemed in vain. Still, I felt all the while that I was sustained by some invisible power. At this solemn moment, I thought I saw a hand from which hung, as it were, a silver hair, and a voice told me that all the hope I had of being saved was no more than a hair; still, pray, and it will be sufficient. I then renewed my struggle, crying for mercy and salvation, until I found that every cry raised me higher and higher, and my head was quite above the fiery pillars. Then I thought I was permitted to look straight forward, and saw the Saviour standing with His hand stretched out to receive me. An indescribably glorious light was *in* Him, and He said, "peace, peace, come unto me." At this moment I felt that my sins were forgiven me, and the time of my deliverance was at hand. I sprang forward and fell at his feet, giving Him all the thanks and highest praises, crying, Thou hast redeemed me—Thou hast redeemed me to thyself. I felt filled with light and love. At this moment I thought my former guide took me again by the hand and led me upward, till I came to the celestial world and to heaven's door, which I saw was open, and while I stood there, a power surrounded me which drew me in, and I saw millions of glorified spirits in white robes. After I had this view, I thought I heard a voice saying, "Art thou willing to be saved?" I said, Yes Lord. Again I was asked, "Art thou willing to be saved in my way?" I stood speechless until he asked me again, "Art thou willing to be saved in my way?" Then I heard a whispering voice say, "If thou art not saved in the Lord's way, thou canst not be saved at all;" at which

I exclaimed, "Yes Lord, in thy own way." Immediately a light fell upon my head, and I was filled with light, and I was shown the world lying in wickedness, and was told I must go there, and call the people to repentance, for the day of the Lord was at hand; and this message was as a heavy yoke upon me, so that I wept bitterly at the thought of what I should have to pass through. While I wept, I heard a voice say, "weep not, some will laugh at thee, some will scoff at thee, and the dogs will bark at thee, but while thou doest my will, I will be with thee to the ends of the earth.

I was at this time not yet thirteen years old. The next day, when I had come to myself, I felt like a new creature in Christ, and all my desire was to see the Saviour.

I lived in a place where there was no preaching, and no religious instruction; but every day I went out amongst the hay-stacks, where the presence of the Lord overshadowed me, and I was filled with sweetness and joy, and was as a vessel filled with holy oil. In this way I continued for about a year; many times while my hands were at my work, my spirit was carried away to spiritual things. One day as I was going to my old place behind the hay-stacks to pray, I was assailed with this language, "Are you going there to weep and pray? what a fool! there are older professors than you are, and they do not take that way to get to heaven; people whose sins are forgiven ought to be joyful and lively, and not be struggling and praying." With this I halted and concluded I would not go, but do as other professors did, and so went off to play; but at this moment the light that was in me became darkened, and the peace and joy that I once had, departed from me.

About this time I was moved back to the farm where my mother lived, and then sold to a stranger. Here I had deep sorrows and plungings, not having experienced a return of that sweet evidence and light with which I had been favoured formerly; but by watching unto prayer, and wrestling mightily with the Lord, my peace gradually returned, and with it a great exercise and weight upon my heart for the salvation of my fellow-creatures; and I was often carried to distant lands and shown places where I should have to travel and deliver the Lord's message. Years afterwards, I found myself visiting those towns and countries that I had seen in the light as I sat at home at my sewing,—places of which I had never heard.

Some years from this time I was sold to a Presbyterian for a term of years, as he did not think it right to hold slaves for life. Having served him faithfully my time out, he gave me my liberty, which was about the thirtieth year of my age.

As I now lived in a neighborhood where I could

attend religious meetings, occasionally I felt moved to speak a few words therein; but I shrank from it—so great was the cross to my nature.

I did not speak much till I had reached my forty-second year, when it was revealed to me that the message which had been given to me I had not yet delivered, and the time had come. As I could read but little, I questioned within myself how it would be possible for me to deliver the message, when I did not understand the Scriptures. Whereupon I was moved to open a Bible that was near me, which I did, and my eyes fell upon this passage, "Gird up thy loins now like a man, and answer thou me. Obey God rather than man," &c. Here I fell into a great exercise of spirit, and was plunged very low. I went from one religious professor to another, enquiring of them what ailed me; but of all these I could find none who could throw any light upon such impressions. They all told me there was nothing in Scripture that would sanction such exercises. It was hard for men to travel, and what would women do? These things greatly discouraged me, and shut up my way, and caused me to resist the Spirit. After going to all that were accounted pious, and receiving no help, I returned to the Lord, feeling that I was nothing, and knew nothing, and wrestled and prayed to the Lord that He would fully reveal His will, and make the way plain.

Whilst I thus struggled, there seemed a light from heaven to fall upon me, which banished all my desponding fears, and I was enabled to form a new resolution to go on to prison and to death, if it might be my portion: and the Lord showed me that it was His will I should be resigned to die any death that might be my lot, in carrying his message, and be entirely crucified to the world, and sacrifice *all* to His glory that was then in my possession, which His witnesses, the holy Apostles, had done before me. It was then revealed to me that the Lord had given me the evidence of a clean heart, in which I could rejoice day and night, and I walked and talked with God, and my soul was illuminated with heavenly light, and I knew nothing but Jesus Christ, and him crucified.

One day, after these things, while I was at my work, the Spirit directed me to go to a poor widow, and ask her if I might have a meeting at her house, which was situated in one of the lowest and worst streets in Baltimore. With great joy she gave notice, and at the time appointed I appeared there among a few coloured sisters. When they had all prayed, they called upon me to close the meeting, and I felt an impression that I must say a few words; and while I was speaking, the house seemed filled with light; and when I was about to close the meeting, and was kneeling, a man came in and stood till

I arose. It proved to be a watchman. The sisters became so frightened, they all went away except the one who lived in the house, and an old woman; they both appeared to be much frightened, fearing they should receive some personal injury, or be put out of the house. A feeling of weakness came over me for a short time, but I soon grew warm and courageous in the Spirit. The man then said to me, "I was sent here to break up your meeting. Complaint has been made to me that the people round here cannot sleep for the racket." I replied, "a good racket is better than a bad racket. How do they rest when the ungodly are dancing and fiddling till midnight? Why are not they molested by the watchmen? and why should we be for praising God, our Maker? Are we worthy of greater punishment for praying to Him? and are we to be prohibited from doing so, that sinners may remain slumbering in their sins?" While speaking these few words I grew warm with *heavenly* zeal, and laid my hand upon him and addressed him with gospel truth, "how do sinners sleep in hell, after slumbering in their sins here, and crying, 'let me rest, let me rest,' while sporting on the very brink of hell? Is the cause of God to be destroyed for this purpose?" Speaking several words more to this amount, he turned pale and trembled, and begged my pardon, acknowledging that it was not his wish to interrupt us, and that he would never disturb a religious assembly again. He then took leave of me in a comely manner and wished us success. After he was gone, I turned to the old sisters who by this time were quite cheered up. You see, said I, if the sisters had not fled, what a victory we might have had on the Lord's side; for the man seemed ready to give up under conviction. If it had not been for their cowardice, we might have all bowed in prayer, and a shout of victory had been heard amongst us.

Our meeting gave great offence, and we were forbid holding any more assemblies. Even the elders of our meeting joined with the wicked people, and said such meetings must be stopped, and that woman quieted. But I was not afraid of any of them, and continued to go, and burnt with a zeal not my own. The old sisters were zealous sometimes, and at other times would sink under the cross. Thus they grew cold, at which I was much grieved. I proposed to them to ask the elders to send a brother, which was concluded upon.

We went on for several years, and the Lord was with us with great power it proved, to the conversion of many souls, and we continued to grow stronger.

I felt at times that I must exercise in the ministry, but when I rose upon my feet I felt ashmed, and so I went under a cloud for some time, and endeav oured to keep silence; but I could not quench the Spirit. I was rejected by the elders and rulers, as Christ was rejected by the Jews before me, and while others were excused in crimes of the darkest dye, I was hunted down in every place where I appointed a meeting. Wading through many sorrows, I thought at times I might as well be banished from this life, as to feel the Almighty drawing me one way, and man another; so that I was tempted to cast myself into the dock. But contemplating the length of eternity, and how long my sufferings would be in that unchangeable world, compared with this, if I endured a little longer, the Lord was pleased to deliver me from this gloomy, melancholy state in his own time; though while this temptation lasted I roved up and down, and talked and prayed.

I often felt that I was unfit to assemble with the congregation with whom I had gathered, and had sometimes been made to rejoice in the Lord. I felt that I was despised on account of this gracious calling, and was looked upon as a speckled bird by the ministers to whom I looked for instruction, and to whom I resorted every opportunity for the same; but when I would converse with them, some would cry out, "You are an enthusiast;" and others said, "the Discipline did not allow of any such division of the work;" until I began to think I surely must be wrong. Under this reflection, I had another gloomy cloud to struggle through; but after awhile I felt much moved upon by the Spirit of the Lord, and meeting with an aged sister, I found upon conversing with her that she could sympathize with me in this spiritual work. She was the first one I had met with, who could fully understand my exercises. She offered to open her house for a meeting, and run the risk of all the church would do to her for it. Many were afraid to open their houses in this way, lest they should be turned out of the church.

I persevered, notwithstanding the opposition of those who were looked upon as higher and wiser. The meeting was appointed, and but few came. I felt much backwardness, and as though I could not pray, but a pressure upon me to arise and express myself by way of exhortation. After hesitating for some time whether I would take up the cross or no, I arose, and after expressing a few words, the Spirit came upon me with life, and a victory was gained over the power of darkness, and we could rejoice together in His love.

As for myself, I was so full I hardly knew whether I was in the body, or out of the body—so great was my joy for the victory on the Lord's side. But the persecution against me increased, and a complaint was carried forward, as was done formerly against Daniel, the servant of God, and the elders came out with indignation for my holding meetings contrary to discipline—being a woman.

Thus we see when the heart is not inspired, and the inward eye enlightened by the Spirit, we are incapable of discerning the mystery of God in these things. Individuals creep into the church that are unregenerate, and after they have been there awhile, they fancy that they have got the grace of God, while they are destitute of it. They may have a degree of light in their heads, but evil in their hearts; which makes them think they are qualified to be judges of the ministry, and their conceit makes them very busy in matters of religion, judging of the revelations that are given to others, while they have received none themselves. Being thus mistaken, they are calculated to make a great deal of confusion in the church, and clog the true ministry.

These are they who eat their own bread, and wear their own apparel, having the form of godliness, but are destitute of the power.

Again I felt encouraged to attend another and another appointment. At one of these meetings, some of the class-leaders were present, who were constrained to cry out, "Surely the Lord has *revealed* these things to her" and asked one another if they ever heard the like? I look upon man as a very selfish being, when placed in a religious office, to presume to resist the work of the Almighty; because He does not work by man's authority. I did not faint under discouragement, but pressed on.

Under the contemplation of these things, I slept but little, being much engaged in receiving the revelations of the Divine will concerning this work, and the mysterious call thereto.

I felt very unworthy and small, notwithstanding the Lord had shown himself with great power, insomuch that conjecturers and critics were constrained to join in praise to his great name; for truly, we had times of refreshing from the presence of the Lord. At one of the meetings, a vast number of the white inhabitants of the place, and many coloured people, attended—many no donbt from curiosity to hear what the old coloured woman had to say. One, a great scripturian, fixed himself behind the door with pen and ink, in order to take down the discourse in short-hand; but the Almighty Being anointed me with such a portion of his Spirit, that he cast away his paper and pen, and heard the discourse with patience, and was much affected, for the Lord wrought powerfully on his heart. After meeting, he came forward and offered me his hand with solemnity on his countenance, and handed me something to pay for my conveyance home.

I returned, much strengthened by the Lord's power, to go on to the fulfilment of His work, although I was again pressed by the authorities ot the church to which I belonged, for imprudency; and so much condemned, that I was sorely tempted by the enemy to turn aside into the wilderness. I was so embarrassed and encompassed, I wondered within myself whether all that were called to be mouth piece for the Lord, suffered such deep wadings as I experienced.

I now found I had to travel still more extensively in the work of the ministry, and I applied to the Lord for direction. I was often *invited* to go hither and thither, but felt that I must wait for the dictates of His Spirit.

At a meeting which I held in Maryland, I was led to speak from the passage, "Woe to the rebellious city," &c. After the meeting, the people came where I was, to take me before the squire; but the Lord delivered me from their hands.

I also held meetings in Virginia. The people there would not believe that a coloured woman could preach. And moreover, as she had no learning, they strove to imprison me because I spoke against slavery: and being brought up, they asked by what authority I spake? and if I had been ordained? I answered, not by the commission of men's hands: if the Lord had ordained me, I needed nothing better.

As I travelled along through the land, I was led at different times to converse with white men who were by profession ministers of the gospel. Many of them, up and down, confessed they did not believe in revelation, which gave me to see that men were sent forth as ministers without Christ's authority. In a conversation with one of these, he said, "You think you have these things by revelation, but there has been no such thing as revelation since Christ's ascension." I asked him where the apostle John got his revelation while he was in the Isle of Patmos. With this, he rose up and left me, and I said in my spirit, get thee behind me Satan.

I visited many remote places, where there were no meeting houses, and held many glorious meetings, for the Lord poured out his Spirit in sweet effusions. I also travelled in Canada, and visited several settlements of coloured people, and felt an open door amongst them.

I may here remark, that while journeying through the different states of the Union, I met with many of the Quaker Friends, and visited them in their families. I received much kindness and sympathy, and no opposition from them, in the prosecution of my labours.

On one occasion, in a thinly settled part of the country, seeing a Friend's meeting house open, I went in; at the same time a Friend and his little daughter followed me. We three composed the meeting. As we sat there in silence, I felt a remarkable overshadowing of the Divine presence, as much so as I ever experienced any where. Toward the close, a few words seemed to be given me, which I expressed, and left the place greatly refreshed in Spirit. From thence I went to Michigan, where I found a wide field of labour amongst my own colour. Here I remained four years. . I established a school for coloured orphans, having always felt the great importance of the religious and moral *agricult*ure of children, and the great need of it, especially amongst the coloured people. Having white teachers, I met with much encouragement.

My eighty-seventh year had now arrived, when suffering from disease, and feeling released from travelling further in my good Master's cause, I came on to Philadelphia, where I have remained until this time, which brings me to my ninety-seventh year. When I went forth, it was without purse or scrip,—and I have come through great tribulation and temptation—not by any might of my own, for I feel that I am but as dust and ashes before my almighty Helper, who has, according to His promise, been with me and sustained me through all, and gives me now firm faith that he will be with me to the end, and, in his own good time, receive me into His everlasting rest.

THE STORY

OF

MATTIE J. JACKSON;

HER PARENTAGE—EXPERIENCE OF EIGHTEEN YEARS IN SLAVERY—
INCIDENTS DURING THE WAR—HER ESCAPE FROM SLAVERY.

A TRUE STORY.

WRITTEN AND ARRANGED BY

DR. L. S. THOMPSON,

(FORMERLY MRS. SCHUYLER,)

AS GIVEN BY MATTIE.

LAWRENCE:
PRINTED AT SENTINEL OFFICE, 123 ESSEX STREET.
1866.

PREFACE

The object in publishing this book is to gain sympathy from the earnest friends of those who have been bound down by a dominant race in circumstances over which they had no control—a butt of ridicule and a mark of oppression; over whom weary ages of degradation have passed. As the links have been broken and the shackles fallen from them through the unwearied efforts of our beloved martyr President Lincoln, as one I feel it a duty to improve the mind, and have ever had a thirst for education to fill that vacuum for which the soul has ever yearned since my earliest remembrance.

Thus I ask you to buy my little book to aid me in obtaining an education, that I may be enabled to do some good in behalf of the elevation of my emancipated brothers and sisters. I have now arrived at the age of twenty. As the first dawn of morning has passed, and the meridian of life is approaching, I know of no other way to speedily gain my object than through the aid and patronage of the friends of humanity.

NOTE Miss Jackson sustains a high moral character— has been much respected since she has been in Lawrence. She is from St. Louis, Missouri, and arrived here on the 11th of April, 1866. To gain the wish of the heart is utterly impossible without more means than she can obtain otherwise. Her friends have borne her expenses to Lawrence, and have and are still willing to render her aid as far their limited means will allow. She was in the same condition of all the neglected and oppressed. Her personal requirements are amply supplied. She now only craves the means to clothe and qualify the intellect. My humble prayer is that she may meet with unlimited success.

This young lady is highly worthy of all the aid our kind friends feel a duty to bestow upon her. She purposes lecturing and relating her story; and I trust she may render due satisfaction and bear some humble part in removing doubts indulged by the prejudices against the natural genius and talent of our race. May God give her grace and speed her on her way.

Respectfully yours,

L. S. T.

MATTIE'S STORY

My ancestors were transported from Africa to America at the time the slave trade flourished in the Eastern States. I cannot give dates, as my progenitors, being slaves, had no means of keeping them. By all accounts my great grandfather was captured and brought from Africa. His original name I never learned. His master's name was Jackson, and he resided in the State of New York. My grandfather was born in the same State, and also remained a slave for some length of time, when he was emancipated, his master presenting him with quite an amount of property. He was true, honest and responsible, and this present was given him as a reward. He was much encouraged by the cheering prospect of better days. A better condition of things now presented itself. As he possessed a large share of confidence, he came to the conclusion, as he was free, that he was capable of selecting his own residence and manage his own affairs with prudence and economy. But, alas, his hopes were soon blighted. More heart rending sorrow and degradation awaited him. He was earnestly invited by a white decoyer to relinquish his former design and accompany him to Missouri and join him in speculation and become wealthy. As partners, they embarked on board a schooner for St. Charles, Mo. On the passage, my grandfather was seized with a fever, and for a while was totally unconscious. When he regained his reason he found himself, near his journey's end, divested of his free papers and all others. On his arrival at St. Charles he was seized by a huge, surly looking slaveholder who claimed him as his

property. The contract had previously been concluded by his
Judas-like friend, who had received the bounty. Oh, what a
sad disappointment. After serving for thirty years to be thrust
again into bondage where a deeper degradation and sorrow
and hopeless toil were to be his portion for the remaining
years of his existence. In deep despair and overwhelmed with
grief, he made his escape to the woods, determined to put an
end to his sorrows by perishing with cold and hunger. His
master immediately pursued him, and in twenty-four hours
found him with hands and feet frost-bitten, in consequence
of which he lost the use of his fingers and toes, and was
thenceforth of little use to his new master. He remained with
him, however, and married a woman in the same station in
life. They lived as happily as their circumstances would
permit. As Providence alloted, they only had one son, which
was my father, Westly Jackson. He had a deep affection for
his family, which the slave ever cherishes for his dear ones.
He had no other link to fasten him to the human family but
his fervent love for those who were bound to him by love
and sympathy in their wrongs and sufferings. My grandfather
remained in the same family until his death. My father,
Westly Jackson, married, at the age of twenty-two, a girl
owned by James Harris, named Ellen Turner. Nothing of
importance occurred until three years after their marriage,
when her master, Harris failed through the extravagance and
mismanagement of his wife, who was a great spendthrift and
a dreaded terror to the poor slaves and all others with whom
she associated in common circumstances, consequently the
entire stock was sold by the sheriff to a trader residing in
Virginia. On account of the good reputation my mother
sustained as a worthy servant and excellent cook, a tyrannical
and much dreaded slaveholder watched for an opportunity to

purchase her, but fortunately arrived a few moments too late, and she was bid off in too poor a condition of health to remain long a subject of banter and speculation. Her husband was allowed to carefully lift her down from the block and accompany her to her new master's, Charles Canory, who treated her very kindly while she remained in his family. Mr. Canory resided in St. Charles County for five years after he purchased my mother. During that time my father and mother were in the same neighborhood, but a short distance from each other. But another trial awaited them. Her master removed twenty miles away to a village called Bremen, near St. Louis, Mo. My father, thereafter, visited my mother once a week, walking the distance every Saturday evening and returning on Sunday evening. But through all her trials and deprivations her trust and confidence was in Him who rescued his faithful followers from the fiery furnace and the lion's den, and led Moses through the Red Sea. Her trust and confidence was in Jesus. She relied on His precious promises, and ever found Him a present help in every time of need. Two years after this separation my father was sold and separated from us, but previous to his delivery to his new master he made his escape to a free State. My mother was then left with two children. She had three during the time they were permitted to remain together, and buried one. Their names were Sarah Ann, Mattie Jane and Esther J. When my father left I was about three years of age, yet I can well remember the little kindnesses my father used to bestow upon us, and the deep affection and fondness he manifested for us. I shall never forget the bitter anguish of my parents' hearts, the sighs they uttered or the profusion of tears which coursed down their sable cheeks. O, what a horrid scene, but he was not her's, for cruel hands had separated them.

The strongest tie of earthly joy that bound the aching heart—
His love was e'er a joyous light that o er the pathway shone—
A fountain gushing ever new amid life's desert wild—
His slightest word was a sweet tone of music round her
    heart—
Their lives a streamlet blent in one. O, Father, must they
    part?
They tore him from her circling arms, her last and fond
    embrace—
O never again can her sad eyes gaze upon his mournful face.
It is not strange these bitter sighs are constant bursting forth.
Amid mirth and glee and revelry she never took a part,
She was a mother left alone with sorrow in her heart.

But my mother was conscious some time previous of the change that was to take place with my father, and if he was sold in the immediate vicinity he would be likely to be sold again at their will, and she concluded to assist him to make his escape from bondage. Though the parting was painful, it afforded her sollace in the contemplation of her husband becoming a free man, and cherishing a hope that her little family, through the aid of some angel of mercy, might be enabled to make their escape also, and meet to part no more on earth. My father came to spend the night with us, according to his usual custom. It was the last time, and sadness brooded upon his brow. It was the only opportunity he had to make his escape without suspicion and detection, as he was immediately to fall into the hands of a new master. He had never been sold from the place of his birth before, and was determined never to be sold again if God would verify his promise. My father was not educated, but was a preacher, and administered the Word of God according to the dictation and revelation of the spirit. His former master had allowed him the privilege of holding meetings in the village within the limits of his pass on the Sundays when he visited my mother. But on this Saturday evening he arrived and gave us all his farewell kiss, and hurried away. My mother's people were aware of my father's intention, but rather than spare my mother, and for fear she might be detected, they secreted his escape. His master called a number of times and enquired for him and strongly pressed my mother to give him an account of my father, but she never gave it. We waited patiently, hoping to learn if he succeeded in gaining his freedom. Many anxious weeks and months passed before we could get any tidings from him, until at length my mother heard that he was in Chicago, a free man and preaching the Gospel. He made every effort to get his family, but all in vain. The spirit of slavery so strongly existed that letters could not reach her; they were all destroyed. My parents had never learned the rescuing scheme of the underground railroad which had borne so many thousands to the standard of freedom and victories. They knew no other resource than to depend upon their own chance in running away and secreting themselves. If caught they were in a worse condition than before.

THEIR ATTEMPT
TO MAKE THEIR ESCAPE

Two years after my father's departure, my mother, with her two children, my sister and myself, attempted to make her escape. After traveling two days we reached Illinois. We slept in the woods at night. I believe my mother had food to supply us but fasted herself. But the advertisement had reached there

before us, and loafers were already in search of us, and as
soon as we were discovered on the brink of the river one of
the spies made enquiries respecting her suspicious appearance.
She was aware that she was arrested, consequently she gave a
true account of herself—that she was in search of her husband.
We were then destitute of any articles of clothing excepting
our wearing apparel. Mother had become so weary that she
was compelled to leave our package of clothing on the way.
We were taken back to St. Louis and committed to prison
and remained there one week, after which they put us in
Linch's trader's yard, where we remained about four weeks.
We were then sold to William Lewis. Mr. Lewis was a very
severe master, and inflicted such punishment upon us as he
thought proper. However, I only remember one severe
contest Mr. Lewis had with my mother. For some slight
offence Mrs. Lewis became offended and was tartly and
loudly reprimanding her, when Mr. L. came in and rashly
felled her to the floor with his fist. But his wife was constantly
pulling our ears, snapping us with her thimble, rapping us
on the head and sides of it. It appeared impossible to please
her. When we first went to Mr. L.'s they had a cowhide
which she used to inflict on a little slave girl she previously
owned, nearly every night. This was done to learn the little
girl to wake early to wait on her children. But my mother
was a cook, as I before stated, and was in the habit of roasting
meats and toasting bread. As they stinted us for food my
mother roasted the cowhide. It was rather poor picking, but
it was the last cowhide my mother ever had an opportunity
to cook while we remained in his family. Mr. L. soon moved
about six miles from the city, and entered in partnership with
his brother-in-law. The servants were then divided and distributed in both families. It unfortunately fell to my lot to

live with Mrs. Larry, my mistress' sister, which rendered my condition worse than the first. My master even disapproved of my ill treatment and took me to another place; the place my mother resided before my father's escape. After a short time Mr. Lewis again returned to the city. My mother still remained as cook in his family. After six years' absence of my father my mother married again a man by the name of George Brown, and lived with her second husband about four years, and had two children, when he was sold for requesting a different kind and enough food. His master considered it a great insult, and declared he would sell him. But previous to this insult, as he called it, my step-father was foreman in Mr. L.'s tobacco factory. He was trusty and of good moral habits, and was calculated to bring the highest price in the human market; therefore the excuse to sell him for the above offence was only a plot. The morning this offence occurred, Mr. L. bid my father to remain in the kitchen till he had taken his breakfast. After pulling his ears and slapping his face bade him come to the factory; but instead of going to the factory he went to Canada. Thus my poor mother was again left alone with two more children added to her misery and sorrow to toil on her weary pilgrimage.

> Racked with agony and pain she was left alone again,
> With a purpose nought could move
> And the zeal of woman's love,
> Down she knelt in agony
> To ask the Lord to clear the way.

> True she said O gracious Lord,
> True and faithful is thy word;
> But the humblest, poorest, may
> Eat the crumbs they cast away.

Though nine long years had passed
Without one glimmering light of day
She never did forget to pray
And has not yet though whips and chains are cast away.

For thus said the blessed Lord,
I will verify my word;
By the faith that has not failed,
Thou hast asked and shall prevail.

We remained but a short time at the same residence when
Mr. Lewis moved again to the country. Soon after, my little
brother was taken sick in consequence of being confined in a
box in which my mother was obliged to keep him. If
permitted to creep around the floor her mistress thought it
would take too much time to attend to him. He was two years
old and never walked. His limbs were perfectly paralyzed
for want of exercise. We now saw him gradually failing, but
was not allowed to render him due attention. Even the
morning he died she was compelled to attend to her usual
work. She watched over him for three months by night and
attended to her domestic affairs by day. The night previous
to his death we were aware he could not survive through the
approaching day, but it made no impression on my mistress
until she came into the kitchen and saw his life fast ebbing
away, then she put on a sad countenance for fear of being
exposed, and told my mother to take the child to her room,
where he only lived one hour. When she found he was dead
she ordered grave clothes to be brought and gave my mother
time to bury him. O that morning, that solemn morning. It
appears to me that when that little spirit departed as though
all heaven rejoiced and angels veiled their faces.

My mother too in concert joined,—
Her mingled praise with them combined.

> Her little saint had gone to God
> Who saved him with his precious blood.

Who said "Suffer little children to come unto me and forbid them not."

THE SOLDIERS, AND OUR TREATMENT DURING THE WAR

Soon after the war commenced the rebel soldiers encamped near Mr. Lewis' residence, and remained there one week. They were then ordered by General Lyons to surrender, but they refused. There were seven thousand Union and seven hundred rebel soldiers. The Union soldiers surrounded the camp and took them and exhibited them through the city and then confined them in prison. I told my mistress that the Union soldiers were coming to take the camp. She replied that it was false, that it was General Kelly coming to re-enforce Gen. Frost. In a few moments the alarm was heard. I told Mrs. L. the Unionists had fired upon the rebels. She replied it was only the salute of Gen. Kelley. At night her husband came home with the news that Camp Jackson was taken and all the soldiers prisoners. Mrs. Lewis asked how the Union soldiers could take seven hundred men when they only numbered the same. Mr. L. replied they had seven thousand. She was much astonished, and cast her eye around to us for fear we might hear her. Her suspicion was correct; there was not a word passed that escaped our listening ears. My mother and myself could read enough to make out the news in the papers. The Union soldiers took much delight in tossing a paper over the fence to us. It aggravated my mistress very much. My mother used to sit up nights and read to keep posted about the war. In a few days my mistress came down to the kitchen again with another bitter complaint that it was a sad affair that the Unionists had taken their delicate citizens who had enlisted and made prisoners of them—that they were babes. My mother reminded her of taking Fort Sumpter and Major Anderson and serving them the same and that turn about was fair play. She then hastened to her room with the speed of a deer, nearly unhinging every door in her flight, replying as she went that the Niggers and Yankees were seeking to take the country. One day, after she had visited the kitchen to superintend some domestic affairs, as she pretended, she became very angry without a word being passed, and said—"I think it has come to a pretty pass, that old Lincoln, with his long legs, an old rail splitter, wishes to put the Niggers on an equality with the whites; that her children should never be on an equal footing with a Nigger. She had rather see them dead." As my mother made no reply to her remarks, she stopped talking, and commenced venting her spite on my companion servant. On one occasion Mr. Lewis searched my mother's room and found a picture of President Lincoln, cut from a newspaper, hanging in her room. He asked her what she was doing with old Lincoln's picture. She replied it was there because she liked it. He then knocked her down three times, and sent her to the trader's yard for a month as punishment. My mistress indulged some hopes till the victory of New Orleans, when she heard the famous Union song sang to the tune of Yankee Doodle:

The rebels swore that New Orleans never should be taken,
But if the Yankees came so near they should not save their bacon.
That's the way they blustered when they thought they were so handy,
But Farragut steamed up one day and gave them Doodle Dandy.

Ben. Butler then was ordered down to regulate the city;
He made the rebels walk a chalk, and was not that a pity?

That's the way to serve them out—that's the way to treat them,
They must not go and put on airs after we have beat them.

He made the rebel banks shell out and pay the loyal people,
He made them keep the city clean from pig's sty to church steeple.
That's the way Columbia speaks, let all men believe her;
That's the way Columbia speaks instead of yellow fever.

He sent the saucy women up and made them treat us well
He helped the poor and snubbed the rich; they thought he was the
    devil,
Bully for Ben. Butler, then, they thought he was so handy;
Bully for Ben Butler then,—Yankee Doodle Dandy.

The days of sadness for mistress were days of joy for us. We shouted and laughed to the top of our voices. My mistress was more enraged than ever—nothing pleased her. One evening, after I had attended to my usual duties, and I supposed all was complete, she, in a terrible range, declared I should be punished that night. I did not know the cause, neither did she. She went immediately and selected a switch. She placed it in the corner of the room to await the return of her husband at night for him to whip me. As I was not pleased with the idea of a whipping I bent the switch in the shape of W, which was the first letter of his name, and after I had attended to the dining room my fellow servant and myself walked away and stopped with an aunt of mine during the night. In the morning we made our way to the Arsenal, but could gain no admission. While we were wandering about seeking protection, the girl's father overtook us and persuaded us to return home. We finally complied. All was quiet. Not a word was spoken respecting our sudden departure. All went on as usual. I was permitted to attend to my work without interruption until three weeks after. One morning I entered Mrs. Lewis' room, and she was in a room adjoining, complaining of something I had neglected. Mr. L. then enquired if I had done my work. I told him I had. She then flew into a rage and told him I was saucy, and to strike me, and he immediately gave me a severe blow with a stick of wood, which inflicted a deep wound upon my head. The blood ran over my clothing, which gave me a frightful appearance. Mr. Lewis then ordered me to change my clothing immediately. As I did not obey he became more enraged, and pulled me into another room and threw me on the floor, placed his knee on my stomach, slapped me on the face and beat me with his fist, and would have punished me more had not my mother interfered. He then told her to go away or he would compel her to, but she remained until he left me. I struggled mightily, and stood him a good test for a while, but he was fast conquering me when my mother came. He was aware my mother could usually defend herself against one man, and both of us would overpower him, so after giving his wife strict orders to take me up stairs and keep me there, he took his carriage and drove away. But she forgot it, as usual. She was highly gratified with my appropriate treatment, as she called it, and retired to her room, leaving me to myself. I then went to my mother and told her I was going away. She bid me go, and added "May the Lord help you." I started for the Arsenal again and succeeded in gaining admittance and seeing the Adjutant. He ordered me to go to another tent, where there was a woman in similar circumstances, cooking. When the General found I was there he sent me to the boarding house. I remained there three weeks, and when I went I wore the same stained clothing as when I was so severely punished, which has left a mark on my head which will ever remind me of my treatment while in slavery. Thanks be to God, though tortured by wrong and goaded by oppression, the hearts that would madden with misery have broken the iron yoke.

MR. LEWIS CALLS AT
THE BOARDING HOUSE

At the expiration of three weeks Mr. Lewis called at my boarding house, accompanied by his brother-in-law, and enquired for me, and the General informed him where I was. He then told me my mother was very anxious for me to come home, and I returned. The General had ordered Mr. Lewis to call at headquarters, when he told him if he had treated me right I would not have been compelled to seek protection of him; that my first appearance was sufficient proof of his cruelty. Mr. L. promised to take me home and treat me kindly. Instead of fulfilling his promise he carried me to the trader's yard, where, to my great surprise, I found my mother. She had been there during my absence, where she was kept for fear she would find me and take my brother and sister and make her escape. There was so much excitement at that time, (1861), by the Union soldiers rendering the fugitives shelter and protection, he was aware that if she applied to them, as he did not fulfill his promise in my case, he would stand a poor chance. If my mother made application to them for protection they would learn that he did not return me home, and immediately detect the intrigue. After I was safely secured in the trader's yard, Mr. L. took my mother home. I remained in the yard three months. Near the termination of the time of my confinement I was passing by the office when the cook of the Arsenal saw and recognized me and informed the General that Mr. L. had disobeyed his orders, and had put me in the trader's yard instead of taking me home. The General immediately arrested Mr. L. and gave him one hundred lashes with the cow-hide, so that they might identify him by a scarred back, as well as his slaves. My mother had the pleasure of washing his stained clothes, otherwise it would not have been known. My master was compelled to pay three thousand dollars and let me out. He then put me to service, where I remained seven months, after which he came in great haste and took me into the city and put me into the trader's yard again. After he received the punishment he treated my mother and the children worse than ever, which caused her to take her children and secrete themselves in the city, and would have remained undetected had it not been for a traitor who pledged himself to keep the secret. But King Whiskey fired up his brain one evening, and out popped the secret. My mother and sister were consequently taken and committed to the trader's yard. My little brother was then eight years of age, my sister sixteen, and myself eighteen. We remained there two weeks, when a rough looking man, called Capt. Tirrell, came to the yard and enquired for our family. After he had examined us he remarked that we were a fine looking family, and bid us retire. In about two hours he returned, at the edge of the evening, with a covered wagon, and took my mother and brother and sister and left me. My mother refused to go without me, and told him she would raise an alarm. He advised her to remain as quiet as possible. At length she was compelled to go. When she entered the wagon there was a man standing behind with his hands on each side of the wagon to prevent her from making her escape. She sprang to her feet and gave this man a desperate blow, and leaping to the ground she made an alarm. The watchmen came to her assistance immediately, and there was quite a number of

Union policemen guarding the city at that time, who rendered her due justice as far as possible. This was before the emancipation proclamation was issued. After she leaped from the wagon they drove on, taking her children to the boat. The police questioned my mother. She told them that Capt. Tirrell had put her children on board the boat, and was going to take them to Memphis and sell them into hard slavery. They accompanied her to the boat, and arrived just as they were casting off. The police ordered them to stop and immediately deliver up the children, who had been secreted in the Captain's private apartment. They were brought forth and returned. Slave speculation was forbidden in St. Louis at that time. The Union soldiers had possession of the city, but their power was limited to the suppression of the selling of slaves to got out of the city. Considerable smuggling was done, however, by pretending Unionism, which was the case with our family.

RELEASED FROM THE TRADER'S YARD AND TAKEN TO HER NEW MASTER

Immediately after dinner my mother called for me to accompany her to our new home, the residence of the Captain, together with my brother and sister. We fared very well while we were there. Mrs. Tirrell was insane, and my mother had charge of the house. We remained there four months. The Captain came home only once a week and he never troubled us for fear we might desert him. His intention was to smuggle us away before the State became free. That was the understanding when he bought us of Mr. Lewis, as it was not much of an object to purchase slaves while the proclamation was pending, and they likely to lose all their property; but they would, for a trifle purchase a whole family of four or five persons to send out of the State. Kentucky paid as much, or more than ever, for slaves. As they pretended to take no part in the rebellion they supposed they would be allowed to keep them without interference. Consequently the Captain's intention was to keep as quiet as possible till the excitement concerning us was over, and he could get us off without detection. Mr. Lewis would rather have disposed of us for nothing than have seen us free. He hated my mother in consequence of her desire for freedom, and her endeavors to teach her children the right way as far as her ability would allow. He also held a charge against her for reading the papers and understanding political affairs. When he found he was to lose his slaves he could not bear the idea of her being free. He thought it too hard, as she had raised so many tempests for him, to see her free and under her own control. He had tantalized her in every possible way to humiliate and annoy her; yet while he could demand her services he appreciated and placed perfect confidence in mother and family. None but a fiendish slaveholder could have rended an honest Christian heart in such a manner as this.

> Though it was her sad and weary lot to toil in slavery
> But one thing cheered her weary soul
> When almost in despair
> That she could gain a sure relief in attitude of prayer

CAPT. TIRRELL REMOVES THE FAMILY—ANOTHER STRATEGY

One day the Captain commenced complaining of the expense of so large a family, and proposed to my mother that we should work out and he take part of the pay. My mother told him she would need what she earned for my little brother's support. Finally the Captain consented, and I was the first to be disposed of. The Captain took me in his buggy and carried me to the Depot, and I was put into a Union family, where I remained five months. Previous to my leaving, however, my mother and the Captain entered into a contract—he agreeing not to sell us, and mother agreeing not to make her escape. While she was carrying out her promise in good faith, he was plotting to separate us. We were all divided except mother and my little brother, who remained together. My sister remained with one of the rebels, but was tolerably treated. We all fared very well; but it was only the calm before the rending tornado. Captain T. was Captain of the boat to Memphis, from which the Union soldiers had rescued us. He commenced as a deck hand on the boat, then attained a higher position, and continued to advance until he became her Captain. At length he came in possession of slaves. Then his accomplishments were complete. He was a very severe slave master. Those mushroom slaveholders are much dreaded, as their severity knows no bounds

> Bondage and torture, scourges and chains
> Placed on our backs indelible stains.

I stated previously, in relating a sketch of my mother's history, that she was married twice, and both husbands were to be sold and made their escape. They both gained their freedom. One was living,—the other died before the war. Both made every effort to find us, but to no purpose. It was some years before we got a correct account of her second husband, and he had no account of her, except once he heard that mother and children had perished in the woods while endeavoring to make their escape. In a few years after his arrival in the free States he married again.

When about sixteen years of age, while residing with her original master, my mother became acquainted with a young man, Mr. Adams, residing in a neighboring family, whom she much respected; but he was soon sold, and she lost trace of him entirely, as was the common occurrence with friends and companions though united by the nearest ties. When my mother arrived at Captain Tirrell's, after leaving the boat, in her excitement she scarce observed anything except her little group so miraculously saved from perhaps a final separation in this world. She at length observed that the servant who was waiting to take her to the Captain's residence in the country was the same man with whom she formed the acquaintance when sixteen years old, and they again renewed their acquaintance. He had been married and buried his wife. It appeared that his wife had been in Captain Tirrell's family many years, and he also, for some time. They had a number of children, and Capt. Tirrell had sold them down South. This cruel blow, assisted by severe flogging and other ill treatment, rendered the mother insane, and finally caused her death.

> In agony close to her bosom she pressed,
> The life of her heart, the child of her breast—
> Oh love from its tenderness gathering might
> Had strengthed her soul for declining age.
>
> But she is free. Yes, she has gone from the land of the slave;
> The hand of oppression must rest in the grave.
> The blood hounds have missed the scent of her way,
> The hunter is rifled and foiled of his prey.

After my mother had left the Captain to take care of herself and child, according to agreement with the Captain, she became engaged to Mr. Adams. He had bought himself previously for a large price. After they became acquainted, the Captain had an excellent opportunity of carrying out his stratagem. He commenced bestowing charity upon Mr. Adams. As he had purchased himself, and Capt. T. had agreed not to sell my mother, they had decided to marry at an early day. They hired a house in the city and were to commence housekeeping immediately. The Captain made him a number of presents and seemed much pleased with the arrangement. The day previous to the one set for the marriage, while they were setting their house in order, a man called and enquired for a nurse, pretending he wanted one of us. Mother was absent; he said he would call again, but he never came. On Wednesday evening we attended a protracted meeting. After we had returned home and retired, a loud rap was heard at the door. My Aunt enquired who was there. The reply was, "Open the door or I will break it down." In a moment in rushed seven men, four watchmen and three traders, and ordered mother to take my brother and me and follow them, which she hastened to do as fast as possible, but we were not allowed time to put on our usual attire. They thrust us into a close carriage. For fear of my mother alarming the citizens they threw her to the ground and choked her until she was nearly strangled, then pushed her into a coach. The night was dark and dreary; the stars refused to shine, the moon to shed her light.

> 'Tis not strange the heavenly orbs
> In silence blushed neath Nature's sable garb
> When woman's gagged and rashly torn away
> Without blemish and without crime.
> Unheeded by God's holy word:—
> Unloose the fetters, break the chain,
> And make my people free again,

And let them breath pure freedom's air
And her rich bounty freely share.
Let Eutopia stretch her bleeding hands abroad;
Her cry of anguish finds redress from God.

We were hurried along the streets. The inhabitants heard our cries and rushed to their doors, but our carriage being perfectly tight, and the alarm so sudden, that we were at the jail before they could give us any relief. There were strong Union men and officers in the city, and if they could have been informed of the human smuggling they would have released us. But oh, that horrid, dilapidated prison, with its dim lights and dingy walls, again presented itself to our view. My sister was there first, and we were thrust in and remained there until three o'clock the following afternoon. Could we have notified the police we should have been released, but no opportunity was given us. It appears that this kidnapping had been in contemplation from the time we were before taken and returned; and Captain Tirrell's kindness to mother,—his benevolence towards Mr. Adams in assisting him to furnish his house,—his generosity in letting us work for ourselves,— his approbation in regard to the contemplated marriage was only a trap. Thus instead of a wedding Thursday evening, we were hurled across the ferry to Albany Court House and to Kentucky through the rain and without our outer garments. My mother had lost her bonnet and shawl in the struggle while being thrust in the coach, consequently she had no protection from the storm, and the rest of us were in similar circumstances. I believe we passed through Springfield. I think it was the first stopping place after we left East St. Louis, and we were put on board the cars and secreted in the gentlemen's smoking car, in which there were only a few rebels. We arrived in Springfield about twelve o'clock at night. When we took the cars it was dark, bleak and cold. It was the 18th of March, and as we were without bonnets and clothing to shield us from the sleet and wind, we suffered intensely. The old trader, for fear that mother might make her escape, carried my brother, nine years of age, from one train to the other. We then took the cars for Albany, and arrived at eight o'clock in the morning. We were then carried on the ferry in a wagon. There was another family in the wagon, in the same condition. We landed at Portland, from thence to Louisville, and were put into John Clark's trader's yard, and sold out separately, except my mother and little brother, who were sold together. Mother remained in the trader's yard two weeks, my sister six, myself four.

THE FARE AT THEIR NEW HOMES

Mother was sold to Captain Plasio. My sister to Benj. Board, and myself to Capt. Ephraim Frisbee. The man who bought my mother was a Spaniard. After she had been there a short time he tried to have my mother let my brother stop at his saloon, a very dissipated place, to wait upon his miserable crew, but my mother objected. In spite of her objections he took him down to try him, but some Union soldiers called at the saloon, and noticing that he was very small, they questioned him, and my brother, child like, divulged the whole matter. The Captain, fearful of being betrayed and losing his property, let him continue with my mother. The Captain paid eight hundred dollars for my mother and brother. We were all sold for extravagant prices. My sister, aged sixteen, was sold for eight hundred and fifty dollars; I was sold for nine hundred dollars. This was in 1863. My mother was cook and fared very well. My sister was sold to a single gentleman, whose intended took charge of her until they were married, after which they took her to her home. She was her waiter, and fared as well as could be expected. I fared worse than either of the family. I was not allowed enough to eat, exposed to the cold, and not allowed through the cold winter to thoroughly warm myself once a month. The house was very large, and I could gain no access to the fire. I was kept constantly at work of the heaviest kind,—compelled to move heavy trunks and boxes,—many times to wash till ten and twelve o'clock at night. There were three deaths in the family while I remained there, and the entire burden was put upon me. I often felt to exclaim as the Children of Israel did: "O Lord, my burden is greater than I can bear." I was then seventeen years of age. My health has been impaired from that time to the present. I have a severe pain in my side by the slightest over exertion. In the Winter I suffer intensely with cold, and cannot get warm unless in a room heated to eighty degrees. I am infirm and burdened with the influence of slavery, whose impress will ever remain on my mind and body. For six months I tried to make my escape. I used to rise at four o'clock in the morning to find some one to assist me, and at last I succeeded. I was allowed two hours once in two weeks to go and return three miles. I could contrive no other way than to improve one of these opportunities, in which I was finally successful. I became acquainted with some persons who assisted slaves to escape by the underground railroad. They were colored people. I was to pretend going to church, and the man who was to assist and introduce me to the proper parties was to linger on the street opposite the house, and I was to follow at a short distance. On Sunday evening I begged leave to attend church, which was reluctantly granted if I completed all my work, which was no easy task. It appeared as if my mistress used every possible exertion to delay me from church, and I concluded that her old cloven-footed companion had impressed his intentions on her mind. Finally, when I was ready to start, my mistress took a notion to go out to ride, and desired me to dress her little boy, and then get ready for church. Extensive hoops were then worn, and as I had attached my whole wardrobe under mine by a cord around my waist, it required considerable dexterity and no small amount of maneuvering to hide the fact from my mistress. While attending to the child I had managed to stand in one corner of the room, for fear she might come in contact with me and thus discover that my hoops were not so elastic as they usually are. I endeavored to conceal my excitement by backing and edging very genteelly out of the door. I had nine pieces of clothing thus concealed on my person, and as the string which fastened them was small it caused me considerable discomfort. To my great satisfaction I at last passed into the street, and my master and mistress drove down the street in great haste and were soon out of sight. I saw my guide patiently awaiting me. I followed him at a distance until we arrived at the church, and there met two young ladies, one of whom handed me a pass and told me to follow them at a square's distance. It was now twilight. There was a company of soldiers about to take passage across the ferry, and I followed. I showed my pass, and proceeded up the stairs on the boat. While thus ascending the stairs, the cord which held my bundle of clothing broke, and my feet became entangled in my wardrobe, but by proceeding, the first step released one foot and the next the other. This was observed only by a few soldiers, who were too deeply engaged in their own affairs to interfere with mine. I seated myself in a remote corner of the boat, and in a few moments I landed on free soil for the first time in my life, except when hurled through Albany and Springfield at the time of our capture. I was now under my own control. The cars were waiting in Jefferson City for the passengers for Indianapolis, where we arrived about nine o'clock.

MATTIE IN INDIANAPOLIS— THE GLORY OF FREEDOM— PRESIDENT LINCOLN'S REMAINS EXHIBITED

My first business, after my arrival at Indianapolis was to find a boarding place in which I at once succeeded, and in a few hours thereafter was at a place of service of my own choice. I had always been under the yoke of oppression, compelled to submit to its laws, and not allowed to advance a rod from the house, or even out of call, without a severe punishment. Now this constant fear and restless yearning was over. It appeared as though I had emerged into a new world, or had never lived in the old one before. The people I lived with were Unionists, and became immediately interested in teaching and encouraging me in my literary advancement and all other important improvements, which precisely met the natural desires for which my soul had ever yearned since my earliest recollection. I could read a little, but was not allowed to learn in slavery. I was obliged to pay twenty-five cents for every letter written for me. I now began to feel that as I was free I could learn to write, as well as others; consequently Mrs. Harris, the lady with whom I lived, volunteered to assist me. I was soon enabled to write quite a legible hand, which I find a great convenience. I would advise all, young, middle aged or old, in a free country to learn to read and write. If this little book should fall into the hands of one deficient of the important knowledge of writing, I hope they will remember the old maxim:—"Never too old to learn." Manage your own secrets, and divulge them by the silent language of your own pen. Had our blessed President considered it too humiliating to learn in advanced years, our race would yet have remained under the galling yoke of oppression. After I had been with Mrs. Harris seven months, the joyful news came of the surrender of Lee's army and the capture of Richmond.

Whilst the country's hearts were throbbing,
　　Filled with joy for victories won;
Whilst the stars and stripes were waving
　　O'er each cottage, ship and dome,
Came upon like winged lightning
　　Words that turned each joy to dread,
Froze with horror as we listened:
　　Our beloved chieftain, Lincoln's dead

War's dark clouds has long held o'er us,
　　They have rolled their gloomy fold's away,
And all the world is anxious, waiting
　　For that promised peaceful day.
But that fearful blow inflicted,
　　Fell on his devoted head,
And from every town and hamlet
　　Came the cry our Chieftain's dead.

Weep, weep, O bleeding nation
　　For the patriot spirit fled,
All untold our country's future—
　　Buried with the silent dead.

God of battles, God of nations to our country send relief
Turn each lamentation into joy whilst we mourn our murdered
     chief.

On the Saturday after the assassination of the President
there was a meeting held on the Common, and a vote taken
to have the President's body brought through Indianapolis,
for the people to see his dear dead face. The vote was taken
by raising the hands, and when the question was put in favor
of it a thousand black hands were extended in the air,
seemingly higher and more visible than all the rest. Nor were
their hands alone raised, for in their deep sorrow and gloom
they raised their hearts to God, for well they knew that He,
through martyred blood, had made them free. It was some
time before the remains reached Indianapolis, as it was near
the last of the route. The body was placed in the centre of
the hall of the State House, and we marched in by fours, and
divided into two on each side of the casket, and passed directly
through the hall. It was very rainy,—nothing but umbrellas
were to be seen in any direction. The multitude were passing
in and out from eight o'clock in the morning till four o'clock
in the afternoon. His body remained until twelve o'clock in
the evening, many distinguished persons visiting it, when
amid the booming of cannon, it moved on its way to Springfield, its final resting-place. The death of the President was
like an electric shock to my soul. I could not feel convinced
of his death until I gazed upon his remains, and heard the
last roll of the muffled drum and the farewell boom of the
cannon. I was then convinced that though we were left to the
tender mercies of God, we were without a leader.

     Gone, gone is our chieftain,
     The tried and the true;
     The grief of our nation the world never knew.

We mourn as a nation has never yet mourned;
The foe to our freedom more deeply has scorned.

In the height of his glory in manhood's full prime,
Our country's preserver through darkest of time;
A merciful being, whose kindness all shared
Shown mercy to others. Why was he not spared?

The lover of Justice, the friend of the slave,
He struck at oppression and made it a grave;
He spoke for our bond-men, and chains from them fell,
By making them soldiers they served our land well.

Because he had spoken from sea unto sea
Glad tidings go heavenward, our country is free,
And angels I'm thinking looked down from above,
With sweet smiles approving his great works of love.

His name with the honor forever will live,
And time to his laurels new lustre will give;
He lived so unselfish, so loyal and true,
That his deeds will shine brighter at every view.

Then honor and cherish the name of the brave,
The champion of freedom, the friend to the slave,
The far-sighted statesman who saw a fair end,
When north land and south land one flag shall defend.

Rest, rest, fallen chieftain, thy labors are o'er,
For thee mourns a nation as never before;
Farewell honored chieftain whom millions adore,
Farewell gentle spirit, whom heaven has won.

SISTER LOST—MOTHER'S ESCAPE

In two or three weeks after the body of the President was
carried through, my sister made her escape, but by some

means we entirely lost trace of her. We heard she was in a free State. In three months my mother also escaped. She rose quite early in the morning, took my little brother, and arrived at my place of service in the afternoon. I was much surprised, and asked my mother how she came there. She could scarcely tell me for weeping, but I soon found out the mystery. After so many long years and so many attempts, for this was her seventh, she at last succeeded, and we were now all free. My mother had been a slave for more than forty-three years, and liberty was very sweet to her. The sound of freedom was music in our ears; the air was pure and fragrant; the genial rays of the glorious sun burst forth with a new lustre upon us, and all creation resounded in responses of praise to the author and creator of him who proclaimed life and freedom to the slave. I was overjoyed with my personal freedom, but the joy at my mother's escape was greater than anything I had ever known. It was a joy that reaches beyond the tide and anchors in the harbor of eternal rest. While in oppression, this eternal life-preserver had continually wafted her toward the land of freedom, which she was confident of gaining, whatever might betide. Our joy that we were permitted to mingle together our earthly bliss in glorious strains of freedom was indescribable. My mother responded with the children of Israel,—"The Lord is my strength and my song. The Lord is a man of war, and the Lord is his name." We left Indianapolis the day after my mother arrived, and took the cars at eleven o'clock the following evening for St. Louis, my native State. We were then free, and instead of being hurried along, bare headed and half naked, through cars and boats, by a brutal master with a bill of sale in his pocket, we were our own, comfortably clothed, and having the true emblems of freedom.

MOTHER'S MARRIAGE

It appeared to me that the city presented an entirely new aspect. The reader will remember that my mother was engaged to be married on the evening after we were kidnapped, and that Mr. Adams, her intended, had prepared the house for the occasion. We now went in search of him. He had moved about five miles into the country. He had carefully preserved his furniture and was patiently awaiting our return. We were gone two years and four months. The clothing and furniture which we had collected were all destroyed. It was over a year after we left St. Louis before we heard from there. We went immediately from the cars to my aunt's, and from there went to Mr. Adams' residence and took him by surprise. They were married in a week after our return. My mother is comfortably situated on a small farm with a kind and affectionate companion, with whom she had formed an early acquaintance, and from whom she had been severed by the ruthless hand of Wrong; but by the divine hand of Justice they were now reunited forever.

MATTIE MEETS HER OLD MASTER— GOES TO SERVICE—IS SENT FOR BY HER STEP-FATHER IN LAWRENCE, MASS.

In a short time I had selected a place of service, and was improving my studies in a small way. The place I engaged was in the family where I was born, where my mother lived when my father Jackson made his escape. Although Mr.

Canory's family were always kind to us, I felt a great
difference between freedom and slavery. After I had been
there a short time my step-father sent for me and my half
brother to come to Lawrence. He had been waiting ever since
the State was free, hoping to get some account of us. He had
been informed, previously, that mother, in trying to make
her escape, had perished by the way, and the children also,
but he was never satisfied. He was aware that my aunt was
permanently in St. Louis, as her master had given her family
their freedom twenty years previous. She was formerly owned
by Major Howe, harness and leather dealer, yet residing in
St. Louis. And long may he live and his good works follow
him and his posterity forever. My father well knew the
deception of the rebels, and was determined to persevere until
he had obtained a satisfactory account of his family. A
gentleman moved directly from Lawrence to St. Louis, who
made particular enquiries for us, and even called at my aunt's.
We then heard directly from my father, and commenced
correspondence. He had not heard directly from us since he
made his escape, which was nine years. He had never heard
of his little son who my mother was compelled by Mrs.
Lewis to confine in a box. He was born eight months after
he left. As soon as possible after my mother consented to let
my little brother go to his father he sent means to assist us to
make preparations for our journey to the North. At first he
only sent for his little son. My mother was anxious about
sending him alone. He was only eleven years old, and
perfectly unused to traveling, and had never been away from
his mother. Finally my father came to the conclusion that, as
my mother had endured such extreme hardships and sufferings during the nine years he was not permitted to participate
or render her any assistance, that it would afford him much

pleasure in sending for us both, bearing our expenses and making us as comfortable as his means would allow. Money was sent us, and our kind friend, Mr. Howe, obtained our tickets and voluntarily assisted us in starting. We left for the North on Monday, April 9th, and arrived safe and sound, on the 11th. We found my step-father's residence about six o'clock in the evening. He was not expecting us till the next day. Our meeting is better imagined than told. I cannot describe it. His little son was only two years old when he left, and I was eleven, and we never expected to meet him again this side of eternity. It was Freedom that brought us together. My father was comfortably situated in a nice white cottage, containing some eight rooms, all well furnished, and attached to it was a fine garden. His wife, who is a physician, was absent, but returned on the following day. The people were kind and friendly. They informed me there was no other colored family in the city, but my step-mother was continually crowded with friends and customers without distinction. My step-mother had buried her only son, who returned from the war in a decline. The white friends were all in deep sympathy with them. I felt immediately at home among such kind and friendly people, and have never felt homesick, except when I think of my poor mother's farewell embrace when she accompanied us to the cars. As soon as my step-mother had arrived, and our excitement was over, they commenced calculating upon placing me in the Sabbath school at the church where my mother belonged. On the next Sabbath I accompanied her and joined the Sabbath school, she occupying a side seat about middle way up the house. I was not reminded of my color except by an occasional loafer or the Irish, usually the colored man's enemy. I was never permitted to attend a white church before, or ride in any public conveyance without being placed in a car for the especial purpose; and in the street cars we were not permitted to ride at all, either South or West. Here I ride where I please, without the slightest remark, except from the ignorant. Many ask me if I am contented. They can imagine by the above contrast. My brother and myself entered the public school, and found a host of interested friends and formed many dear acquaintances whom I shall never forget. After attending school a month the term closed. I advanced in my studies as fast as could be expected. I never attended school but one month before. I needed more attention than my kind teacher could possibly bestow upon me, encumbered as she was by so many small children. Mother then proposed my entering some select school and placing myself entirely under its discipline and influence. I was much pleased with the idea, but as they had already been to so much expense for me, I could not wish to place them under any heavier contribution. I had previously told my step-mother my story, and how often my own mother had wished she could have it published. I did not imagine she could find time to write and arrange it, but she immediately proposed writing and publishing the entire story, by the sale of which I might obtain the aid towards completing my studies. I am glad I came to the old Bay State, the people of which the rebels hate with an extreme hatred. I found it just such a place as I had imagined by the appearance of the soldiers and the kindness they manifested.

> New England, that blessed land,
> All in a happy Union band;
> They with the needy share their bread
> And teach the weak the Word of God.

We never heard from my sister Hester, who made her escape from Kentucky, except when she was on the cars, though we have no doubt she succeeded in gaining her freedom.

SUMMARY

On my return to St. Louis I met my old master, Lewis, who strove so hard to sell us away that he might avoid seeing us free, on the street. He was so surprised that before he was aware of it he dropped a bow. My mother met Mrs. Lewis, her old mistress, with a large basket on her arm, trudging to market. It appeared she had lived to see the day when her children had to wait upon themselves, and she likewise. The Yankees had taken possession, and her posterity were on an equality with the black man. Mr. Lewis despised the Irish, and often declared he would board at the hotel before he would employ Irish help, but he now has a dissipated Irish cook. When I was his slave I was obliged to keep away every fly from the table, and not allow one to light on a person. They are now compelled to brush their own flies and dress themselves and children. Mr. Lewis' brother Benjamin was a more severe slave master than the one who owned me. He was a tobacconist and very wealthy. As soon as the war commenced he turned Unionist to save his property. He was very severe in his punishments. He used to extend his victim, fastened to a beam, with hands and feet tied, and inflict from fifty to three hundred lashes, laying their flesh entirely open, then bathe their quivering wounds with brine, and, through his nose, in a slow rebel tone he would tell them "You'd better walk a fair chalk line or else I'll give yer twice as much." His former friends, the guerrillas, were aware he only turned Union to save his cash, and they gave those persons he had abused a large share of his luxury. They then, in the presence of his wife and another distinguished lady, tortured him in a most inhuman manner. For pretending Unionism they placed him on a table and threatened to dissect him alive if he did not tell them where he kept his gold. He immediately informed them. They then stood him against the house and fired over his head. From that, they changed his position by turning him upside down, and raising him two feet from the floor, letting him dash his head against the floor until his skull was fractured, after which he lingered awhile and finally died. There was a long piece published in the paper respecting his repentance, benevolence, & c. All the slaves who ever lived in his family admit the Lord is able to save to the uttermost. He saved the thief on the cross, and perhaps he saved him.

When I made my escape from slavery I was in a query how I was to raise funds to bear my expenses. I finally came to the conclusion that as the laborer was worthy of his hire, I thought my wages should come from my master's pocket. Accordingly I took twenty-five dollars. After I was safe and had learned to write, I sent him a nice letter, thanking him for the kindness his pocket bestowed to me in time of need. I have never received any answer to it.

When I complete my education, if my life is spared, I shall endeavor to publish further details of our history in another volume from my own pen.

CHRISTIANITY

Christianity is a system claiming God for its author, and the welfare of man for its object. It is a system so uniform, exalted and pure, that the loftiest intellects have acknowledged its influence, and acquiesced in the justness of its claims. Genius has bent from his erratic course to gather fire from her altars, and pathos from the agony of Gethsemane and the sufferings of Calvary. Philosophy and science have paused amid their speculative researches and wonderous revelations, to gain wisdom from her teachings and knowledge from her precepts. Poetry has culled her fairest flowers and wreathed her softest, to bind her Author's "bleeding brow." Music has strung her sweetest lyres and breathed her noblest strains to celebrate His fame; whilst Learning has bent from her lofty heights to bow at the lowly cross. The constant friend of man, she has stood by him in his hour of greatest need. She has cheered the prisoner in his cell, and strengthened the martyr at the stake. She has nerved the frail and sinking heart of woman for high and holy deeds. The worn and weary have rested their fainting heads upon her bosom, and gathered strength from her words and courage from her counsels. She has been the staff of decrepit age, and the joy of manhood in its strength. She has bent over the form of lovely childhood, and suffered it to have a place in the Redeemer's arms. She has stood by the bed of the dying, and unveiled the glories of eternal life; gilding the darkness of the tomb with the glory of the resurrection.

Christianity has changed the moral aspect of nations. Idolatrous temples have crumbled at her touch, and guilt owned its deformity in her presence. The darkest habitations of earth have been irradiated with heavenly light, and the death shriek of immolated victims changed for ascriptions of praise to God and the Lamb. Envy and Malice have been rebuked by her contented look, and fretful Impatience by her gentle and resigned manner.

At her approach, fetters have been broken, and men have

risen redeemed from dust, and freed from chains. Manhood has learned its dignity and worth, its kindred with angels, and alliance to God.

To man, guilty, fallen and degraded man, she shows a fountain drawn from the Redeemer's veins; there she bids him wash and be clean. She points him to "Mount Zion, the city of the living God, to an innumerable company of angels, to the spirits of just men made perfect, and to Jesus the Mediator of the new Covenant," and urges him to rise from the degradation of sin, renew his nature and join with them. She shows a pattern so spotless and holy, so elevated and pure, that he might shrink from it discouraged, did she not bring with her a promise from the lips of Jehovah, that he would give power to the faint, and might to those who have no strength. Learning may bring her ample pages and her ponderous records, rich with the spoils of every age, gathered from every land, and gleaned from every source. Philosophy and science may bring their abstruse researches and wonderous revelations—Literature her elegance, with the toils of the pen, and the labors of the pencil—but they are idle tales compared to the truths of Christianity. They may cultivate the intellect, enlighten the understanding, give scope to the imagination, and refine the sensibilities; but they open not, to our dim eyes and longing vision, the land of crystal founts and deathless flowers. Philosophy searches earth; Religion opens heaven. Philosophy doubts and trembles at the portals of eternity; Religion lifts the veil, and shows us golden streets, lit by the Redeemer's countenance, and irradiated by his smile. Philosophy strives to reconcile us to death; Religion triumphs over it. Philosophy treads amid the pathway of stars, and stands a delighted listener to the music of the spheres; but Religion gazes on the glorious palaces of God, while the harpings of the blood-washed, and the songs of the redeemed, fall upon her ravished ear. Philosophy has her place; Religion her important sphere; one is of importance here, the other of infinite and vital importance both here and hereafter.

Amid ancient lore the Word of God stands unique and pre-eminent. Wonderful in its construction, admirable in its adaptation, it contains truths that a child may comprehend, and mysteries into which angels desire to look. It is in harmony with that adaptation of means to ends which pervades creation, from the polypus tribes, elaborating their coral homes, to man, the wonderous work of God. It forms the brightest link of that glorious chain which unites the humbles work of creation with the throne of the infinite and eternal Jehovah. As light, with its infinite particles and curiously blended colors, is suited to an eye prepared for the alterations of day; as air, with its subtle and invisible essence, is fitted for the delicate organs of respiration; and, in a word, as this material world is adapted to man's physical nature; so the word of eternal truth is adapted to his moral nature and mental constitution. It finds him wounded, sick and suffering, and points him to the balm of Gilead and the Physician of souls. It finds him stained by transgressions and defiled with guilt, and directs him to the "blood that cleanseth from all unrighteousness and sin." It finds him athirst and faint, pining amid the deserts of life, and shows him the wells of salvation and the rivers of life. It addresses itself to his moral and spiritual nature, makes provision for his wants and weaknesses, and meets his yearnings and aspirations. It is adapted to his mind in its earliest stages of progression, and its highest state of intellectuality. It provides light for his darkness, joy for his anguish, a solace for his woes, balm for his wounds, and heaven for his hopes. It unveils the unseen world, and reveals him who is the light of creation, and the joy of the universe, reconciled through the death of His Son. It promises the faithful a blessed re-union in a land undimmed with tears, undarkened by sorrow. It affords a truth for the living and a refuge for the dying. Aided by the Holy Spirit, it guides us through life, points out the shoals, the quicksands and hidden rocks which endanger our path, and at last leaves us with the eternal God for our refuge, and his everlasting arms for our protection.

Struggles · for · Freedom.

*Yours Truly
Lucy A Delaney*

FROM THE

DARKNESS COMETH THE LIGHT

⇒ OR ⇐

STRUGGLES FOR FREEDOM.

ST. LOUIS, MO.
PUBLISHING HOUSE OF J. T. SMITH,
No. 11, Bridge Entrance.

Dedication.

———

To those who by their valor have made their name immortal, from whom we are daily learning the lessons of patriotism, in whom we respect the virtues of charity, patience and friendship as displayed towards the colored race and to those

> "Whose deeds crowd History's pages
> And Time's great volume make,"

is this little volume reverently dedicated—

THE GRAND ARMY OF THE REPUBLIC.

Preface.

———

So many of my friends have urged me to give a short sketch of my varied life that I have consented, and herewith present it for the consideration of my readers. Those who were with me in the days of slavery will appreciate these pages, for though they cannot recur with any happiness to the now "shadowy past, or renew the unrenewable," the unaccountable longing for the aged to look backward and review the events of their youth will find an answering chord in this little book.

Those of you who have never suffered as we have, perhaps may suppose the case, and therefore accept with

interest and sympathy the passages of life and character
here portrayed and the lessons which should follow from
them.

If there is a want of unity or coherence in this work,
be charitable and attribute it to lack of knowledge and
experience in literary acquirements. As this is a world
of varied interests and many events, although we are each
but atoms, it must be remembered, that we assist in making the grand total of all history, and therefore are excus-
able in making our affairs of importance to ourselves, and
endeavoring to impress them on others. With this reason
of my seeking your favor, I leave you to the perusal of
my little tale.   L. A. D.

STRUGGLES FOR FREEDOM.

CHAPTER I.

"Soon is the echo and the shadow o'er,
Soon, soon we lie with lid-encumbered eyes
And the great fabrics that we reared before
Crumble to make a dust to hide who dies."

In the year 18——, Mr. and Mrs. John
Woods and Mr. and Mrs. Andrew Posey lived
as one family in the State of Illinois. Living
with Mrs. Posey was a little negro girl, named
Polly Crocket, who had made it her home
there, in peace and happiness, for five years.
On a dismal night in the month of September,
Polly, with four other colored persons, were
kidnapped, and, after being securely bound
and gagged, were put into a skiff and carried
across the Mississippi River to the city of

St. Louis. Shortly after, these unfortunate negroes were taken up the Missouri River and sold into slavery. Polly was purchased by a farmer. Thomas Botts, with whom she resided for a year, when, overtaken by business reverses, he was obliged to sell all he possessed, including his negroes.

Among those present on the day set apart for the sale was Major Taylor Berry, a wealthy gentleman who had travelled a long distance for the purpose of purchasing a servant girl for his wife. As was the custom, all the negroes were brought out and placed in a line, so that the buyers could examine their good points at leisure. Major Berry was immediately attracted by the bright and alert appearance of Polly, and at once negotiated with the trader, paid the price agreed upon, and started for home to present his wife with this flesh and blood commodity, which money could so easily procure in our vaunted land of freedom.

Mrs. Fanny Berry was highly pleased with Polly's manner and appearance, and concluded to make a seamstress of her. Major Berry had a mulatto servant, who was as handsome as an Apollo, and when he and Polly met each other, day after day, the natural result followed, and in a short time, with the full consent of Major Berry and his wife, were married. Two children were the fruit of this marriage, my sister Nancy and myself, Lucy A. Delaney.

While living in Franklin county, Major Berry became involved in a quarrel with some gentleman, and a duel was resorted to, to settle the difficulty and avenge some fancied insult. The major arranged his affairs and made his will, leaving his negroes to his wife during her life-time and at her death they were to be free; this was his expressed wish.

My father accompanied Major Berry to New Madrid, where the fatal duel was fought, and stayed by him until the end came, received his last sigh, his last words, and closed his dying eyes, and afterwards conveyed the remains of his best friend to the bereaved family with a sad heart. Though sympathizing deeply with them in their affliction, my father was much disturbed as to what disposition would be made of him, and after Major Berry was consigned with loving hands to his last resting place, these haunting thoughts obtruded, even in his sleeping hours.

A few years after, Major Berry's widow married Robert Wash, an eminent lawyer, who afterwards became Judge of the Supreme Court. One child was born to them, who, when she grew to womanhood, became Mrs. Francis W. Goode, whom I shall always hold in grateful remembrance as long as life lasts, and God bless her in her old age, is my fervent prayer for her kindness to me, a poor little slave girl!

We lived in the old "Wash" mansion some

time after the marriage of the Judge, until
their daughter Frances was born.   How well I
remember those happy days!   Slavery had no
horror then for me, as I played about the place,
with the same joyful freedom as the little
white children.   With mother, father and
sister, a pleasant home and surroundings, what
happier child than I!

As I carelessly played away the hours,
mother's smiles would fade away, and her
brow contract into a heavy frown. I wondered much thereat, but the time came—ah!
only too soon, when I learned the secret of
her ever-changing face!

CHAPTER II.

Mrs. Wash lost her health, and, on the advice of a physician, went to Pensacola, Florida, accompanied by my mother. There she died, and her body was brought back to St. Louis and there interred. After Mrs. Wash's death, the troubles of my parents and their children may be said to have really commenced.

Though in direct opposition to the will of Major Berry, my father's quondam master and friend, Judge Wash tore my father from his wife and children and sold him "way down South!"

Slavery! cursed slavery! what crimes has it invoked! and, oh! what retribution has a righteous God visited upon these traders in human flesh! The rivers of tears shed by us helpless

ones, in captivity, were turned to lakes of
of blood! How often have we cried in our
anguish, "Oh! Lord, how long, how long?"
But the handwriting was on the wall, and
tardy justice came at last and avenged the
woes of an oppressed race! Chickamauga,
Shiloh, Atlanta and Gettysburgh, spoke in
thunder tones! John Brown's body had
indeed marched on, and we, the ransomed
ones, glorify God and dedicate ourselves to
His service, and acknowledge His greatness
and goodness in rescuing us from such
bondage as parts husband from wife, the
mother from her children, aye, even the babe
from her breast!

Major Berry's daughter Mary, shortly after,
married H. S. Cox, of Philadelphia, and they
went to that city to pass their honeymoon,
taking my sister Nancy with them as wait-
ing-maid. When my father was sold South,
my mother registered a solemn vow that her
children should not continue in slavery all

their lives, and she never spared an opportunity to impress it upon us, that we must
get our freedom whenever the chance offered.
So here was an unlooked-for avenue of escape
which presented much that was favorable in
carrying out her desire to see Nancy a free
woman.

Having been brought up in a free State,
mother had learned much to her advantage,
which would have been impossible in a slave
State, and which she now proposed to turn to
account for the benefit of her daughter. So
mother instructed my sister not to return with
Mr. and Mrs. Cox, but to run away, as soon
as chance offered, to Canada, where a friend
of our mother's lived who was also a runaway slave, living in freedom and happiness
in Toronto.

As the happy couple wandered from city to
city, in search of pleasure, my sister was constantly turning over in her mind various
plans of escape. Fortune finally favored

Nancy, for on their homeward trip they stopped at Niagara Falls for a few days. In her own words I will describe her escape:

"In the morning, Mr. and Mrs. Cox went for a drive, telling me that I could have the day to do as I pleased. The shores of Canada had been tantalizing my longing gaze for some days, and I was bound to reach there long before my mistress returned. So I locked up Mrs. Cox's trunk and put the key under the pillow, where I was sure she would find it, and I made a strike for freedom! A servant in the hotel gave me all necessary information and even assisted me in getting away. Some kind of a festival was going on, and a large crowd was marching from the rink to the river, headed by a band of music. In such a motley throng I was unnoticed, but was trembling with fear of being detected. It seemed an age before the ferry boat arrived, which at last appeared, enveloped in a gigantic wreath of black smoke. Hastily I embarked, and as the boat stole away into the misty twilight and among crushing fields of ice, though the air was chill and gloomy, I felt the warmth of freedom as I neared the Canada shore. I landed, without question, and found my mother's friend with but little difficulty, who assisted me to get work and support myself. Not long afterwards, I married a prosperous farmer, who provided me with a happy home, where I brought my children into the world without the sin of slavery to strive against."

On the return of Mrs. Cox to St. Louis she sent for my mother and told her that Nancy had run away. Mother was very thankful, and in her heart arose a prayer of thanksgiving, but outwardly she pretended to be vexed and angry. Oh! the impenetrable mask of these poor black creatures! how much of joy, of sorrow, of misery and anguish have they hidden from their tormentors!

I was a small girl at that time, but remember how wildly mother showed her joy at Nancy's escape when we were alone together. She would dance, clap her hands, and, waving them above her head, would indulge in one of those wierd negro melodies, which so charm and fascinate the listener.

Mrs. Cox commenced housekeeping on a grand and extended scale, having a large acquaintance, she entertained lavishly. My mother cared for the laundry, and I, who was living with a Mrs. Underhill, from New York, and was having rather good times, was compelled to go live with Mrs. Cox to mind the baby. My pathway was thorny enough, and though there may be no roses without thorns, I had thorns in plenty with no roses.

I was beginning to plan for freedom, and was forever on the alert for a chance to escape and join my sister. I was then twelve years old, and often talked the matter over with mother and canvassed the probabilities of both of us getting away. No schemes were too wild for us to consider! Mother was especially restless, because she was a free woman up to the time of her being kidnapped, so the injustice and weight of slavery bore more heavily upon her than upon me. She did not dare to talk it over with anyone for fear that they would sell her further down the river, so I was her only confidant. Mother was always planning and getting ready to go, and while the fire was burning brightly, it but needed a little more provocation to add to the flames.

CHATER III.

Mrs. Cox was always very severe and exacting with my mother, and one occasion, when something did not suit her, she turned on mother like a fury, and declared, "I am just tired out with the 'white airs' you put on, and if you don't behave differently, I will make Mr. Cox sell you down the river at once."

Although mother turned grey with fear, she presented a bold front and retorted that "she didn't care, she was tired of that place, and didn't like to live there, nohow." This so infuriated Mr. Cox that he cried, "How dare a negro say what she liked or what she did not like; and he would show her what he should do."

So, on the day following, he took my mother to an auction-room on Main Street and sold

her to the highest bidder, for five hundred and
fifty dollars. Oh! God! the pity of it! "In
the home of the brave and the land of the
free," in the sight of the stars and stripes—
that symbol of freedom—sold away from her
child, to satisfy the anger of a peevish
mistress!

My mother returned to the house to get her
few belongings, and straining me to her
breast, begged me to be a good girl, that she
was going to run away, and would buy me as
soon as she could. With all the inborn faith
of a child, I believed it most fondly, and when
I heard that she had actually made her
escape, three weeks after, my heart gave an
exultant throb and cried, "God is good!"

A large reward was offered, the bloodhounds (curse them and curse their masters)
were set loose on her trail. In the day time
she hid in caves and the surrounding woods,
and in the night time, guided by the wondrous
North Star, that blessed lodestone of a slave

people, my mother finally reached Chicago, where she was arrested by the negro-catchers. At this time the Fugitive Slave Law was in full operation, and it was against the law of the whole country to aid and protect an escaped slave; not even a drink of water, for the love of the Master, might be given, and those who dared to do it (and there were many such brave hearts, thank God!) placed their lives in danger.

The presence of bloodhounds and "nigger-catchers" in their midst, created great excitement and scandalized the community. Feeling ran high and hundreds of people gathered together and declared that mother should not be returned to slavery; but fearing that Mr. Cox would wreak his vengeance upon me, my mother finally gave herself up to her captors, and returned to St. Louis. And so the mothers of Israel have been ever slain through their deepest affections!

After my mother's return, she decided to

sue for her freedom, and for that purpose employed a good lawyer. She had ample testimony to prove that she was kidnapped, and it was so fully verified that the jury decided that she was a free woman, and papers were made out accordingly.

In the meanwhile, Miss Martha Berry had married Mr. Mitchell and taken me to live with her. I had never been taught to work, as playing with the babies had been my sole occupation; therefore, when Mrs. Mitchell commanded me to do the weekly washing and ironing, I had no more idea how it was to be done than Mrs. Mitchell herself. But I made the effort to do what she required, and my failure would have been amusing had it not been so appalling. In those days filtering was unknown and the many ways of clearing water were to me an unsolved riddle. I never had to do it, so it never concerned me how the clothes were ever washed clean.

As the Mississippi water was even muddier

than now, the results of my washing can be better imagined than described. After soaking and boiling the clothes in its earthy depths, for a couple of days, in vain attempt to get them clean, and rinsing through several waters, I found the clothes were getting darker and darker, until they nearly approximated my own color. In my despair, I frantically rushed to my mother and sobbed out my troubles on her kindly breast. So in the morning, before the white people had arisen, a friend of my mother came to the house and washed out the clothes. During all this time, Mrs. Mitchell was scolding vigorously, saying over and over again, "Lucy, you do not want to work, you are a lazy, good-for-nothing nigger!" I was angry at being called a nigger, and replied, "You don't know nothing, yourself, about it, and you expect a poor ignorant girl to know more than you do yourself; if you had any feeling you would get somebody to teach me, and then I'd do well enough."

She then gave me a wrapper to do up, and told me if I ruined that as I did the other clothes, she would whip me severely. I answered, "You have no business to whip me. I don't belong to you."

My mother had so often told me that she was a free woman and that I should not die a slave, I always had a feeling of independence, which would invariably crop out in these encounters with my mistress; and when I thus spoke, saucily, I must confess, she opened her eyes in angry amazement and cried:

"You *do* belong to me, for my papa left you to me in his will, when you were a baby, and you ought to be ashamed of yourself to talk so to one that you have been raised with; now, you take that wrapper, and if you don't do it up properly, I will bring you up with a round turn."

Without further comment, I took the wrapper, which was too handsome to trust to an inexperienced hand, like Mrs. Mitchell very well knew I was, and washed it, with the same direful results as chronicled before. But I could not help it, as heaven is my witness. I was entirely and hopelessly ignorant! But of course my mistress would not believe it, and declared over and over again, that I did it on purpose to provoke her and show my defiance of her wishes. In vain did I disclaim any such intentions. She was bound to carry out her threat of whipping me.

I rebelled against such government, and would not permit her to strike me; she used shovel, tongs and broomstick in vain, as I disarmed her as fast as she picked up each weapon. Infuriated at her failure, my opposition and determination not to be whipped, Mrs. Mitchell declared she would report me to Mr. Mitchell and have him punish me.

When her husband returned home, she immediately entered a list of complaints against me as long as the moral law, including my failure to wash her clothes properly, and her

inability to break my head for it; the last in-
dictment seemed to be the heaviest she could
bring against me. I was in the shadow of the
doorway as the woman raved, while Mr.
Mitchell listened patiently until the end of his
wife's grievances reached an appeal to him to
whip me with the strength that a man alone
could possess.

Then he declared. "Martha, this thing of
cutting up and slashing servants is something
I know nothing about, and positively will not
do. I don't believe in slavery, anyhow; it is
a curse on this land, and I wish we were well
rid of it."

"Mr. Mitchell, I will not have that saucy
baggage around this house, for if she finds
you won't whip her, there will be no living
with her, so you shall just sell her, and I in-
sist upon it."

"Well, Martha," he answered, "I found the
girl with you when we were married, and as
you claim her as yours, I shall not interpose

any objections to the disposal of what you choose to call your property, in any manner you see fit, and I will make arrangements for selling her at once."

I distinctly overheard all that was said, and was just as determined not to be sold as I was not to be whipped. My mother's lawyer had told her to caution me never to go out of the city, if, at any time, the white people wanted me to go, so I was quite settled as to my course, in case Mr. Mitchell undertook to sell me.

Several days after this conversation took place, Mrs. Mitchell, with her baby and nurse, Lucy Wash, made a visit to her grand-mother's, leaving orders that I should be sold before her return; so I was not surprised to be ordered by Mr. Mitchell to pack up my clothes and get ready to go down the river, for I was to be sold that morning, and leave, on the steamboat Alex. Scott, at 3 o'clock in the afternoon.

"Can't I go see my mother, first?" I asked.

"No," he replied, not very gently, "there is no time for that, you can see her when you come back. So hurry up and get ready, and let us have no more words about it!"

How I did hate him! To hear him talk as if I were going to take a pleasure trip, when he knew that if he sold me South, as he intended, I would never see my dear mother again.

However, I hastily ran up stairs and packed my trunk, but my mother's injunction, "never to go out of the city," was ever present in my mind.

Mr. Mitchell was Superintendent of Indian Affairs, his office being in the dwelling house, and I could hear him giving orders to his clerk, as I ran lightly down the stairs, out of the front door to the street, and with fleet foot, I skimmed the road which led to my mother's door, and, reaching it, stood trembling in every limb with terror and fatigue.

I could not gain admittance, as my mother

was away to work and the door was locked. A white woman, living next door, and who was always friendly to mother, told me that she would not return until night. I clasped my hands in despair and cried, "Oh! the white people have sold me, and I had to run away to keep from being sent down the river."

This white lady, whose name I am sorry I cannot remember, sympathized with me, as she knew my mother's story and had written many letters for her, so she offered me the key of her house, which, fortunately, fitted my mother's door, and I was soon inside, cowering with fear in the darkness, magnifying every noise and every passing wind, until my imagination had almost converted the little cottage into a boat, and I was steaming down South, away from my mother, as fast as I could go.

Late at night mother returned, and was told all that had happened, and after getting sup

per, she took me to a friend's house for con-
cealment, until the next day.

As soon as Mr. Mitchell had discovered my
unlooked-for departure, he was furious, for he
did not think I had sense enough to run
away; he accused the coachman of helping
me off, and, despite the poor man's denials,
hurried him away to the calaboose and put
him under the lash, in order to force a con-
fession. Finding this course unavailing, he
offered a reward to the negro catchers, on the
same evening, but their efforts were equally
fruitless.

CHAPTER IV.

On the morning of the 8th of September, 1842, my mother sued Mr. D. D. Mitchell for the possession of her child, Lucy Ann Berry. My mother, accompanied by the sheriff, took me from my hiding-place and conveyed me to the jail, which was located on Sixth Street, between Chestnut and Market, where the Laclede Hotel now stands, and there met Mr. Mitchell, with Mr. H. S. Cox, his brother in-law.

Judge Bryant Mullanphy read the law to Mr. Mitchell, which stated that if Mr. Mitchell took me back to his house, he must give bond and security to the amount of two thousand dollars, and furthermore, I should not be taken out of the State of Missouri until I had a chance to prove my freedom.   Mr. H. S. Cox became his security and Mr. Mitchell gave bond accordingly, and then demanded that I should be put in jail.

"Why do you want to put that poor young girl in jail?" demanded my lawyer. "Because," he retorted, "her mother or some of her crew might run her off, just to make me pay the two thousand dollars; and I would like to see her lawyer, or any other man, in jail, that would take up a d—— nigger case like that."

"You need not think, Mr. Mitchell," calmly replied Mr. Murdock, "because my client is colored that she has no rights, and can be cheated out of her freedom. She is just as free as you are, and the Court will so decide it, as you will see."

However, I was put in a cell, under lock and key, and there remained for seventeen long and dreary months, listening to the

"—— foreign echoes from the street,
Faint sounds of revel, traffic, conflict keen—
And, thinking that man's reiterated feet

Have gone such ways since e'er the world has been,
I wondered how each oft-used tone and glance
Retains its might and old significance."

My only crime was seeking for that freedom which was my birthright! I heard Mr. Mitchell tell his wife that he did not believe in slavery, yet, through his instrumentality, I was shut away from the sunlight, because he was determined to prove me a slave, and thus keep me in bondage. Consistency, thou art a jewel!

At the time my mother entered suit for her freedom, she was not instructed to mention her two children, Nancy and Lucy, so the white people took advantage of this flaw, and showed a determination to use every means in their power to prove that I was not her child.

This gave my mother an immense amount of trouble, but she had girded up her loins for the fight, and, knowing that she was right, was resolved, by the help of God and a good lawyer, to win my case against all opposition.

After advice by competent persons, mother went to Judge Edward Bates and begged him to plead the case, and, after fully considering the proofs and learning that my mother was a poor woman, he consented to undertake the case and make his charges only sufficient to cover his expenses. It would be well here to give a brief sketch of Judge Bates, as many people wondered that such a distinguished statesman would take up the case of an obscure negro girl.

Edward Bates was born in Belmont, Goochland county, Va., September, 1793. He was of Quaker descent, and inherited all the virtues of that peace-loving people. In 1812, he received a midshipman's warrant, and was only prevented from following the sea by the influence of his mother, to whom he was greatly attached. Edward emigrated to Missouri in 1814, and entered upon the practice of law, and, in 1816, was appointed prosecuting lawyer for the St. Louis Circuit. Toward the close of the same year, he was appointed Attorney General for the new State of Missouri, and in 1826, while yet a young man, was elected representative to congress as an anti-Democrat, and served one term. For the following twenty-five years, he devoted himself to his profession, in which he was a shining light. His probity and uprightness attracted to him a class of people who were in the right and only sought justice, while he repelled, by his virtues, those who traffic in the miseries or mistakes of unfortunate people, for they dared not come to him and seek counsel to aid them in their villainy.

In 1847, Mr. Bates was delegate to the Convention for Internal Improvement, held in Chicago, and by his action he came prominently before the whole country. In 1850, President Fillmore offered him the portfolio of Secretary of War, which he declined. Three years later, he accepted the office of Judge of St. Louis Land Court.

When the question of the repeal of the Missouri Compromise was agitated, he earnestly opposed it, and thus became identified with the "free labor" party in Missouri, and united with it, in opposition to the admission of Kansas under the Lecompton Constitution. He afterwards became a prominent anti-slavery man, and in 1859 was mentioned as a candidate for the presidency. He was warmly supported by his own State, and for a time it seemed that the opposition to Governor Seward might concentrate on him. In the National Republican Convention, 1860, he received forty-eight votes on the first ballot, but when it became apparent that Abraham Lincoln was the favorite, Mr. Bates withdrew his name. Mr. Lincoln appointed Judge Bates Attorney General, and while in the Cabinet he acted a dignified, safe and faithful part. In 1864, he resigned his office and returned to his home in St. Louis, where he died in 1869, surrounded by his weeping family.

"——loved at home, revered abroad.
Princes and lords are but the breath of kings;
'An honest man's the noblest work of God.'"

On the 7th of February, 1844, the suit for my freedom began. A bright, sunny day, a day which the happy and care-free would drink in with a keen sense of enjoyment. But my heart was full of bitterness; I could see only gloom which seemed to deepen and gather closer to me as I neared the court-room. The jailer's sister-in-law, Mrs. Lacy, spoke to me of submission and patience; but I could not feel anything but rebellion against my lot. I could not see one gleam of bright-ness in my future, as I was hurried on to hear my fate decided.

Among the most important witnesses were Judge Robert Wash and Mr. Harry Douglas, who had been an overseer on Judge Wash's farm, and also Mr. MacKeon, who bought my mother from H. S. Cox, just previous to her running away.

Judge Wash testified that "the defendant,

Lucy A. Berry, was a mere infant when he came in possession of Mrs. Fannie Berry's estate, and that he often saw the child in the care of its reputed mother, Polly, and to his best knowledge and belief, he thought Lucy A. Berry was Polly's own child."

Mr. Douglas and Mr. MacKeon corroborated Judge Wash's statement. After the evidence from both sides was all in, Mr. Mitchell's lawyer, Thomas Hutchinson, commenced to plead. For one hour, he talked so bitterly against me and against my being in possession of my liberty that I was trembling, as if with ague, for I certainly thought everybody must believe him; indeed I almost believed the dreadful things he said, myself, and as I listened I closed my eyes with sickening dread, for I could just see myself floating down the river, and my heart-throbs seemed to be the throbs of the mighty engine which propelled me from my mother and freedom forever!

Oh! what a relief it was to me when he

finally finished his harangue and resumed his
seat! As I never heard anyone plead before,
I was very much alarmed, although I knew in
my heart that every word he uttered was a
lie! Yet, how was I to make people believe?
It seemed a puzzling question!

Judge Bates arose, and his soulful eloquence
and earnest pleading made such an impression on my sore heart, I listened with renewed
hope. I felt the black storm clouds of doubt
and despair were fading away, and that I was
drifting into the safe harbor of the realms of
truth. I felt as if everybody *must* believe
him, for he clung to the truth, and I wondered
how Mr. Hutchinson could so lie about a poor
defenseless girl like me.

Judge Bates chained his hearers with the
graphic history of my mother's life, from the
time she played on Illinois banks, through
her trials in slavery, her separation from her
husband, her efforts to become free, her
voluntary return to slavery for the sake of her

child, Lucy, and her subsequent efforts in securing her own freedom. All these incidents he lingered over step by step, and concluding, he said:

"Gentlemen of the jury, I am a slave-holder myself, but, thanks to the Almighty God, I am above the base principle of holding anybody a slave that has as good right to her freedom as this girl has been proven to have; she was free before she was born; her mother was free, but kidnapped in her youth, and sacrificed to the greed of negro traders, and no free woman can give birth to a slave child, as it is in direct violation of the laws of God and man!"

At this juncture he read the affidavit of Mr. A. Posey, with whom my mother lived at the time of her abduction; also affidavits of Mr. and Mrs. Woods, in corroboration of the previous facts duly set forth. Judge Bates then said:

"Gentleman of the jury, here I rest this case,

as I would not want any better evidence for one of my own children. The testimony of Judge Wash is alone sufficient to substantiate the claim of Polly Crockett Berry to the defendant as being her own child."

The case was then submitted to the jury, about 8 o'clock in the evening, and I was returned to the jail and locked in the cell which I had occupied for seventeen months, filled with the most intense anguish.

CHAPTER V.

"There's a joy in every sorrow,
  There's a relief from every pain;
Though to-day 'tis dark to-morrow
  HE will turn all bright again."

Before the sheriff bade me good night he told me to be in readiness at nine o'clock on the following morning to accompany him back to court to hear the verdict. My mother was not at the trial. She had lingered many days about the jail expecting my case would be called, and finally when called to trial the dear, faithful heart was not present to sustain me during that dreadful speech of Mr. Hutch. inson. All night long I suffered agonies of fright, the suspense was something awful, and could only be comprehended by those who have gone through some similar ordeal.

I had missed the consolation of my mother's presence, and I felt so hopeless and alone!

Blessed mother ! how she clung and fought for me. No work was too hard for her to undertake. Others would have flinched before the obstacles which confronted her, but undauntedly she pursued her way, until my freedom was established by every right and without a questioning doubt!

On the morning of my return to Court, I was utterly unable to help myself. I was so overcome with fright and emotion,—with the alternating feelings of despair and hope—that I could not stand still long enough to dress myself. I trembled like an aspen leaf ; so I sent a message to Mrs. Lacy to request permission for me to go to her room, that she might assist me in dressing. I had done a great deal of sewing for Mrs. Lacy, for she had showed me much kindness, and was a good Christian. She gladly assisted me, and under her willing hands I was soon made ready, and, promptly at nine o'clock, the sheriff called and escorted me to the courthouse.

On our way thither, Judge Bates overtook us. He lived out a short distance in the country, and was riding on horseback. He tipped his hat to me as politely as if I were the finest lady in the land, and cried out, "Good morning Miss Lucy, I suppose you had pleasant dreams last night!" He seemed so bright and smiling that I was inbued with renewed hope; and when he addressed the sheriff with "Good morning Sir." I don't suppose the jury was out twenty minutes were they?" and the sheriff replied "oh! no, sir," my heart gave a leap, for I was sure that my fate was decided for weal or woe.

I watched the judge until he turned the corner and desiring to be relieved of suspense from my pent-up anxiety, I eagerly asked the sheriff if I were free, but he gruffly answered that "he didn't know." I was sure he did know, but was too mean to tell me. How could he have been so flinty, when he must have seen how worried I was.

At last the courthouse was reached and I had taken my seat in such a condition of helpless terror that I could not tell one person from another. Friends and foes were as one, and vainly did I try to distinguish them. My long confinement, burdened with harrowing anxiety, the sleepless night I had just spent, the unaccountable absence of my mother, had brought me to an indescribable condition. I felt dazed, as if I were no longer myself. I seemed to be another person—an onlooker—and in my heart dwelt a pity for the poor, lonely girl, with down-cast face, sitting on the bench apart from anyone else in that noisy room. I found myself wondering where Lucy's mother was, and how she would feel if the trial went against her; I seemed to have lost all feeling about it, but was speculating what Lucy would do, and what her mother would do, if the hand of Fate was raised against poor Lucy! Oh! how sorry I did feel for myself!

At the sound of a gentle voice, I gathered courage to look upward, and caught the kindly gleam of Judge Bates' eyes, as he bent his gaze upon me and smilingly said, "I will have you discharged in a few minutes, Miss Lucy!"

Some other business occupied the attention of the Court, and when I had begun to think they had forgotten all about me, Judge Bates arose and said calmly, "Your Honor, I desire to have this girl, Lucy A. Berry, discharged before going into any other business."

Judge Mullanphy answered "Certainly!" Then the verdict was called for and rendered, and the jurymen resumed their places. Mr. Mitchell's lawyer jumped up and exclaimed: "Your Honor, my client demands that this girl be remanded to jail. He does not consider that the case has had a fair trial, I am not informed as to what course he intends to pursue, but I am now expressing his present wishes?"

Judge Bates was on his feet in a second and cried: "For shame! is it not enough that this girl has been deprived of her liberty for a year and a half, that you must still pursue her after a fair and impartial trial before a jury, in which it was clearly proven and decided that she had every right to freedom? I demand that she be set at liberty at once!"

"I agree with Judge Bates," responded Judge Mullanphy, "and the girl may go!"

Oh! the overflowing thankfulness of my grateful heart at that moment, who could picture it? None but the good God above us! I could have kissed the feet of my deliverers, but I was too full to express my thanks, but with a voice trembling with tears I tried to thank Judge Bates for all his kindness.

As soon as possible, I returned to the jail to bid them all good-bye and thank them for their good treatment of me while under their care. They rejoiced with me in my good fortune and wished me much success and happiness in years to come.

I was much concerned at my mother's prolonged absence, and was deeply anxious to meet her and sob out my joy on her faithful bosom. Surely ⁙ was the hands of God which prevented mother's presence at the trial, for broken down with anxiety and loss of sleep on my account, the revulsion of feeling would have been greater than her over-wrought heart could have sustained.

As soon as she heard of the result, she hurried to meet me, and hand in hand we gazed into each others eyes and saw the light of freedom there, and we felt in our hearts that we could with one accord cry out: "Glory to God in the highest, and peace and good will towards men."

Dear, dear mother! how solemnly I invoke your spirit as I review these trying scenes of my girlhood, so long agone! Your patient face and neatly-dressed figure stands ever in the foreground of that checkered time; a figure showing naught to an on-looker but the common place virtues of an honest woman!

Never would an ordinary observer connect these virtues with aught of heroism or greatness, but to me they are as bright rays as ever emanated from the lives of the great ones of earth, which are portrayed on historic pages —to me, the qualities of her true, steadfast heart and noble soul become "a constellation, and is tracked in Heaven straightway."

CHAPTER VI.

After the trial was over and my mother had at last been awarded the right to own her own child, her next thought reverted to sister Nancy, who had been gone so long, and from whom we had never heard, and the greatest ambition mother now had was to see her child Nancy. So, we earnestly set ourselves to work to reach the desired end, which was to visit Canada and seek the long-lost girl. My mother being a first-class laundress, and my-self an expert seamstress, it was easy to pro-cure all the work we could do, and command our own prices. We found, as well as the whites, a great difference between slave and free labor, for while the first was compulsory, and, therefore, at the best, perfunctory, the latter must be superior in order to create a demand, and realizing this fully, mother and

I expended the utmost care in our respective callings, and were well rewarded for our efforts.

By exercising rigid economy and much self-denial, we, at last, accumulated sufficient to enable mother to start for Canada, and oh! how rejoiced I was when that dear, over-worked mother approached the time, when her hard-earned and long-deferred holiday was about to begin. The uses of adversity is a worn theme, and in it there is much of weak cant, but when it is considered how much of sacrifice the poverty-stricken must bear in order to procure the slightest gratification, should it not impress the thinking mind with amazement, how much of fortitude and patience the honest poor display in the exercise of self-denial! Oh! ye prosperous! prate of the uses of adversity as poetically as you please, we who are obliged to learn of them by bitter experience would greatly prefer a change of surroundings.

Mother arrived in Toronto two weeks after she left St. Louis, and surprised my sister Nancy, in a pleasant home. She had married a prosperous farmer, who owned the farm on which they lived, as well as some property in the city near by. Mother was indescribably happy in finding her child so pleasantly situated, and took much pleasure with her bright little grandchildren; and after a long visit, returned home, although strongly urged to remain the rest of her life with Nancy; but old people are like old trees, uproot them, and transplant to other scenes, they droop and die, no matter how bright the sunshine, or how balmy the breezes.

On her return, mother found me with Mrs. Elsie Thomas, where I had lived during her absence, still sewing for a livelihood. Those were the days in which sewing machines were unknown, and no stitching or sewing of any description was allowed to pass muster, unless each stitch looked as if it were a part of the

cloth. The art of fine sewing was lost when
sewing machines were invented, and though
doubtless they have given women more
leisure, they have destroyed that extreme
neatness in the craft, which obtained in the
days of long ago.

Time passed happily on with us, with no
event to ruffle life's peaceful stream, until
1845, when I met Frederick Turner, and in a
few short months we were made man and wife.
After our marriage, we removed to Quincy,
Ill., but our happiness was of short duration,
as my husband was killed in the explosion of
the steamboat Edward Bates, on which he
was employed. To my mind it seemed a
singular coincidence that the boat which bore
the name of the great and good man, who
had given me the first joy of my meagre life
—the precious boon of freedom—and that his
namesake should be the means of weighting
me with my first great sorrow; this thought
seemed to reconcile me to my grief, for that

name was ever sacred, and I could not speak it without reverence.

The number of killed and wounded were many, and they were distributed among friends and hospitals; my husband was carried to a friend's, where he breathed his last. Telegraphs were wanting in those times, so days passed before this wretched piece of news reached me, and there being no railroads, and many delays, I reached the home of my friend only to be told that my husband was dead and buried. Intense grief was mine, and my repining worried mother greatly; she never believed in fretting about anything that could not be helped. My only consolation from her was, "Cast your burden on the Lord." *My* husband is down South, and I don't know where he is; he may be dead; he may be alive; he may be happy and comfortable; he may be kicked, abused and half-starved. *Your* husband, honey, is in heaven; and mine —God only knows where he is!"

In those few words, I knew her burden was heavier than mine, for I had been taught that there was hope beyond the grave, but hope was left behind when sold "down souf"; and so I resolved to conceal my grief, and devote myself to my mother, who had done so much and suffered so much for me.

We then returned to St. Louis, and took up the old life, minus the contentment which had always buoyed us up in our daily trials, and with an added sorrow which cast a sadness over us. But Time, the great healer, taught us patience and resignation, and once more we were

"Waiting when fortune sheds brightly her smile,
There always is something to wait for the while."

CHAPTER VII.

Four years afterward, I became the wife of
Zachariah Delaney, of Cincinnati, with whom
I have had a happy married life, continuing
forty-two years.   Four children were born to
us, and many were the plans we mapped out for
their future, but two of our little girls were
called from us while still in their childhood.
My remaining daughter attained the age of
twenty-two years, and left life behind, while
the brightest of prospects was hers, and my
son, in the fullness of a promising youth, at
the age of twenty-four, "turned his face to the
wall."   So my cup of bitterness was full to
the brim and overflowing; yet one consolation
was always mine!   Our children were born
free and died free!   Their childhood and my
maternity were never shadowed with a thought
of separation.   The grim reaper did not spare

them, but they were as "treasures laid up in heaven." Such a separation one could accept from the hand of God, with humble submission, "for He calleth His own!"

Mother always made her home with me until the day of her death; she had lived to see the joyful time when her race was made free, their chains struck off, and their right to their own flesh and blood lawfully acknowledged. Her life, so full of sorrow, was ended. full of years and surrounded by many friends, both black and white, who recognized and appreciated her sufferings and sacrifices and rejoiced that her old age was spent in freedom and plenty. The azure vault of heaven bends over us all, and the gleaming moonlight brightens the marble tablet which marks her last resting place, "to fame and fortune unknown," but in the eyes of Him who judgeth us, hers was a heroism which outvied the most famous.

  * * * * * * *

I frequently thought of father, and wondered if he were alive or dead; and at the time
of the great exodus of negroes from the
South, a few years ago, a large number arrived in St. Louis, and were cared for by the
colored people of that city. They were shel-
tered in churches, halls and private houses,
until such time as they could pursue their
journey. Methought, I will find him in this
motley crowd, of all ages, from the crowing
babe in its mother's arms, to the aged and
decrepit, on whom the marks of slavery were
still visible. I piled inquiry upon inquiry,
until after long and persistent search, I learned that my father had always lived on the
same plantation, fifteen miles from Vicks-
burg. I wrote to my father and begged him
to come and see me and make his home with
me; sent him the money, so he would be to
no expense, and when he finally reached St.
Louis, it was with great joy that I received
him. Old, grizzled and gray, time had dealt

hardly with him, and he looked very little like the dapper master's valet, whose dark beauty won my mother's heart.

Forty-five years of separation, hard work, rough times and heart longings, had perseveringly performed its work, and instead of a man bearing his years with upright vigor, he was made prematurely old by the accumulation of troubles. My sister Nancy came from Canada, and we had a most joyful reunion, and only the absence of our mother left a vacuum, which we deeply and sorrowfully felt. Father could not be persuaded to stay with us, when he found his wife dead; he longed to get back to his old associations of forty-five years standing, he felt like a stranger in a strange land, and taking pity on him, I urged him no more, but let him go, though with great reluctance.

* * * * * * *

There are abounding in public and private libraries of all sorts, lives of people which fill our minds with amazement, admiration, sympathy, and indeed with as many feelings as there are people, so I can scarcely expect that the reader of these episodes of my life will meet with more than a passing interest, but as such I will commend it to your thought for a brief hour. To be sure, I am deeply sensible that this story, as written, is not a very striking performance, but I have brought you with me face to face with but only a few of the painful facts engendered by slavery, and the rest can be drawn from history. Just have patience a little longer, and I have done

I became a member of the Methodist Episcopal Church in 1855; was elected President of the first colored society, called the "Female Union," which was the first ever organized exclusively for women; was elected President of a society known as the "Daughters of Zion"; was matron of "Siloam Court," No. 2, three years in succession; was Most Ancient Matron of the "Grand Court of Missouri," of which only the wives of Masons are allowed to become members. I am at present, Past Grand Chief Preceptress of the "Daughters of the Tabernacle and Knights of Tabor," and also was Secretary, and am still a member, of Col. Shaw Woman's Relief Corps, No. 34, auxiliary to the Col. Shaw Post, 343, Grand Army of the Republic.

Considering the limited advantages offered me, I have made the best use of my time, and what few talents the Lord has bestowed on me I have not "hidden in a napkin," but used them for His glory and to benefit those for whom I live. And what better can we do than to live for others?

Except the deceitfulness of riches, nothing is so illusory as the supposition of interest we assume that our readers may feel in our affairs; but if this sketch is taken up for just a moment of your life, it may settle the problem in your mind, if not in others, "Can the negro race succeed, proportionately, as well as the

whites, if given the same chance and an equal
start ?"

"The hours are growing shorter for the millions who are toiling;
And the homes are growing better for the millions yet to be;
And we all shall learn the lesson, how that waste and sin are
        spoiling
The fairest and the finest of a grand humanity.

It is coming! it is coming! and men's thoughts are growing
        deeper;
They are giving of their millions as they never gave before;
They are learning the new Gospel; man must be his brother's
        keeper,
And right, not might, shall triumph, and the selfish rule no
        more."

Finis.

A Slave Girl's
Story

Being an Autobiography of
KATE DRUMGOOLD.

❧ ❧ ❧ ❧

BROOKLYN–NEW YORK.

CHAPTER I

Once a slave girl, I have endeavored to fill the pages with some of the most interesting thoughts that my mind is so full of, and not with something that is dry.

This sketch is written for the good of those that have written and prayed that the slaves might be a freed people, and have schools and books and learn to read and write for themselves; and the Lord, in His love for us and to us as a race, has ever found favor in His sight, for when we were in the land of bondage He heard the prayers of the faithful ones, and came to deliver them out of the Land of Egypt.

For God loves those that are oppressed, and will save them when they cry unto him, and when they put their trust in Him.

Some of the dear ones have gone to the better land, but this is one of the answers to their prayers.

We, as the Negro Race, are a free people, and God be praised for it. We as the Negro Race, need to feel proud of the race, and I for one do with all my heart and soul and mind, knowing as I do, for I have labored for the good of the race, that their children might be the bright and shining lights. And we can see the progress that we are making in an educational way in a short time, and I think that we should feel very grateful to God and those who are trying to help us forward. God bless such with their health, and heart full of that same love, that this world can not give nor taketh away.

There are many doors that are shut to keep us back as a race, but some are opened to us, and God be praised for those that are opened to the race, and I hope that they will be true to their trust and be of the greatest help to those that have given them a chance.

There are many that have lost their lives in the far South in trying to get an education, but there are many that have done well, and we feel like giving God all the praise.

I was born in Old Virginia, in or near the Valley, the other side of Petersburg, of slave parents, and I can just call to mind the time when the war began, for I was not troubled then about wars, as I was feeling as free as any one could feel, for I was sought by all of the rich whites of the neighborhood, as they all loved me, as noble whites will love a child, like I was in those days, and they would send for me if I should be at my play and have me to talk for them, and all of their friends learned to love me and send me presents, and I would stand and talk and preach for some time for them.

My dear mother was sold at the beginning of the war, from all of her little ones, after the death of the lady that she belonged to, and who was so kind to my dear mother and all of the rest of the negroes of the place; and she never liked the idea of holding us as slaves, and she always said that we were all that she had on the earth to love; and she did love me to the last.

The money that my mother was sold for was to keep the rich man from going to the field of battle, as he sent a poor white man in his stead, and should the war end in his favor, the poor white man should have given to him one negro, and that would fully pay for all of his service in the army. But my God moves in a way unknown to men, and they can never understand His ways, for He can plant His footsteps on the North, the South, the East, the West, and outride any man's ideas; and how wonderful are all of his ways. And if we, as a race, will only put our trust in Him, we shall gain the glorious victory, and be a people whose God is the God of all this broad earth, and may we humble ourselves before Him and call Him, Blessed.

I told you that my white mother did not like the idea of calling us her slaves, and she always prayed God that I should never know what slavery was, for she said I was never born to serve as did the slaves of some of the people that owned them.

And God, in His love for me and to me, never let me know of it, as did some of my own dear sisters, for some of them were hired out after the old home was broken up.

My mother was sold at Richmond, Virginia, and a gentleman bought her who lived in Georgia, and we did not know that she was sold until she was gone; and the saddest thought was to me to know which way she had gone, and I used to go outside and look up to see if there was anything that would direct me, and I saw a clear place in the sky, and it seemed to me the way she had gone, and I watched it three and a half years, not knowing what that meant, and it was there the whole time that mother was gone from her little ones.

On one bright Sunday I asked my older sister to go with me for a nice walk and she did so, for she was the one that was so kind to the rest of us—and we saw some sweet flowers on the wayside and we began to have delight in picking them, when all at once I was led to leave her alone with the flowers and to go where I could look up at that nice, clear spot, and as I wanted to get as near to it as I could, I got on the fence, and as I looked that way I saw a form coming to me that looked like my dear mother's, and calling to my sister Frances to come at once and see if that did not look like my dear

mother and she came to us, so glad to see us, and to ask after
her baby that she was sold from that was only six weeks old
when she was taken from it; and I would that the whole world
could have seen the joy of a mother and her two girls on that
heaven-made day—a mother returning back to her own once
more, a mother that we did not know that we should ever see
her face on this earth more. And mother, not feeling good
over the past events, had made up her mind that she would
take her children to a part of this land where she thought
that they would never be in bondage any more on this earth.

So she sought out the head man that was placed there by
the North to look after the welfare of lately emancipated
negroes of the South, to see that they should have their rights
as a freed people.

This gentleman's name was Major Bailley, who was a
gentleman of the highest type, and it was this loving man
that sent my dear mother and her ten little girls on to this
lovely city, and the same time he informed the people of
Brooklyn that we were on the way and what time we should
reach there; and it seemed as though the whole city were out
to meet us. And as God would have it, six of us had homes
on that same day, and the people had their carriages there to
take us to our new homes.

This God-sent blessing was of a great help to mother, as
she could get the money to pay her rent, which was ten
dollars per month, and God bless those of my sisters who
could help mother to care for her little ones, for they had not
been called home then, and God be praised for all that we
have ever did for her love and comfort while she kept house.

The subject was only a few years old, when she saw her
heart so fixed that she could not leave me at my mother's any
longer, so she took me to be her own dear, loving child, to

eat, drink, sleep and to go wherever she went, if it was for months, or even years; I had to be there as her own and not as a servant, for she did not like that, but I was there as her loving child for her to care for me, and everything that I wanted I had; truly do I feel grateful to my Heavenly Father for all of those blessings that came to me in the time that I needed so much of love and care.

This dear lady, Mrs. Bettie House, my white mother, died at the beginning of the war and then the time came for poor me to go to my own dear mother again for awhile, and soon the time came for us to be parted asunder, where we did not see one another any more until after the war of 1865. And we all thought that mother was dead, for we did not hear any tidings of her after she had reached the far South.

I shall never forget that lovely Sunday morning when I saw my dear mother returning again to her own native home and her own dear ones once more, but mother would not go to the house with us, as she did not want to take the law in her own hands. So she told sister and I where she was stopping and told us to come to her after we had told the gentleman where we lived, and I went to him and told him that mother had come back and wanted to have us to come where she was staying. He, Mr. House, did not want us to go, and I took my oldest sister and marched out to go where mother was and he did not like that freedom, and he tried to find which way that we had gone to the place, but he did not find us, and we had been to the place where the people were that had homes, and that they would kill us at first sight, and that was all that I wanted to see, and I did not find one thing true of their sayings.

Mother now has to tell the gentleman where to find all of her own dear ones whom God in His love for had kept for her, and she should have been very grateful to Him that her life had been prolonged and all that she had left alive were still alive, awaiting for her to return, and finding that her children were all over in different places, and now she has to tell where to find them, through the help of the Lord. And when she had gone for them and was told that some of her own were dead, she said that she would go and dig up their bones; but they were not dead, as was said, and she sent the soldiers after them and sometimes they were told the same as mother was, and some of the little ones had to be sent for two or three times before they were brought. My oldest sister knew where they all were, so she could help to get the rest.

One of my sisters who lived at the same place where we were living was detained and the soldiers had go three times before they could get her, for they said that she had died since we had left, for I would not stay at the place as he, Mr. House, did not want us to go on Monday to see my mother, on whom I should look to, as she had come to claim her own. I told my oldest sister that we would leave, and my sister Annie was at one of Mr. House's sons, who found that we were going to see mother and she came with us, so that left three there yet; that was sister Lavinia and the baby, sister Rosa, and they let mother have the baby, as it was a sickly child; and she had to send there three times before she could get sister Lavinia, and the last time the soldiers, with horses, went, and the House's took off all of her clothing and put them into water to keep them from taking her, and they had to take blankets and wrap her in them, and bring her to mother, and she took sick from that time from the long ride, and getting cold she nearly died.

One they hid in the garden; one they put in the cellar, and so these were hard times for mother and us, who were in the road one night walking to find some place to get out of the rain and let those wet garments get dried, for it was so dark that we could not see a hand before us.

But after all the hard trials we reached this lovely city, where there are those that love and fear God, and who love the souls of the negro as well as those of the white, the red, the yellow or brown races of the earth, for we have ever found some of the people who do not forget us day or night in their prayers, that God will send a blessing to us as a race.

To my story of a life of slavery:

My dear mother had a dear husband that she was sold from also, and he, not knowing that he should ever see my mother any more, as the times were then, he waited for a while and then he found him another wife, and when mother came and found that he was married to another she tried to get him, but she could do nothing about it; so having to leave him behind to look after the last one and her family, although it seemed hard for her to do so.

My mother had a large family to take care of, but the Lord was good to her and helped her, for she had laid some of them away, and then there were ten little girls to care for. My brother was lost to us and to mother also, as he was sent to the war to do service for his owner, and we did not know if he was alive or not, and he was my mother's only boy, as this is a girl family that you do not see or hear of every day, for that made seventeen girls to have battle through life had they all have lived to this time.

CHAPTER II

My mother did not know where my brother was before she was sold, for we heard that he had tried to get over to the Northern side and had been taken to Richmond, Va., and put into Castle Thunder, and that was the last that we heard of him during the war. When, to our surprise, we were on our way North we learned that he was going to school; that the Northern people had teachers there in the South to teach them to read and to write; and he learning that we had gone North made himself ready and came on, but he did not know where to find us, so getting a place to work, and the same time telling those that he worked for that his people were here somewhere, they found mother and got her to go to the place where he was, and sure enough there was her dead and lost boy, and the joy and love that came to that dear, loving mother and her only son on that day will never be known on this side of the grave, as they have both gone to the land of the blest, for my brother never used any bad language in his life, and when he took the Lord for his own, it was his meat and his drink to live for Him and to follow where He led, and he died a true child of the King.

A few years later and mother's name was enrolled in the Lambs' Book of Life, for she gladly answered to the roll call and fell asleep in the arms of Jesus.

Well, my first place was in Adelphi street, with a family by the name of Hammond, and I was there to help do the work, and when they found that I liked to work so well they wanted me to do so much that I left that place and got me another, for I did not get out to church or to Sunday-school, and that was not the way that I had been trained, for when I was three years old my white mother had taken me to church with her on horseback.

Well, I said that I saw these children going to school on every week day but Saturdays and on Sundays to Sunday-school, and I there at work as if it were not the Lord's day, and I never shall like to work on that day as I was born on Sunday morning.

Well, I left there not knowing what to do, and a white lady took me in and told me to stay there until I could get another place, and I helped her girl on the next day to finish all of the work and I made ready to look for a place, and God did help me to find one and I shall never forget Him as long as I live, for that was with a fine family and they showed me love at once and I showed them love in return.

They were members of the Washington Avenue Baptist Church, and a more beloved family never lived. This was the Bailley family—Mr. and Mrs. Bailley, Miss Abbey Bailley, Mr. Bailley's sister, a young lady in her teens, Miss Ella Bailley, and a nice boy by the name of Johnny Bailley, and they were a nice family and they took me to church on Sunday morning and sent me to Sunday-school in the afternoon with their children, and what a heaven it seemed to me from the place where I was living at first.

I shall always remember my dear white mother, of whom I spoke of in the first part, and whom I shall call your attention to in many more pages of this little Life Book, and shall always remember her with love and the kindest feeling. She was a member of the true Methodist Church and was never seen by her darling child from the House of God since I could remember, for I was with her at all times on the family horse, Kimble, and when I got large enough to ride alone she bought me a fine black that had all the metal that a horse could have, and his name was Charlie Engrum, and she paid a large price for him, and he was the grandest horse I ever saw, and it was my delight to be near a horse or horses when I was a child, for I did not have any fear of any kind of horse, and I would take a ride the first thing in the morning, even before I would have my breakfast, and my dear white mother would save it for me as she knew that I would have that ride first; for it always made her feel proud to see how well I had learned to ride, and she was the one that had taught me how to ride, for she had me on the horse when I was three years old and from that time until she went home to come out no more forever.

I was two and a half years, as near as I can remember, when my own slave mother's house was burned to the ground, and I shall never forget that Saturday night. My mother's husband had gone to a dance and mother was there alone with her little ones, and we all came near getting burned up. We were all asleep when I awoke and found the house in a blaze. I did not know enough or I was so much scared that I did not call to my mother, but I think that she heard me when I rolled out of the bed, and she was out of the bed quick as could be and getting the feather beds she threw them out of the door and got the children and threw them out, and she, finding that she did not have them all, said, "My God! I have not all of my little ones;" and she ran in the house to look and she found me under the bed, for I saw so much fire that I was getting out of it, and God be praised that I was saved from that fire, and I have not had the time to run after any fires since, for that fire was all the fire I want.

I had not to stay there then, for the time is near at hand when I shall go to my white mother's to live, for she is in Tennessee and will come home soon to be with her darling child; and when she shall start again I shall go, and now the times are all well for me as then, but the time has come that the Lord has called her away from her child to be with Him, and how could I live without her? And she was to leave her sick child there for her own mother to care for, and God will raise up friends in this lonely world to look after those that cry unto heaven, believing that He is a hearer of the true prayer. I shall always remember that Saturday afternoon when

I was lying so sick when my dearly beloved white mother took so sick, and they had the doctor there for me, and he had to see after her the same time, and she was getting so much worse all the time and the doctor had not any hopes of her, and they took me from the room where she was, to a room upstairs and she had them to take me down to look at her once more. That was on Sunday and on Monday she heard the call to her to come up to that blessed land where she should be forever with the Lord and her dear husband.

What a glory it must be for those that have washed their robes and made them white in the blood of the Lamb.

I can call to mind when she the blessed one, that I call my white mother, went to get me some shoes and a fine hat, and the one that sold them told her, as she looked at a hat I wanted, that its price was twenty dollars, but I was not thinking of the prices then as I do now, and I cried to have that hat and did not want any of the others, and he told my white mother that was too much for to spend on a hat for me, but she told him nothing would cost too much for her to get for me, and she got that fine hat for me and he had his money; so you can see how much she loved me. And now that dear one is gone from me, and it seemed the dearest one on this earth, and I did not think then that I could have lived without her whom God had given to me for this world, but God, in His wonderful love for me and to me, raised up friends for me and helped me to find favor in the sight of all the people, for they seemed to love me for her sake, and I did not get well for a long time.

This subject came to this dear lady, Mrs. Bettie House, when but three years old, and from the day she came to that house she walked in her footsteps, for she, Mrs. House, could not move, but she was right in the way; and when she used to set me down for my play at certain times in the day, when she was going in her room for prayer, she would find me near before she was through; and if ever there was a loving woman she was one, and I own my love to God for such a one as she was to care for me all of those nights of watching by my bed, while the angels watched from above to see that I should rise from that bed and live to be a woman that would live for God and bless His name in all the earth, knowing that I am tempted and tried on every hand. But trusting in His omnipotent power I shall reach the land of the blest where that dear one has gone to come out no more forever.

Well, to my story:

Dear public, hoping that this little life will be read with the greatest love for humanity, and I am sure that if you have any love for the God of heaven you can not fail to find a love for this book, and I hope you will find a fullness of joy in reading this life, for if your heart was like a stone you would like to read this little life.

I had many a hard spell of sickness since the death of this lady and the doctors said that I could not live beyond a certain time, but every time they said so Doctor Jesus said she shall live, for because I live she shall live also; and He came to me and laid His strong arm around me and raised me up by the power of His might, and to see the salvation of our God in the land of the living. And to-day I can praise His name for His wonderful love to the children of man.

I told you that my brother was the oldest child of eighteen and he was in his teens when he was sent to the war; and it was a great thing to him when he found himself in the hands of a people that were so kind and good to him and showing such love for him, after being knocked around by those he had been staying with, and it seemed like a heaven to him; and he did learn fast, and he felt so glad to learn to read and to write, and he would sit at nights when he was through with his daily toil and write, so that he could let some one look at it and see how well he was getting along, and I saw how anxious he was to get an education. I asked my lady to let him come there and wait on the table, and have time to go every day to school, and she did so, and he would go to No. 1 School to Mr. C. Dosey, and he did nicely in his studies, and God be praised that he had that much to take home with him, and I shall always feel glad that I gave him that much.

I was thinking of my dear brother when the news reached me that he was in this city, and I can never tell any one how glad that I was to see the only boy that my mother ever had, for we all loved him dearly, as he cared for all the rest of the children and it was no more than natural that we should; and my mother thought so much of him that she often would say if we were all boys she would not have to worry, for boys could do so much better than girls. But I think that she found that the girls were the best in her old age, for if one could not be near her the other would, and if there is a time in the life of a parent it is when they are helpless, and a boy is not any good to care for a sick parent and they have to go without care.

But God be praised for all of the love and honor that was bestowed on mother before she went home, for God has told us to honor our fathers and our mothers that their days may be long upon the land which the Lord, thy God, giveth thee; and we can not do them enough honor for the love and the all night watching that we have when we are babies, and if we have all of the love and care that I had, I am sure that a

mother has her hands full; and when now I think of the care
and the worry that it was to take care of my sick body, I can
not help telling some one of it, that they may feel as grateful
as I feel, for God did give them love for me, and if there is
one that should feel grateful it is this feeble-bodied slave girl,
for I was such a slave to sickness, and God was so good to
raise me, even me, and I will say, praise His name.

I was telling you of my white mother being so true to the
attendance in the services of God, and I only wish that you
would have known her as I did, for she was more like one
of the heavenly host than she was like us, who are such sinful
creatures. Now, it seems like sometimes that we have not
much love for the One who had so much love for us that He
gave all the dear One that He had to bring us to Himself,
that we should taste of those joys which He has for those who
have washed their robes and made them white in the Blood
of the Lamb.

The Lord helped me to find love and favor with all after
my white mother was gone from this earth, when I felt that
I would soon follow the darling one to the blessed mansion;
and I would look to see her come to me, and I went as soon
as I was well to the house and lay on the steps, and it was
not until we had left the dear old place before I could be kept
from there; and I wish that the whole world could have seen
how much she was like an angel, and I would to God she
could see me to-day; it would do you good. Lord, lead me
on day by day, and help my feeble life to be formed like
her's, for when I think how she used to watch by my bed at
nights, while the angels watched by my bed from on high to
see that I should rise; and is not God the One that I should
serve? And I love to serve Him and honor Him, for He is
my all in all; for she has shown me how great her love was

for me and all of humanity, and I love to think of her love and to know how wonderful it would be to see her sweet face on this green earth, and it does seem to me as if I could almost see her by thinking of her so much.

I have said that we came to this lovely city in the year of our Lord 1865, and in that year I went to live with a good family that were members of the church, where the Lord spoke peace to my soul, under the preaching of the Rev. David Moore, then the beloved leader of the noblest band of God's children on this earth, and a more beloved people never lived. They were always on the lookout for any strangers that might come in the church; and they soon found me out as I was a stranger in the Monday night meeting. The dear pastor came to me the first one, for he did not stop to think whether I was an African or what nation I had come from, but he saw in me a soul, and he wanted to find out if there was any room for Jesus to live or what I should do with Jesus, or what should I do for Him, who had done so much for me; and my poor heart was ready and waiting for some one to come to its rescue. It was then and there that I yielded my life and my all to the one that can save to the uttermost all that come unto Him by the Lord Jesus Christ.

I followed my Lord and Master in the Jordan in the year of our Lord 1866, and those sweet moments have never left me once. As the years go by they seem to be the more sweet to my sinful soul, and I am trying to wing my way to these bright mansions above, where I shall meet those dear ones who have gone before.

I have had some of the darkest days of my life while on this voyage of life, but when it is dark Jesus says, "Peace, be still and fear not, for I will pilot thee."

And then my heart can sing:

> "Jesus, Saviour, pilot me
>   Over life's tempestuous sea,
> Unknown waves before me roll,
>   Hiding rocks and treacherous shoals
> Chart and compass come from Thee,
>   Jesus, Saviour, pilot me."

I know that He has led me through paths seen and unseen and has been my pilot, for we have been called to pass through many a dark trial, but God has been able for it all.

My dear mother had four of her children called home to heaven within a short time. Some of them left her for the land of love in the same month, and there seemed like nothing but God's displeasure on us, but it was God's love to us, for we know that they are safe from all harm and danger in this world of sin and distress. Some of them I never saw more after landing in this city, but I shall see them and know them when I shall have fought the blessed battle on this side, and the victory shall be on the Lord's side. Then I can sing with the angels above:

> "Crown Him, Crown Him, angels.
> Crown Him, Crown Him, King of Kings.
> Crown Him, Crown Him, angels.
> Crown Him, Crown Him, Crown the Saviour King of Kings."

What joy there will be to crown Him as our Heavenly King and to know that we are the inhabitants of that kingdom.

CHAPTER III

I was baptized by the Rev. David Moore, the pastor of the Washington Avenue Church, who is one of the best beloved ones on this earth, for he never overlooked me in the time that my soul needed the Lord Jesus Christ to save me from my sins and make me a child of the King, which makes me what I am to day. I bless God that he ever put it in my dear mother's mind to come to this place, for she was not a Christian, and the heaviest burden that I have carried was praying for one that was the head of the great family where she should have been a leader of her dear ones to the Lamb of God, that taketh away the sins of the world. But God be praised for a little one to lead so many, for of all the people of mothers there was not one that knew of this love of God, and how many were the souls given for me to work for. I told my mother that I had found Jesus and was going to follow Him. She said. "My child, you are too young. I am afraid that you will not hold out." And I said, "Mother, if I should look to myself I should fail, but I look to Jesus. I have given my life and He can hold me in the power of His might and can keep me from failing; so I can not go against your will, but I must follow Him, for you know how He has saved me from sickness so many times, and now the time has come for me to pay my vows unto Him for making me His own." I went forward in the way that He marked out for me and then to pray that she might be saved.

My grandma was almost one hundred years old, and when she heard that the Lord had saved me and that I was praying for her she saw her own sins and asked me to come on to visit all of my people, and I, getting ready, got my oldest sister to go with me. I found that the way was opened for work, as there we began the work, and they were looking to see something that they would never see in this world, and sweetly they were all brought to the Saviour. Grandma went home to carry the good news and some of the rest have gone with the same good news.

Later years some of my sisters came and some did not

come. Then some got tired and went back to the world, but I have no joy like the joy there is in the Lord.

My dear mother found the peace in Jesus before she went to that land of song. When the Lord sent the death angel to call her name she was ready to answer, "Here am I ready to go in, to come out no more."

My mother left us on the 28th day of February, 1894, in the triumph of faith in the Lord Jesus Christ. What a blessed thought that I shall soon be with her on the other side of the river to help her "Crown Him Lord of all."

To my story:

The subject of this sketch, as I said, was born again under the preaching of Rev. David Moore, of the Washington Avenue Baptist Church, which is one of the noblest churches of this city, and it has some of the best people in it of any church in the world, for there is more done for those in need in other lands. When I became a member of that church I could not read in any book, for I did not know a letter. There was a gentleman in the church by the name of Mr. Lansberry, who finding that I was one of those that was going to learn, went to a store and bought me a First Reader and gave it to me, and I did not lose any of my time at nights. I went to the meetings every night and came back and got a lady, who was a sister of Mr. Bailey, to be my teacher, and sometimes she used to be so very sleepy that she could not keep her eyes open and I would shake her and say that my lesson was to be learned, and it was always well learned. Then I went to the Sunday-school to let my Sunday-school teacher hear it on Sundays, and he, Mr. Ward, always said that he was sure that I would learn so fast I would soon catch up with his Bible Class. It was not long before I could lay my Reader down and take my lessons in the Bible, and I can bless God for all of this, for the love and the kindness that I received of all that knew me was a token of His great love for me, and I know that He was near me all the time to bring me nearer to the Light. My mind was then fixed that I should some day go to school and I could not rest night or day I was so anxious to go to school; but my dear mother could not send me. She had poor health and no one to help her to take care of the younger children, and I had to work and do the best I could with my books, hoping that the time would come that I should see myself sitting in some school studying, the same time asking mother to let two of the other children go to school every day. She did let them go for awhile, but some one came and wanted her to let them go to work out again and she let them go out to work:

Well, I said that I would go to school some day, and they had a fine time laughing at my high ideas and I let them laugh all that they wanted to, but I worked hard and long to get the means that I might be able to go, as I said, to some pay school, where I could not be stopped at any time. When I was almost ready to leave for some school the smallpox took me, and I was laid aside for three or four years; that is, I was not well, and thought that my plans were all broken. I still trusted in God, for I knew that He would do all things for me as long as I put my trust in Him.

Well, as time rolled on I found myself improving slowly and I was then living with a dear, good lady by the name of Miss L. A. Pousland, who is one of the loveliest ladies that ever lived, for she loves me to-day as a mother, though she is in eightieth odd year and is doing well for an old lady.

We were living in South Oxford street when I took sick of the smallpox and she did not want me taken away from there, as she wanted to take care of me herself, but I felt that it would be too much for her to wait on me, so the doctor said that it was only a heavy cold that I had taken and would be all right in a week or so. But I knew that I had a fever of some kind, so I asked that I might go to my mother's house, and she sent for the carriage and I went home.

When I had reached my mother's I felt somewhat better, only to grow worse all the time, and my eyes getting so that I could not see when it was day or night. I had a nurse that knew all about the disease and a good doctor that the city health doctor let take charge of the case after he had been out there to see me: and knowing that the case was taking, that no one should get it he let me remain at home for nine days, and then I went to the hospital and was there till the symptoms were well dried.

When the doctor found out that I was able to come out he, Dr. Schenck, wrote to my lady to send a carriage out. She did so at once and I was at my mother's for awhile, and then my lady came to see me and told me how the woman did the people in the house, so I told her how bad my limbs were, and she said that if I could go home with her and tell her what to do, she would get on without the woman and let her go. My mother made me ready in a little while and I was soon at the dear old home, 344 Carlton avenue.

God be praised for the way he has led me since I was three years old until this day, for it was His hand that taught me to remember all of these long years. I have in my mind the time at the old home when they put me on the fine dressing table in front of the large mirror, while the Rev. Mr. Walker baptized me in the name of the Father and the Son and the Holy Ghost, according to the Methodist tests in those days, and I always thought that was to give me my Christian name; but when the Lord had spoken peace to my soul He led me to follow in his footsteps, and I gladly followed Him to be buried to the world—that is, to be put out of sight, and that is what the word means. I have found it to be one of those times when the Father was pleased with His own dear beloved Son, and I know that He will be pleased whenever we do please Him, for God so loved the world of sinful men that He gave His only begotten Son that whosoever believeth in Him should have everlasting life, for God sent not His Son into the world to condemn it, but that through Him all might believe in Him and have everlasting life.

I wish that I could know that the whole world was receiving this life, and that we all could help to crown Him, as the angels are crowning Him, the King of Kings and Lord of Heaven and of this earth.

It is a blessed hope to know that God is love, and they that worship Him must worship Him in spirit and in truth.

I joined the church in 1866 and began to try and follow in this good old way that leads from earth to glory, and it has not always been a path of the sweetest flowers, but I have never failed to find my all in the Lord Jesus Christ.

He led me on day by day, and after awhile I found that He had led me to go away from home that I might get ready for the work that my heart was so full of, for every time that I saw the newspaper there was some one of our race in the far South getting killed for trying to teach and I made up my mind that I would die to see my people taught. I was willing to go to prepare to die for my people, for I could not rest till my people were educated. Now they are in a fair way to be the people that God speaks of in the Holy Word, as He says that Ethopia shall yet stretch forth her hand and all nations shall bow unto her. I long to see the day that the Ethiopians shall all bow unto God as the One that we should all bow unto, for it is to Him that we all owe our homage and to be very grateful to Him for our deliverance as a race. If we should fail to give him the honor due there would a curse come to us as a race, for we remember those of olden times were of the same descent of our people, and some of those that God honored most were of the Ethiopians, such as the Unica and Philop, and even Moses, the law-giver, was of the same seed.

And not long ago darkness hung over the face of this race and God moved upon the face of this dark earth and the light came forth.

How wonderfully solemn and yet grand are these inspired thoughts and words of a race whose God is so loving and forgiving, and we, contemplating the grand mystery of the world beyond this vale of tears, for God does preserve all that He has planted on this earth.

No subject can surely be a more delightful study than the history of a slave girl, and the many things that are linked to this life that man may search and research in the ages to come, and I do not think there ever can be found any that should fill the mind as this book.

This is a perfect representation of things as I can remember them, and to think how wonderful are these most beneficent streams of God's providence to all those of our race that have prayed that their loving children might feel the warm streams of an education flowing through every child. Tens of thousands of miles, North, South, West and East, God has thrown His mantle of love all around us, and it is that which should make us love and fear Him, who is able to destroy both soul and body; for His searching eye rests on all of the negro race, to see what use they are going to make of their time and talent, and I hope that nature will teach them that all of our talent belongs to the great God who gave us our being.

Nature awakens in our being a feeling that we must lay at His feet that we may get the blessed approval, for we are so changeable, but God is unchanging. He is omnipotent, and all else is transition. Yet God rules the oceans, the mountains, the valleys, and all that walks the broad earth.

Well, now I shall tell you something more of my working in the City of Brooklyn. I lived with the Bailey family the first year, and when they went away in the summer, as all of the rich used to do, I stayed in the house for the summer and they went across the ocean and were away for some time. The next year I did not like to stay in the house alone, so Mrs. Bailey got me a place with a nice friend of hers, and when she came home, thought that she was going to have me to come back to live with her but I stayed with her friend as there were but three in the family and the work was not hard, and it gave me more time to study, and Mrs. Stafford's son, Willie, was so glad to have me as his pupil that I had not any trouble to get my lessons ready for him. He went to school every day and he could not get through his head how it was that I could not go to school every day as he did. His mother told him how it was and his eyes would fill with tears and he would ask his mother and father to let him stay at home on Sundays to read the Bible to me while I should get the dinner ready, and they would let him stay, for he wanted to see me going to the House of God on Sundays as they did and was willing to have anything to eat that I might have the opportunity of attending the church and Sunday-school. His mother would let me go to the Sunday-school on every Sunday, for they were good people and were of the kind that delighted in their help and they were members of the Church of The Messiah, and they were a very happy family. They did not think that anything was too good for my enjoyment and that is the reason that I stayed with them and did not go back to the lady as she wanted me to do. I could not tell which seemed to love me most, and then her son was so willing to teach me, as Miss Abbie Bailey had, so I made up my mind that as I had more time there for study I would remain, and I had some of the best days of my life when I began to learn so fast, and he would bring me before his mother and father that they might hear me recite my lessons and see how well I was doing under him as my teacher. They felt the more glad to see how much he was interested in teaching me. Later on in years I was taken sick with the smallpox and was carried away to the hospital. He was taken sick while I was away and his mother said that he would call for me about the last one on this earth, and she tried to find me, but she did not know where I was for some time after his death, and then she felt so bad to think that he was gone and did not see me, for he always loved to be with me that he might hear me sing, as I was always on the wings of song if I were at my work; and that is the way that I have been all of my life.

When I got well of the smallpox, as I said, I went back to the place where I was living when I took the malady, and there I tried to work, but was very feeble for a long time and under the doctor's care all of the time and spending more than I could make, for some of the doctors charged me two dollars a visit, and that will use up a poor person's earnings very soon.

But all of this time I kept in mind the idea that I should save every cent that I could that I might send myself to school some day. That day did come when it seemed as dark as any night I had ever seen, when I should go away to boarding school and spend that little and should not have enough to finish; but I went, taking the Lord as the guide of my life, and the way began to grow bright before me and I could see all the clouds rolling away and the brightness shining forth. I went to Washington, D. C., and entered the Wayland Seminary, under the leadership of Professor G. M. P. King, of Bangor, Maine, with his other teachers and professors under him; all of whom are a noble band of teachers. And the way the Lord did help me in my studies is a blessing to the dear ones that I had under me for the eleven years that I was in the school work, and the way they progressed.

I said that I attended the Wayland Seminary for three years, of eight months, making it in all of my stay there twenty-four months, which may seem long to some, but it seems short to me, though I am very glad that I had that much time there for it was a fountain of blessing to my soul.

I left Washington, D. C., in the year of 1878 and came to Brooklyn and went to work again to earn money to go off to school, and when I did go it was another school in the Blue Ridge, Alleghany Mountains, where the very air of heaven seemed to fan the whole hill sides, and there never was a more lovely place on this earth for one to learn a lesson, for we could see the key to all lessons where nature had designed for a grand school of learning. At this place was to be found one of the best schools of learning that has been built by man. And I think of the hundreds and thousands of teachers and preachers and lawyers and doctors that these two schools have turned out in the different parts of this country, and many of them are in other parts of the world.

And all of this has been done through the churches, and God be praised for those that have given of their means.

At Harper's Ferry I spent four years and they were years

of hard labor, but they were just as sweet as they could well be, for the Lord went with me and I found favor with all of the teachers. When I had spent the first eight months there I learned to have the greatest love for my beloved teachers, and when the time came for me to leave the teachers I thought that my poor heart would break. Though I was coming to my own people in Brooklyn, I felt that I was leaving my best friends on the earth and so did all of the students.

Well, now the Summer had passed and gone and the Fall came when God permitted all of the loving ones to come together once more to take up the cares of studies again. So the time of the winter season was always a blessing to all, and some found it the happiest time of their lives, for they found Jesus precious to their souls and could study so much better than they could before.

CHAPTER IV

There were sometimes as many as sixty or seventy brought to the knowledge of the Truth, and sometimes we had to go out of the class-room into the prayer-room, for the Lord was among us in the Spirit's power.

When in 1886 I went out for good, that I might be of some use to my own people I started in the strength of the Lord, and He did give me the greatest victory as a school teacher, for all of the people sought me to take their children in my school and give them a start. I had my hands full of work, but I let them come in for the Board always sent them to me find out if I could find room and time, and I always made the time for when scholars find that a teacher loves them they will do any amount of hard studying.

And so the time rolled on, with everything to make me feel like hard work, in the strength of the blessed Lord.

I was three years old when I was leaving my own dear mother's home to go to my new mother's home, or I should say to my white mother's home, to live with her, and I left my mother's as happy as any child could leave her own home, for this lovely lady was always at my mother's to see me ever since I could remember anything, and she was the joy of my little life and I seemed to be all the joy of her sweet life. She had learned to love me from the time that I came into the world.

She had watched me in my cradle and longed for the day to come when I should be able to walk, for she knew that I would follow her everywhere she should go. She said to all of the friends around that if I should live to remember her that would be all that she would ask.

And so she read her blessed Bible and prayed until she saw her prayers answered, and then she went to her home in glory, where she has watched and waited and longed to see the good old ships of those who have washed their robes and made them white in the Blood of the Lamb.

I can never tell any one how many happy hours that I had, for the only trial that I had was that of sickness, which caused me to be of a great care to her all of her life. It was her delight to wait on me and to have her cousin, the doctor, to be always ready to come at any moment she should send for him. He was a good doctor by the name of Sims, and I always liked him, too, until I had the typhoid fever and I had to take some oil. I did not like to take it and he held my hands so that they could pour that in me, and he and I fell out.

My white mother used to give it to me, but she did not let me know what she was giving me, for she put some molasses in the oil and cooked them, so I should not know. I would not have known if I had not seen her one night have the old bottle in her hand putting the oil in the kettle, which she was making ready for me, and I looked up and saw what it was and, as young ones will do, did not want to take molasses and butter which I had been taking so long, for I had to take it on every night or I could not speak.

Later on she moved from the place where she was and bought another farm where it was not near the water, as the doctor thought that was not a good place for me to be, and I was not sick so much as I had been at the former.

The first hard spell of sickness on this farm was the fever that I was sick of at the time that she took sick of the yellow jaundice, and she turned as yellow as anything could be. She went home with that awful malady, thinking of me and of what my future should be in God's hands, to love and bless the world in which I should live if it should be the will of Him who knows the future of all the people that live on this earth.

So God has been a father and a loving mother and all else to me, and sometimes there has been enough of trials in this life to make me almost forget that I had this strong arm to save me from these trials and temptations; but when I fly to Him I find all and in all in Him.

He is my rock and my hiding place in the time of trials, for a child that had all of the love and comfort of a queen was now left to her own dear mother, who had so many more and had to work so hard to take care of us all that I have seen sit up all night long working for her little ones. I used to feel sorry to see her sitting up alone at her work. I would get up out of the bed and sit with her till daylight; for I was always near mother after the dear one had been plucked from this earth to await my arrival.

I have found that learning is to refine and elevate the mind, so we should cultivate our hearts and minds and live to bless those we meet. We should neither flatter nor despise those that are rich or great.

It was not long after this dear one had been called away before we were all in different places, and to share the fate that comes to those that are left behind those that have been good and kind. Then the time is coming that mother is to be taken from the whole family of little ones and they are to be left in the hands of others. That is one of the saddest times of life for children when they do not know if they shall ever see her face on this green earth any more; and if to-day we should hear the cries of those little lambs it surely would break the heart of a stone, for remember that we have the same feelings for our mothers as any race of people and our hearts will melt as easily as the richest ones on this earth.

But God in His great love to us meant that we should see the return of our dear mother to her own and that he would send her and the children out of the Land of Egypt as He did of old when He had tried to teach the rulers how wrong it was to sell and buy human flesh, and this was one of those awful sins that had to be repented of by those that could and would not see the truth. When the wrath of God came upon them and took all of the slaves away from them they could see nothing but tears and curses to the God of Heaven, and some of them cursed the earth, the stars, the moon. The negroes that had prayed so hard to God said that was the cause of the war, for they could see something in their prayers that seemed to reach up to heaven, and the answer had come for their deliverance.

Is not this a great God who can hear the prayers of the faithful ones when they pray? Do not we owe our lives and our all to this great and good God the Father, God the Son and God the Holy Ghost? And if we should fail to recognize Him we should have a worse sin fall on us than ever any one race had.

Well, to my story:

My brother James was my mother's oldest child. He was sent away to the war to keep his master at home, and we did not hear from him for a long time, but we made up our minds that if he did not get killed he would go over to the Northern side as soon as he should get the chance, though we did not see him to tell him to do so, for all of my mother's children were like herself in the love of freedom. My mother was one that the master could not do anything to make her feel like a slave and she would battle with them to the last that she would not recognize them as her lord and master and she was right.

My brother did try to get away, but he was caught and locked up in Richmond, Va., and for a awhile we heard them say that he would be killed, but God was there to help him, so he came out all right and went to work on the breastworks, and when he did try again he got over on the Northern side. They almost caught him again, but as the Lord was his leader at night, he made his escape, and to hear him tell of that river that he crossed and how he walked on the water and he was so scared that he did not know he got wet; but I know that he did get wet, though. He said the Lord carried him over the river without letting him get wet. I am sure that I could not help laughing at my brother to hear of such a thing, for there never was a time that I have read of since the time of Peter that any one was called to walk on the water. The Lord was there Himself to show Peter how small his strength was when he trusted in his own strength, and Peter would have failed entirely if his Lord and Master had not been there.

And so it would have been with my dear brother. He would have been taken by the Southerners, and that would have been his last trial on this side of the grave.

My sister Frances was hired out and we did not see her from one Christmas to the other, for she was a good way off where she could not get home. She was treated very badly by some of those where she lived and her limbs had been sprained so that she could hardly move on them. When later on the Lord had it so arranged that she was taken home to live, where she could be cared for, she soon got better and was able to go about helping mother, with the rest of the children, for my brother who had to help her to care for the children was gone, and she was all the help that my mother had, for I was not large enough to do much and had not been put to mind the children.

The gentleman that my dear brother belonged to was a Methodist and a minister. He did not want to go to the war and so he sent my poor brother to defend what belonged to him, and he did not get the good of it after all, for my brother was determined that he would gain his freedom if he could and he tried and did not get tired of trying.

Then my sister Annie was given to the gentleman's married son and she was not with us, and sister Tempy Green was with the minister, and she was one of the dead ones that mother had a time to get. Maggie, Susie, Martha and Mary were at the same place where mother was sold from, and she went and got them at once. It was like a dream to them to see how far she had been sold and to see her back there again.

Sister Lavinia was at the same place where I was and she was treated very badly by the man's own daughter, for she would whip her without cause. Sister Rosa was at the same place and she was three and a half years on mother's return. As I told you, she was six weeks old when mother was sold and that made it three years and three months that mother was gone from her own native home to a part of the country where she did not know any one, not even the great God who had been so good to her all of those years when she was gone; and all of her whole life God was watching over her and giving to the world one child who was to help to educate the down-trodden race which was, through Abraham Lincoln, to be God's leader for the children that were in Egypt in the South, and God with this leader and the race, they came through fire and smoke, and now they can see the light of another day. Some of the race say that they are sometimes, in their thoughts, ashamed that they belong to a race that has been in bondage, but I have never felt that way, for I am glad that things have been as they were, for God has moved in a way that is unknown to men and His wonders He has performed, and has planted His footsteps in the South, the West, the East and in the North, and is watching the people and asking them what doors are they opening for the Ethiopian.

Father Abraham is calling to the Ethiopians to know what has been the result of the great emancipation, and can we not send the echo back with a jubilee, that we are marching on in education in double file, and longing to see the day that not one of your sons and daughters of this broad earth but what shall learn to read and write; though it may bless the earth with a tenfold blessing that they will not forget to bless God with a hundred fold.

Three cheers for this great Emancipator.

And while he may sleep yonder, forgotten may be by some, his name has a green spot in my heart and shall ever keep green while on this side I stay.

And there is another one who sleeps yonder whom I shall not forget and that is Father John Brown, whose ashes are as dear to me as the apple of mine eye; and how can I forget him after four years of study at the dear old place where he was taken from and hanged, because he saw the wrath of God upon the nation and came forth to save his people.

Another one who will ever be shining bright in the hearts and minds of the whole negro race, and what shall I say of him who led us to the greatest victory the world has ever known—Ulysses S. Grant, the loved of all nations and the pride of all lands; he whom the world admires, to call the blessed, who mourned for this land to see the end, and God did help him in ways that man knew not, save himself and his God.

And there is another dear one that God will help me to remember with all of the love and gratitude, and it makes me feel sad as I have to speak of her once more and it may be that I shall have to speak of her many times, as she was the one that brought me on to this lovely city, and that is my mother, who has gone to that land of song where there is no more of sickness or sorrow and where God will dry every tear.

There is another I remember and that is Father Charles Sumner, who for years wrote and also fought and spoke, as never man spoke, for the race and the Civil Rights Bill, that it might not die, but it should be a rock for the defence of the race.

And there is another that I shall not leave out of this book, for if I did the book would be incomplete, and that is Frederick Douglass, the greatest of men among the negro race of this country or of any land on the globe. He wrote and spoke and went all over to try to do all he could for his race, and who could forget such men as these? I would say in true lines, may the earth fail to move sooner than I forget those noble lives. Honored be their memories and honored be their ashes, for their lives shall live in the memories of all coming generations and their ashes will make rich the soil whereon they lie.

May God give us some more of such men as these for they are few, and we need so many now to go forth and speak the truth.

And there is dear Doctor David Moore, that my pen, I fear, would fail to move, if I did not do him honor. He was beloved and honored to the last day of his stay in the Washington Avenue Baptist Church, and it was on account of sickness that he had to leave this city and go up in the northern part of this State that he might be able to preach the Word, and God did make him well after he had left Brooklyn; and his work has been crowned with great success.

God did use him in this city to His own glory in saving men, women and children from the very door of sin and the dread of the life which is to come. And may the God of Heaven and the Ruler of this earth be with him as he comes near the Jordan to make its waters calm, and enter in the gate and hear the blessed "Well done, good and faithful servant, enter thou in the joys of thy Lord."

J. D. Fulton is one that will have one of the highest places at God's right hand, for he started out to look after the Ethiopian's rights when he was only seventeen years of age. What can be said of a long life like his, that has written and traveled and spoke to such large crowds of hearers in the interest of the race which I represent. How I have seen those silvery locks fly as his warm heart melted to tears as he pleaded for the down-trodden of the Ethiopians; and if God has ever heard a prayer I know that He hears the prayer of this dear good man, for I have seen the answer come in mighty power, in many ways, to the saving of precious souls, and the way that he wrote about the negro in this country and its problem.

He was called to the Hanson Place Church to preach and he worked hard, with God's help, and improved the church and many were brought to the Saviour through the Word, such as the Lord will own and bless at the last day.

Doctor Fulton is one of the best men on this broad earth to love and labor for humanity and I do not think that my race, the noble Ethiopians, should ever forget him as long as God shall spare his life. When the time shall come when the dear blessed one shall be called to the world above, and that active form is stilled in death and when that silvery voice is no longer heard in the defence of the down-trodden Ethiopians and the oppressed of any land, that he will hear the "Well done, good and faithful servant, enter thou into the joy of thy Lord."

And to think of one who has written so long never more to wield the pen in the cause of the church and God's children is a sad thought to the writer, for she has loved him as a father and he shall ever have a green spot in my heart for I shall never forget his kind words to me in my lonely hours.

Dr. J. D. Fulton's first wife was one of the loveliest women

that ever lived, for I have been to their house to dine with
the family and I found that Mrs. Sarah Fulton and family
were the same that they were in the church. There was the
sweetest home that I ever saw in all my life, for the father
and the mother were all love, and then take Miss Jennie, the
eldest child, and she was a lovely girl, and there was Miss
Nellie, another lovely girl, and Sadie, the youngest girl, and
she was her father all the way, and the boy Justin, who came
to the family while I was away. I think he has a large heart
like his dear father, and I do know that if he only is a good
man like his father God will own and bless him.

Dr. Fulton's second wife, Aunt Laura, was a lovely woman,
for we all learned to love her when her first husband was
living.

Miss L. A. Pousland was one of the best ladies I have
seen in this city, for it was from her house that I went to the
Wayland Seminary in 1875, and to her love I owe a love of
gratitude, and to all that may come to me as worldly goods I
shall always think of Miss L. A. Pousland and of her love
to me when I was getting ready for school and the letters full
of love to me all the time while I was prosecuting my studies.
Oh, how she longed to see me out in the world doing my
Master's will and helping to teach, for she is a Boston lady,
and they are a learned people and like to see all others learn,
and that is the way, like the old Pilgrim Fathers were, that
there should be a grand common level for all after them.

To my story of child in House's family:

This Mr. John House had the largest sum offered to him
for a girl as I was that was ever offered for any one and he
would not accept the whole world of money, on account of
the one that had loved me and cared for me, for he well
knew that after all of those prayers that he would be sinning;

and he would not have had my mother sold away from her children if his brother would have let him know it in time. He went away to attend court and to his surprise found that my mother was sold. He came home at once to let us know of it, and he was the one that called in my sister Frances and sister Annie and sister Rosa, for the two oldest that I speak of fell to a dead brother who had drank himself to death, and these were sold to pay for his drink. He had been dead for some time and those that he owed now came in to get their pay, which was their only chance; and the money that they got did not do them much good, thanks to God, for it was in the time of the war and the money was of the Confederate money, and it was during the great struggle when this money was called in never more to be the money of these United States, for this Union needs the kind of money that will be good in all lands, and I am glad that the people can see it now as they never saw it before.

CHAPTER V

I am glad that the dear Lord has laid it in my heart at this time in life to let the world hear something of a life that they will all be filled with a love for one whom it has been a delight to meet at any and all times.

Mrs. Sarah Potter, who is a beloved and dear lady, who is the bright morning star of the Washington Avenue Baptist Church, and who is one of the brightest lights that this city has or ever will have, for she is all over this city looking after the needy ones, comes from a noble family and all of the family have been foreign missionaries. She has been a home missionary for many years and God has blessed her and her labors, and her dear father was doing missionary work in India for fifty years, and God blessed his work there. Now that his dear work has been finished in this world and he has gone to his reward, his works do follow him, for the number that have been saved through his preaching eternity will tell.

His form will no more walk out on the field of battle for the Lord, and who can fill the place of such a life-work as this child of the King has filled? And to go home to his beloved and blessed Master with his arms full of blessed sheaves; and as we think of him, how we wonder in our daily walks if we shall go to the Saviour with our hands full or shall we go empty-handed and thus to meet our Saviour so; not one soul with which to greet Him, must we empty-handed go?

I have heard of Mr. Mason as one of the first to go among the Coreans, and I have seen some of them, that have taken the Lord for their all and in all, come to this land of ours to fit themselves for the blessed work among their own people. God be praised for such a man as Dr. Mason and all of his loving children, who have had the same spirit that their father had, and he was filled with the Holy Ghost and with the power of the Lord.

Mrs. Sarah W. Potter was the beloved wife of a sea captain, Mr. William Potter, and he owned a ship that sailed the Indian Ocean, and he was washed overboard one night while his wife, Mrs. Potter, was sick, and she did not know that he had a watery grave until the next day. They had one son, who is now married, by the name of Frank, whom I held as an idol, as he always called to me when in trouble, for his dear mother taught him the love of the Bible, and he would not fight any boy, let them do him as they would. He knew that I would go after the boys for blocks, as I was one of those soldiers that was not afraid to fight. As he grew older I told him that he had to go out into the world to fight his way and I wanted him to begin it at once, and he did learn to battle for himself. He married a lovely girl by the name of Miss Katie Harvey and they have two children, the eldest a girl and the youngest a boy, which is the lovely little man of the home.

I have seen that mother sit up at nights waiting for her son to come that she might ask a blessing on him before he should sleep, and how could that boy go astray after all these prayers and entreaties? May he lead his lambs to the blessed Master, and have the "Well done, good and faithful servant, enter thou into the joys of thy Lord."

To my story of work in the City of Brooklyn:

The lady, Miss L. A. Pousland, whom I spoke of in the preceding pages, is the place where I found myself living in 1875, after twelve or thirteen years of service. It was there that I met Mrs. Sarah Potter. She has been all of a mother to me to give me all the encouragement she could bestow on me. For all of this kindness I am more than grateful to my Heavenly Father, for I know that all goodness comes from Him. He surely has shown His love to her in sparing her to see me go from her home to Washington to school and spend three years and then go to Harper's Ferry and spend four years, and to see me out in the world teaching for eleven years, and to break down while at my post and now at home to serve in another way. Is not this not God's love to me, as a poor, humble servant of His? I should never forget to give the love and honor due Him.

God knows my heart and He will bless the work in my hands, as the writer of this book.

When I found that I could get through school in a given

time as I had studied hard, if I had the money, I told Miss L. A. Pousland, that I would not be there to work any more, as I had a place in Saratoga Springs for the Summer. She felt bad to lose me, but as she knew that I could make more money for three months at the Springs she wanted me to have my heart's desire, so I came on from school and went to see her and then made ready for the Springs, getting one of my sisters to go with me and taking such things as we could. We were there too soon and we had to wait for work, and I went around and made myself known to the white people. They soon called on me to come and do work for them, and the first was a Mrs. Carpenter, a good lady. She then got her married daughter to have me to work for her family and they were a fine family. Her daughter's husband was a grand studio man on Broadway, doing a good business. Then she sent me to another friend of hers, and my sister and I could live for a while. When the rush came I did not forget the one who had helped me, but went to her two days out of a week, for she had her house filled with boarders, and the Summer was all a blessing to her and her family.

There was Mrs. Purdy, who was another one of my friends, for I did work for her laundry for three years, and she said whenever I came to the Springs and wanted work to come to her; if the house was filled there was room for me. So you see how God did open the way for me in that strange and lonely place, where there are so many that go there for the Summer looking for work. I went out of the house where we were stopping and got the washing and brought it home to my sister, for she would not go out of the house as she had not been from the place where she lived before. I got her to go with me to help me with the work, and it was coming in so fast I had to get a white lady to help us to get through, for the colored people said that we would not get work as the laws were passed to keep the New York workers out, and I told them that they would have to pass laws to keep the rich people of New York from coming there to board if they should keep the workers out; so I did not hear to that, and found the way for I had the will, and where there is a will there is always a way. So much for the first Summer.

Well, the second time I went up alone. I say alone, I mean that my sister did not go, but the Lord did go with me that Summer, for I did not go to the house where my sister and I was for they tried to discourage us the first time. I always mark one that is an enemy to me and shake the dust off of my feet and let the Lord do for that one what He thinks is best.

Well, for the third year I was there with the Lord and He was surely there with me. I did not do any work on the Lord's Day, but tried to teach them. When they made me an offer of larger pay for the work done on the Lord's Day, I told them that in six days the Lord made the heavens and the earth and He rested on the seventh day, and I felt that if He needed rest on that day I was sure that I must have rest. So the Sunday work was not carried on any more in that laundry. He said that the Lord had sent me to that laundry for the bettering of all in it. The gentleman was from Philadelphia and his name was Mr. Cheek.

So you see how the Lord preached His word through me, a feeble one of the dust, and what can not the Lord help us to do if we only trust in Him and if we strive to live for His honor and glory while on this side of Jordan?

Mrs. Purdy had one daughter, and a lovely girl in music, and her name was Kittie Purdy. She was sought to play everywhere as she was a fine player, and everyone thinks her a very pretty girl. Her mother is a perfect lady, for she used to be so kind to her help. She never was late in any of her meals for the help and she always sat down with us and eat with us. She was as jolly as any one at the table and she always called me her bird, for I was on the wing of song from the time I began my work until my work was finished, and then I would start home as happy as any one could be. Then I would be the first to greet her in the mornings always and she used to say that I brought to her a great deal of comfort each hour and drove all of her business cares away. I used to feel glad that I, although a working girl, could be of some love and comfort to some one, and it makes me feel glad to-day that God in His love to me and for me can own such a feeble one.

My next start was for Asbury Park to do work for Mrs. Haseltine, another lovely lady, who was a Boston lady and whom I learned to love as a mother. I worked for her two years and was to have worked for her the third year if she had not taken sick at the time she did. A gentleman came on from Philadelphia and she got me to work for him and I found him a fine gentleman. I praise God for all that came to me while I was pursuing my studies, and to-day I do feel like saying,

> "Blessed assurance, Jesus is mine,
>   Oh! what a foretaste of glory divine;
>   Heir of salvation, purchase of God,
>   Born of His spirit, washed in His blood.
>   This is my story, this is my song,
>   Praising my Saviour all the day long,
>   This is my story, this is my song,
>   Praising my Saviour all the day long."

To my story: Mrs. Haseltine, I said, had to go to the Saratoga Springs for the Summer and she used to let me hear from her, but my work in school was so great that I lost sight of her and I do not know if she is in Florida or not. Wherever she is I love her and she has my heart. She did all that she could all the time that I worked for her to let me do extra work for the boarders so that I might earn money outside of what she paid me, and the ladies used to come to the laundry and talk to me, for some of these ladies went to school as I did and some of them waited at the large hotels in the Summer time to pay their board. The gentleman that had Mrs. Haseltine's house took me in at evening time to entertain the guests, and they all helped me. When I came home to make ready for school I was at our own church one evening when dear Dr. J. D. Fulton was giving us one of his grand lectures, and he gave me time to sing, read and speak. The church took a grand collection for me, which amounted to seventeen dollars and seventy-three cents. I was better fixed that year than I had been at any year since I had been going to school, for I had worked all of the Summer and would not spend any of my money as I wanted it all for school, but the Evil one came and stole it from me and I was left without a dollar, and I had the heavy heart one is sure to have when they need money as I did. Then I had to borrow money to leave for the school, and you may think how one feels after a Summer's work, and to have some one else to use the money that has not been gotten with their own labor.

Well, I did not know what I should do, so I made up my mind that I had done all that lay in my power—that is, I had earned the money, and some one had taken it from me and I was left to go without. So I took the Lord for it, and could not board as I had done, but I bought some little things to use and boarded myself, and I was up sometimes at the late hours of night, when all of the people were asleep, cooking for the next day, that I might not be late at school. So you can see how loving God was to me.

My life in school was one of joy to me and to my mother and sisters and brother and brothers-in-law, and all of the time that I was in school they were sending me their mites to help me along. My sister, Mrs. E. F. Rodwell and Mr. G. W. Rodwell, and my sister, Mrs. Annie Lindsey and Mr. F. P. Lindsey were the ones that never for once forgot me, and at Christmas time I was like a child looking for something. Everybody was good to me. Praise the Lord for all of the love that came to me in the time of need.

Well, my work ended in 1886, though I taught in 1885, and had the blessing of God with me in this school. There were twenty-five out of the school brought to the knowledge of the truth, such as the Lord will own and bless at the last day. God be the glory. Amen and Amen.

The place was Woodstock, Shenandoah County, Va., and I was called from that school to go West where they needed me to teach in a place where the teachers had made the pupils almost hate to go to a school. My heart was in that work, which no one liked, so I went there trusting in the Lord. I lost that place, but they got me another one where they built me a new house, and the Lord did bless me in this place, although I was not able to go to the Baptist Church only once a month, for there was not any nearer than ten or fourteen miles. When the next year came I helped the people build a church and it was all paid for before I left there. How God did pour out His spirit there in the salvation of souls, and He did add unto the dear church such as will be saved at the day when He shall come to make up his jewels; and I can praise His name for such a Saviour.

Well, to my story: As a teacher in the same place for eleven years, or I should say I was connected with the same school for that length of time, and all the way the Saviour led me. Sometimes it was not all flowers and sweetness, but in it all I can see the hand of the Blessed One; and it used to make me say to myself, Praise the Lord, Oh, my soul, and all that is within me praise His holy name!

After being there for sometime I was taken sick and was there sick and could not teach my school for that Winter. It made me feel very bad, but my good Dr. Ford said that he thought all of the county were sorry to learn of my illness and all were losing a good teacher. I would not be able to do any school work for sometime to come as the nerves were all overworked, and that had brought on other troubles which were of a dangerous nature. So my heart was heavy indeed, and if I had not had my hope built in Jesus Christ I would not have stood, for I felt that all other ground was to me a sinking sand. I stayed there all of the Winter and then came on home to Brooklyn, and the Lord was so good to make me well; I went back to my work and taught all that Winter, and when my school was out I then went down to the county seat, which is ten miles from the station and is about fourteen from my school, where I spoke of.

Hinton is a lovely little town on the Chesapeake and Ohio Railroad and in the Blue Ridge and Alleghany Mountains, and is one of the greatest places on the road, as all of the trains from the West, East, South and North stop there. It is a lovely town and they have a roundhouse there where they build locomotives. They have a fine Y. M. C. there. There are a number of men employed at this place. They have two nice Baptist Churches and a Baptist Mission, two Methodist Churches, one Episcopalian, one Congregational, one Presbyterian and one Roman Catholic and one college, a number of private schools and a number of public schools and the county is doing a good work in education, and to the Lord be all the praise for all of this good work.

Hinton I said was a lovely place. Like Harper's Ferry, that I spoke of in the preceding chapter, it is situated on Camp Hill in a lovely place, between the Potomac River on one side and the Shenandoah River on the other, and it has two of the most beautiful bridges I ever saw. When you see the trains coming and going it looks lovely.

The Wayland Seminary is in a lovely spot on Meredian Hill, between Fifteenth and Sixteenth streets, and you can see all over the City of Washington. It is lovely to behold with all of its fine buildings and art galleries, though I do not like it as well as Harper's Ferry, for I was not well the whole time I was there and I had so much better health at the Ferry. I bless God that I made the change when I did or I might have been gone to my long home before I had the time to see so much of God's love to me in the way He has led me through paths that I did not see then. I can truly say unto Him, Lord, Thou hast been my dwelling place in all of these years of trial and has been my rock in a weary land and my shelter in the times of storm.

Well, I came home last October a year ago, 1895, and made up my mind to stay for the time being. Some of the people found out that I was here and they sent for me to come to see them. I went to Mrs. Murphy's the next week and I was there nearly a year and found that I could not do much lifting, so I did not feel well for quite a while, and I had a heavy day of it the last time that I was there. So I told her daughter I should not come any more as I had gone early that I should get home early. It was nearly six o'clock when I stopped. They are a lovely family of four men and four girls, all of whom are are very fine indeed; two sons married, and children, and one daughter married and she has two little ones. Miss Josephine is a school teacher. Miss Alice is the housekeeper, as the mother is not very well at times. One of the lovely girls is a Sister in a convent.

I also did work for her daughter, Mrs. Nellie Chester, and she is a lovely woman. I had to lose her work as she had to get her a girl.

I also worked for fine families by the names of Mrs. Handford and Mrs. Taylor, but they went away from this city.

CHAPTER VI

I am now doing work for a lovely family by the name of Mrs. Coddington, as her husband has died not long since, and he was a nice man and they have two lovely girls that teach school. I also work for Mrs. White, who is a lovely lady, and all of her family.

At the Pells and the Powells. Mrs. Pell is a lovely woman, with two children, one a lovely young lady and full of the sweetest music the ear ever heard, for I do not think that there ever was any one that could play sweeter music than her. The other is a boy, a nice youngster of promise.

Mrs. Powell is the sister of the first Mrs. Pell and she has one daughter, who is a Mrs. Pell, whom I have to call Mrs. E. Pell to let each one know which one I mean. There are

other ladies in the mansion that are very nice to me. Mrs.
Pell No. 1 is the head of the house and is a fine lady, and in
telling you of those that I have worked for and I am doing
work for I mean to tell that it is by the day that I work for
some of them; as you will see as you read this that I have had
very few places where I lived out by the month, and staying
a good while in a place.

I did work for Mrs. Johnson, but as her business is not
so good at times she has me whenever she can feel as if she
can spare the money. So this little life of mine has been
almost locked up in a nutshell, and Jesus has come to me in
the spirit's power that I should tell the world of His wonderful
love to me a poor sinner of the dust. And what can not the
Lord do for those who put their trust in Him? We feel like
saying to the blessed One, how amiable are all of Thy works,
oh Lord, and our eyes are seeing Thy salvation in many parts
of the earth.

I can remember the first time that it was my pleasure to
hear dear Dr. J. D. Fulton. It was on Thanksgiving Day
when he first came to this city to preach at the Hanson Place
Church, as their pastor. The Rev. David Moore had him to
preach the Thanksgiving sermon at the Washington Avenue
Baptist Church, and we were all delighted at hearing him on
that day. I loved him on hearing that sermon, for I felt the
spirit power on that day, through his preaching. I shall always
think of the Doctor and his loving family, for we, as the
negro race, have not such a friend on earth as Dr. Fulton. I
am not afraid to say it to his dear honor as he is not dead,
and I wish every negro knew him as I do for then they would
all feel toward him as I feel. I hope that he will long live to
tell the truth as he has in days gone by; and if he was in this
city where the evil is so strong, we should hear him sounding

the watchword, and that is the reason that those that loved the ways of sin did not like him, for they felt that he had cause to trouble them while they were yet in their sins.

But I hope that the day will come when I shall hear him again in this city, and I hope that God will give him long life and that he may see the travel of his soul and be satisfied, for I know that he tries to do God's will in this love that he has for humanity and that is why the Lord will bless him in all the work that his hands find to do.

I was not at home when he left this city and I felt sad when I found that he was gone, for we shall ever miss him. My prayer is to God that he may live to a good old age and that when he shall be called to come up higher that he may be caught up in the air to meet his Lord and Master and all of those that have gone on before, and be ready to Crown Him King of Kings and Lord of Lords.

Progress of Church Work

A speech to a crowded church, in the year of our Lord 1888, in Talcott, Summers Co., W. V. I was asked to have this published out there, but I wanted to have it brought to my home in Brooklyn. I was into so much work out there, and my people were not there to see what the Lord did help me to do:

Dear friends, we are here to-night to commemorate this grand occasion, and our watchword is Onward and Upward to the Prize!

This is a time that we should all shout the Jubilee and to send the glad tidings to all the world and to let all the nations know that we are on our march to that happy land of song.

Dear friends, let us look for a few moments and think of

the time when you had not a church where you could worship God. I told you that God would give you this lovely place, where no one could drive you out, and to see what great things He has done for you in a little time, and how great things can He not do if we will only trust Him? We have those of our race that have held places of greatest trust and God bless them in those places. Why should we give up the fight and lay our armor by when there is so much for us to do? No, no, we can not and we will not lay the grand old armor down, for the Lord is on our side and we shall surely conquer if we look to Him whose arm is so large and strong. Then let us take fresh courage and march on until we reach the goal, and then we shall be glad and rejoice for the Lord has spoken good to His people, the Ethiopians.

Oh, ye colored people, why not take this as yours and begin now to rejoice ye in your own race and feel proud of the race, but not ones that can dance the best on the ball-room floor, for there is very little in that when it is all summed up in a whole. Let us thank all the good people who have shown any love to us while we have been in this work of building and may they all find favor in the sight of God. You have a dear good pastor who is willing to give his life to the Lord and the church. Let us take fresh courage and march into His service, for we shall gain if we only trust in God and do the right He will help us to persevere.

Time would fail me and my pen would fail to move if I should try to enumerate all of the blessings that have come to us as a race. I hope that we, as the hated negro race, will make a fresh start from this night and do all that we can to forward the work in this church, and God will send us a blessing.

Etiquette of Young Men

I was wondering a few days since if the men of the present day had lost the respect that men used to have for the women. I was carried back to the year of 1884 while in school with so many of the young men of my own race, when I saw so much of the respect that they showed to us girls and that was what caused me to write this to their honor. I think that true etiquette is one of the greatest blessings that young men can have for the women, for it is to them that we look to for the protection and love, and if we fail to find it in them where shall we look? This is one of the greatest fortunes that one can have, and it is that which makes a young man what he ought to be. We, as the women, need so many of such ones and the world needs them fully as much, and the God who made them looks for more and when he does not find it in the dear creatures that He has made it makes Him feel sad.

I found a number of young men that used to attend the Wayland Seminary that had the greatest regard for the girls, and I could not but notice them in this respect and their kind acts while there, although I was not in the same classes with them, but I never saw them make any difference while I was in school. I always found good friends among them and I never saw a young man meet one of the young ladies but they lifted their hats, and that made the people of Washington, D. C., always speak of it in the kindest terms. One never loses anything in this way, and their virtues are greater than gold.

When the weather was very bad one day and I was coming from school and a young man saw me fall down, he came to help me home and I felt very grateful and I feel that wherever that young man shall go he will have favor in the eyes of all, and God will be his leader for he has made a good beginning.

School Life

While at the Harper's Ferry school I found the loveliest teachers that ever were in a school. Professor Brackett, the head of the school, is a fine gentleman, and his wife, Mrs. W. Brackett, is a lovely lady and she is one of the finest teachers that ever lived. She has three nice children, two of them are girls and one boy, who is a young man by this time, for I have not seen him since he went to Maine to attend school, which is the Bates'. It is a fine school of Latin, and a number of the students went to that same school.

Mr. W. P. Curtis was one of the professors. He was my Sunday-school teacher and he was fine.

Mr. D. M. Wilson was a dear professor, whom we loved. Miss Caroline Franklin was a lovely teacher and we all loved her. Miss C. Brackett was one of the lovely teachers, and one whom every one of the other teachers loved, for she was one of the finest readers that ever lived, let it be man or woman. They used to have her read nearly every afternoon when the school was out, and sometimes they would call to Professor Curtis to read to the school. He was a very good reader, but Miss C. L. Franklin was the grand trainer of the whole school. They had a grand reading circle there at nights for the rich of the Ferry, and she was the one to do the fine reading. All of the noble people of the place loved her and she will ever be loved and remembered by all who knew her. She is now in Washington, D. C., teaching, and the people have learned to love her as we did. I do not think that any one could help loving her for her love and fidelity to the race which she represents.

Miss C. L. Franklin's mother, who is a lovely woman whom we all love as a mother, for she had many of the students at her house to board, like Mrs. William Lovett, and she was so very kind to all of them that she will be remembered by us all, for we love those in our school life that would say a kind word to us. It was to help us along in our daily toil.

Mrs. Julia Robinson was one of the lovely ladies at the Ferry, also, and all of the teachers boarded there. She has a number of the students that board with her and she is much beloved.

Mrs. Bell was one of the ladies that kept boarders and she is much beloved. Mr. W. M. Bell is one of the teachers and all love him as a teacher.

Mr. J. Trinkle, who keeps one of the halls in the Summer time has a number of boarders, and does well all of the Summer months and in the Winter he teaches in or near the Ferry. With it all they are all doing what they can to help to forward the interest or an education in all of that section, and I really think that part of the country will show a larger percentage of those that have been educated through the churches than could have been taught in the public schools, for the terms are so very short that it is hard for the people to get a start.

But God has wonderfully blessed the teachers that have been sent on there from the North to look after the interests of the negroes. They love the work of the school-room, and it is their meat and their drink daily to give away what they have received. The Word says that it is more blessed to give than to receive, and we are always ready to receive from the hands of our earthly friends, and it is much greater to receive from God.

Mr. Thomas Lovett has two lovely little girls, named, respectively, Florence, the eldest, and the other Shoelett, and they are very smart. Mr. Lovett has built a hill-top house in a lovely place. It is filled in the Summer time, while he has music for the boarders. That makes it pleasant during the warm weather of the Summer months, and it is one of the loveliest places that can be found on the B. & O. Railroad, and the white people go their from all parts.

I had the pleasure of stopping there on my way home in 1895, and it did my soul good to find such a fine house built by one of the colored gentlemen and one that I had known, for I was at his mother's boarding house for the whole time that I was at the Ferry. He was teaching school then in the Winter time and looking after his mother's business in the Summer time. So I am glad that some of my people are trying to make an honest living. He is one among the many at the Ferry that are keeping boarding houses; and I am thankful for all that comes to us as a race. I hope, as I have often heard dear Dr. Fulton say that he wanted to see the race go forward, and I pray that the time is not far distant when all of the friends of the negroes shall see them making men and women of themselves, and then the grand problem will be solved. Then we shall be glad, for I am grieved night and day for my own people, and I feel so grateful to God for letting me see and to know that I have such a good friend as Dr. Fulton is. He shall be loved by me as long as I live, and I hope that he will ever be loved by all that shall read this life of mine, for he has been a father to me and I am one that always remembers a kindness as long as any one will do one for me. God will bless those that will think of me in love.

As this day has been one of quiet to me I have wondered what it would be to me if I could look into those bright mansions above and see my two mothers' faces. What a joy there would be at the sight of them seeing me and of me seeing them, and we all singing,

> Holy, holy, holy, Lord God Almighty.
>   Early in the morning our songs shall rise to Thee;
> Holy, holy, merciful and mighty,
>   Casting down their golden crowns around the glassy sea.

And what a glory it will be for all that have washed their robes and made them white in the blood of the Lamb; and I know that two darling mothers have washed their robes and made them white, and to God be all the praise for the great love that He has shown to poor me, who feels so lonely on this lovely Lord's day. How much have I found in His service, too, and if I could be able to go there to-night I feel that I should be blessed, but I have to stay at home to-night as I have not been well for a month or more. I feel grateful as can be that I could be out this morning, and I will pay vows unto my God as long as I shall live, for He is my rock and my hiding place in the time of trouble. I have had a storm of them and it is to Him I fly to shield my soul from the evil one, and knowing as do how many hard spells I have had, it is right for me to be as careful as I can, taking the Lord for my healer. How He has blessed me so many times when there were no other hopes for me to build on, I have found that I could trust in His almighty power.

I shall not forget the kind care of Dr. Matthews, of this

lovely city, whom God gave to me when I was very low and the three times a day that he paid his visits to see how I was getting along. He was so kind in his words to comfort me and to give my mother cheer I shall always think of him kindly, for the snow was so deep that a horse could not travel very well and he had to walk it three times a day. I had not my white mother then to care for me, but my own mother did what she could for me and I know that she has her reward in heaven for all that she has ever done for me in the times when I needed the most care.

There is good Dr. Reeves, a good Quaker doctor, and I had to have him to attend me. He was very kind and gentle in his treatment of me and I am very glad that I found such a friend in him, for he was like a father to me? I shall not overlook dear Dr. Warmsley, who was a good doctor to me and he was kind as he could be, and I shall not forget him, although I have not seen him for a long time.

What shall I say of the last doctor that I was under out West, and that is Dr. J. W. Ford, who was so kind to me as a stranger. He would come when he was sent for. It made no difference what time of day or night. It might be you would find him on his way where he was sent for and sometimes he would be on the road all night long, for he is the best doctor in the county, and I was going to say the best in the State of West Virginia. They all send for him; far and near, where they have any fever, and he is so good in fevers, through the Lord, he is sure to bring them out of if they do as he tells them. May the Lord give him a good long life to do the will of Him who is the greatest doctor after all. And if we only put our trust in Him we shall find that He will make our sick bed easy for us and He will carry us all the way while we are sick, for He has borne our sorrows and sickness.

To my story as a school girl: It was full of sweet love and regard, for I gained favor with all of the teachers and professors and all of the pupils. The Lord be praised for all of this love and joy that came to me in my school days. Then the love that came from the Washington Avenue Baptist Church of sending me the sum of twenty or thirty dollars to help me in paying my expenses was of the greatest love for one in a school, as I wanted to pay as I went, and then the Sunday-school would send me their money, one of the dear, loving favors of God's love, and naming each time from which the money came and sending it through the Board at Chicago. Then Mrs. Conley or Mrs. Connell sent it to me and the Board sent the same way when my own beloved church sent me money. It was in the time of Mrs. Sarah Fulton and she did not forget me when I was in school. The Mission Band of our church sent me some money every year after the first year that I went to school. Sometimes it was to the answer of my prayers that the money came at the time I needed it to pay my board and God be praised for those who from the bottom of their hearts contributed in the grand and good work of education. For all that I shall do in this life to help some one that needs help, I shall think of the Lord's love to me and try and do what I can to bring them to the Lamb of God that taketh away the sins of the world, and to God I owe my life and my all, and if I should fail to love and honor Him I know that He will not remember me before His dear Father in heaven.

Mr. William Lovett, the father of a large family, is one of the finest gentlemen anywhere around the whole country, and is much beloved by all who know him. The white people who board with him in the Summer time all liked him, for he was so nice and quiet. He has a large family of girls and boys and all are smart. He sent two of them to the Hillsdale College when they had finished at the Ferry, and one was John Lovett, who studied law, and the other one, Miss Etta Lovett, was a fine school teacher and a music teacher.

I have just learned that the last one of the girls has married, and that is the youngest of the family. They all have good partners for life, which does not come to all large families. God bless such a father and mother, who have taken such good care of the training of their children.

Mr. John Lovett was one of the teachers of whom I shall speak of, as I boarded in their house for four years. A more lovely woman never lived than his mother. She is known far and wide as one of the best ladies to keep boarders and she has a lovely family of girls and boys. Mr. Thomas Lovett is a doctress, who is one of the finest ladies that lives. She is from the North and she has some of the best people of the Northern cities that she waited on, and they love her to-day for the kind care that she had for them.

Miss Emma Carter is one of the teachers, and Miss Lizzie Sims, Miss Frances Sims, Mr. Burrell and Mr. C. H. Plummer; and of later years Miss Mary Brackett has gone there as one of its teachers and there are others that have gone there as teachers. The dear good work is going on in the strength of the Lord and I hope that He will still bless his work. The same that I said of Miss C. L. Franklin I will say of Miss Lulia Brackett, who is married now and is still one of its beloved teachers. She loves the work of teaching the negroes better than her own life and all that she has in Maine. God bless those dear teachers, as they labor there for my own dear people whom God has blessed in getting an education.

Miss Lulia Brackett married a Mr. Loughtner, who is a school master for the whites at the Ferry, and who is a fine school teacher and whom the people like very much. It is a joy to meet him on his way to his school-house.

Mr. William Bell is one of the the teachers whom we all love dearly, and he taught school outside for a while before he came to teach at the college. He had the greatest success as a teacher. May God bless those faithful ones as they are far from their homes, family, friends and loving ones.

I had the pleasure of working for a fine family in Brooklyn by the name of Davis, and I found them all a lovely family. I had the pleasure of going away in the country one Summer to a place called Flemington, N. J., and we had a fine time as it was his father and mother's home, and they had a dairy farm and all of the nice things that one finds in the country. I was not well while there as it was low land, and one of their daughters was not well, so I feeling that I would be better to come home they got ready and come on home, and I left them and went to my home where I could rest. In the Fall I was so much better that I was able to go back out West and take up my work again. When I had finished my public school I taught a pay school for the Summer and had a large number of scholars, and they progressed well. Some of them would go without their food all day to study extra lessons.

It would be all of a joy to the whole world to have seen how well all of the girls, boys, young men and young ladies did in all of the schools where I have had the pleasure of teaching.

I have never taught in any school with any other teacher or teachers, and I was so much more blessed, for all teachers have a way of their own. The new teacher always makes so much change in a school and in the pupils, I found that to do good work in school I should stay long in one place, that I might bring the scholar near to me. Sometimes I have had it rough, but in it all I can see the hand of God leading me to do all that I could to help forward the great cause of education in those parts where there was so much need.

I have just learned that the Rev. J. D. Fulton has had a stroke and I cannot tell how he is at this time, but I can not do any work until I hear from him, as I have had my mind on him for some time, as he was somewhere in Massachusetts and I had not heard from him for some time. The last time that I heard from him he was not well, and I knew that he was so great for working that I feared he would break down.

So I wrote to Mrs. Wamsley, his daughter, and shall wait to hear how he is, for I know she will let me know at once as she is there with her father.

I have heard from her and he is better, thank God, and not dead, as so many thought, for he does so much work that no one thought that he could get over it.

And here on this 20th day of January I fell sick myself and have not been able to take up my work until the 4th day of March, and once more in the strength of the Lord I have taken up this work and hope to push it as fast I can, and I hope to finish it in the near future if the Lord wills. I hope that all who will may have the pleasure of knowing of something of the joys and of the sorrows that have crowned this little life of mine, but in and through it all I have seen the blessed hand of Him who is wise.

March 4th, 1897.

Memories of Childhood's Slavery Days

Memories of Childhood's Slavery Days

By

Annie L. Burton

BOSTON
ROSS PUBLISHING COMPANY
1909

RECOLLECTIONS OF A HAPPY LIFE

The memory of my happy, care-free childhood days on the plantation, with my little white and black companions, is often with me. Neither master nor mistress nor neighbors had time to bestow a thought upon us, for the great Civil War was raging. That great event in American history was a matter wholly outside the realm of our childish interests. Of course we heard our elders discuss the various events of the great struggle, but it meant nothing to us.

On the plantation there were ten white children and fourteen colored children. Our days were spent roaming about from plantation to plantation, not knowing or caring what things were going on in the great world outside our little realm. Planting time and harvest time were happy days for us. How often at the harvest time the planters discovered cornstalks missing from the ends of the rows, and blamed the crows! We were called the " little fairy devils." To the sweet potatoes and peanuts and sugar cane we also helped ourselves.

Those slaves that were not married served the food from the great house, and about half-past eleven they would send the older children with food to the workers in the fields. Of course, I followed, and before we got to the fields, we had eaten the food nearly all up. When the workers returned home they complained, and we were whipped.

The slaves got their allowance every Monday night of molasses, meat, corn meal, and a kind of flour called " dredgings " or " shorts." Perhaps this allowance would be gone before the next Monday night, in which case the slaves would steal hogs and chickens. Then would come the whipping-post. Master himself never whipped his slaves; this was left to the overseer.

We children had no supper, and only a little piece of bread or something of the kind in the morning. Our dishes consisted of one wooden bowl, and oyster shells were our spoons. This bowl served for about fifteen children, and often the dogs and the ducks and the peafowl had a dip in it. Sometimes we had buttermilk and bread in our bowl, sometimes greens or bones.

Our clothes were little homespun cotton slips,

with short sleeves. I never knew what shoes were until I got big enough to earn them myself.

If a slave man and woman wished to marry, a party would be arranged some Saturday night among the slaves. The marriage ceremony consisted of the pair jumping over a stick. If no children were born within a year or so, the wife was sold.

At New Year's, if there was any debt or mortgage on the plantation, the extra slaves were taken to Clayton and sold at the court house. In this way families were separated.

When they were getting recruits for the war, we were allowed to go to Clayton to see the soldiers.

I remember, at the beginning of the war, two colored men were hung in Clayton; one, Cæsar King, for killing a blood hound and biting off an overseer's ear; the other, Dabney Madison, for the murder of his master. Dabney Madison's master was really shot by a man named Houston, who was infatuated with Madison's mistress, and who had hired Madison to make the bullets for him. Houston escaped after the deed, and the blame fell on Dabney Madison, as he was the only slave of his master and mistress. The clothes of the two victims were hung on two pine trees, and no colored person would touch them. Since I have grown up, I have seen the skeleton of one of these men in the office of a doctor in Clayton.

After the men were hung, the bones were put in an old deserted house. Somebody that cared for the bones used to put them in the sun in bright weather, and back in the house when it rained. Finally the bones disappeared, although the boxes that had contained them still remained.

At one time, when they were building barns on the plantation, one of the big boys got a little brandy and gave us children all a drink, enough to make us drunk. Four doctors were sent for, but nobody could tell what was the matter with us, except they thought we had eaten something poisonous. They wanted to give us some castor oil, but we refused to take it, because we thought that the oil was made from the bones of the dead men we had seen. Finally, we told about the big white boy giving us the brandy, and the mystery was cleared up.

Young as I was then, I remember this conversation between master and mistress, on master's return from the gate one day, when he had received the latest news: " William, what is the news from the seat of war? " " A great battle was fought at Bull Run, and the Confederates won," he replied. " Oh, good, good," said mistress, " and what did Jeff Davis say?" " Look out for the blockade. I do not know what the end may be soon," he answered. " What does Jeff Davis mean by that?" she asked. " Sarah Anne, I don't know, unless he means that the niggers will be free." " O, my God, what shall we do?" " I presume," he said, " we shall have to put our boys to work and hire help." " But," she said, " what will the niggers do if they are free? Why, they will starve if we don't keep them." " Oh, well," he said, " let them wander, if they will not stay with their owners. I don't doubt that many owners have been good to their slaves, and they would rather remain with their owners than wander about without home or country."

My mistress often told me that my father was a planter who owned a plantation about two miles from ours. He was a white man, born in Liverpool, England. He died in Lewisville, Alabama, in the year 1875.

I will venture to say that I only saw my father a dozen times, when I was about four years old; and those times I saw him only from a distance, as he was driving by the great house of our plantation. Whenever my mistress saw him going by, she would take me by the hand and run out upon the piazza, and exclaim, " Stop there, I say! Don't you want to see and speak to and caress your darling child? She often speaks of you and wants to embrace her dear father. See what a bright and beautiful daughter she is, a perfect picture of yourself. Well, I declare, you are an affectionate father." I well remember that whenever my mistress would speak thus and upbraid him, he would whip up his horse and get out of sight and hearing as quickly as possible. My mistress's action was, of course, intended to humble and shame my father. I never spoke to him, and cannot remember that he ever noticed me, or in any way acknowledged me to be his child.

My mother and my mistress were children together, and grew up to be mothers together. My mother was the cook in my mistress's household. One morning when master had gone to Eufaula, my mother and my mistress got into an argument, the consequence of which was that my mother was whipped, for the first time in her life. Whereupon, my mother refused to do any more work, and ran away from the plantation. For three years we did not see her again.

Our plantation was one of several thousand acres, comprising large level fields, upland, and considerable forests of Southern pine. Cotton, corn, sweet potatoes, sugar cane, wheat, and rye were the principal crops raised on the plantation. It was situated near the P—— River, and about twenty-three miles from Clayton, Ala.

One day my master heard that the Yankees were coming our way, and he immediately made preparations to get his goods and valuables out of their reach. The big six-mule team was brought to the smoke-house door, and loaded with hams and provisions. After being loaded, the team was put in the care of two of the most trustworthy and valuable slaves that my master owned, and driven away. It was master's intention to have these things taken to a swamp, and there concealed in a pit that had recently been made for the purpose. But just before the team left the main road for the by-road that led to the swamp, the two slaves were surprised by the Yankees, who at once took possession of the provisions, and started the team toward Clayton, where the Yankees had headquarters. The road to Clayton ran past our plantation. One of the slave children happened to look up the road, and saw the Yankees coming, and gave warning. Whereupon, my master left unceremoniously for the woods, and remained concealed there for five days. The niggers had run away whenever they got a chance, but now it was master's and the other white folks' turn to run.

The Yankees rode up to the piazza of the great house and inquired who owned the plantation. They gave orders that nothing must be touched or taken away, as they intended to return shortly and take possession. My mistress and the slaves watched for their return day and night for more than a week, but the Yankees did not come back.

One morning in April, 1865, my master got the news that the Yankees had left Mobile Bay and crossed the Confederate lines, and that the Emancipation Proclamation had been signed by President Lincoln. Mistress suggested that the slaves should not be told of their freedom; but master said he would tell them, because they would soon find it out, even if he did not tell them. Mistress, however, said she could keep my mother's three children, for my mother had now been gone so long.

All the slaves left the plantation upon the news of their freedom, except those who were feeble or sickly. With the help of these, the crops were gathered. My mistress and her daughters had to go to the kitchen and to the washtub. My little half-brother, Henry, and myself had to gather chips, and help all we could. My sister, Caroline, who was twelve years old, could help in the kitchen.

After the war, the Yankees took all the good mules

and horses from the plantation, and left their old army stock. We children chanced to come across one of the Yankees' old horses, that had " U. S." branded on him. We called him " Old Yank " and got him fattened up. One day in August, six of us children took " Old Yank " and went away back on the plantation for watermelons. Coming home, we thought we would make the old horse trot. When " Old Yank " commenced to trot, our big melons dropped off, but we couldn't stop the horse for some time. Finally, one of the big boys went back and got some more melons, and left us eating what we could find of the ones that had been dropped. Then all we six, with our melons, got on " Old Yank " and went home. We also used to hitch " Old Yank " into a wagon and get wood. But one sad day in the fall, the Yankees came back again, and gathered up their old stock, and took " Old Yank " away.

One day mistress sent me out to do some churning under a tree. I went to sleep and jerked the churn over on top of me, and consequently got a whipping.

My mother came for us at the end of the year 1865, and demanded that her children be given up to her. This, mistress refused to do, and threatened to set the dogs on my mother if she did not at once leave the place. My mother went away, and remained with some of the neighbors until supper time. Then she got a boy to tell Caroline to come down to the fence. When she came, my mother told her to go back and get Henry and myself and bring us down to the gap in the fence as quick as she could. Then my mother took Henry in her arms, and my sister carried me on her back. We climbed fences and crossed fields, and after several hours came to a little hut which my mother had secured on a plantation. We had no more than reached the place, and made a little fire, when master's two sons rode up and demanded that the children be returned. My mother refused to give us up. Upon her offering to go with them to the Yankee headquarters to find out if it were really true that all negroes had been made free, the young men left, and troubled us no more.

The cabin that was now our home was made of logs. It had one door, and an opening in one wall, with an inside shutter, was the only window. The door was fastened with a latch. Our beds were some straw.

There were six in our little family; my mother, Caroline, Henry, two other children that my mother had brought with her upon her return, and myself.

The man on whose plantation this cabin stood,

hired my mother as cook, and gave us this little home. We children used to sell blueberries and plums that we picked. One day the man on whom we depended for our home and support, left. Then my mother did washing by the day, for whatever she could get. We were sent to get cold victuals from hotels and such places. A man wanting hands to pick cotton, my brother Henry and I were set to help in this work. We had to go to the cotton field very early every morning. For this work, we received forty cents for every hundred pounds of cotton we picked.

Caroline was hired out to take care of a baby.

In 1866, another man hired the plantation on which our hut stood, and we moved into Clayton, to a little house my mother secured there. A rich lady came to our house one day, looking for some one to take care of her little daughter. I was taken, and adopted into this family. This rich lady was Mrs. E. M. Williams, a music teacher, the wife of a lawyer. We called her " Mis' Mary."

Some rich people in Clayton who had owned slaves, opened the Methodist church on Sundays, and began the work of teaching the negroes. My new mistress sent me to Sunday school every Sunday morning, and I soon got so that I could read. Mis' Mary taught me every day at her knee. I soon could read nicely, and went through Sterling's Second Reader, and then into McGuthrie's Third Reader. The first piece of poetry I recited in Sunday school was taught to me by Mis' Mary during the week. Mis' Mary's father-in-law, an ex-judge, of Clayton, Alabama, heard me recite it, and thought it was wonderful. It was this:

> "I am glad to see you, little bird,
> It was your sweet song I heard.
> What was it I heard you say?
> Give me crumbs to eat today?
> Here are crumbs I brought for you.
> Eat your dinner, eat away,
> Come and see us every day."

After this Mis' Mary kept on with my studies, and taught me to write. As I grew older, she taught me to cook and how to do housework. During this time Mis' Mary had given my mother one dollar a month in return for my services; now as I grew up to young womanhood, I thought I would like a little money of my own. Accordingly, Mis' Mary began to pay me four dollars a month, besides giving me my board and clothes. For two summers she " let me out " while she was away, and I got five dollars a month.

While I was with Mis' Mary, I had my first sweetheart, one of the young fellows who attended Sunday school with me. Mis' Mary, however, objected to the young man's coming to the house to call, because she did not think I was old enough to have a sweetheart.

I owe a great deal to Mis' Mary for her good training of me, in honesty, uprightness and truthfulness. She told me that when I went out into the world all white folks would not treat me as she had, but that I must not feel bad about it, but just do what I was employed to do, and if I wasn't satisfied, to go elsewhere; but always to carry an honest name.

One Sunday when my sweetheart walked to the gate with me, Mis' Mary met him and told him she thought I was too young for him, and that she was sending me to Sunday school to learn, not to catch a beau. It was a long while before he could see me again, — not until later in the season, in watermelon time, when Mis' Mary and my mother gave me permission to go to a watermelon party one Sunday afternoon. Mis' Mary did not know, however, that my sweetheart had planned to escort me. We met around the corner of the house, and after the party he left me at the same place. After that I saw him occasionally at barbecues and parties. I was permitted to go with him some evenings to church, but my mother always walked ahead or behind me and the young man.

We went together for four years. During that time, although I still called Mis' Mary's my home, I had been out to service in one or two families.

Finally, my mother and Mis' Mary consented to our marriage, and the wedding day was to be in May. The winter before that May, I went to service in the family of Dr. Drury in Eufaula. Just a week before I left Clayton I dreamed that my sweetheart died suddenly. The night before I was to leave, we were invited out to tea. He told me he had bought a nice piece of poplar wood, with which to make a table for our new home. When I told him my dream, he said, "Don't let that trouble you, there is nothing in dreams." But one month from that day he died, and his coffin was made from the piece of poplar wood he had bought for the table.

After his death, I remained in Clayton for two or three weeks with my people, and then went back to Eufaula, where I stayed two years.

My sweetheart's death made a profound impression on me, and I began to pray as best I could. Often I remained all night on my knees.

Going on an excursion to Macon, Georgia, one time, I liked the place so well that I did not go back to Eufaula. I got a place as cook in the family of an Episcopal clergyman, and remained with them eight years, leaving when the family moved to New Orleans.

During these eight years, my mother died in Clayton, and I had to take the three smallest children into my care. My oldest sister was now married, and had a son.

I now went to live with a Mrs. Maria Campbell, a colored woman, who adopted me and gave me her name. Mrs. Campbell did washing and ironing for her living. While living with her, I went six months to Lewis' High School in Macon. Then I went to Atlanta, and obtained a place as first-class cook with Mr. E. N. Inman. But I always considered Mrs. Campbell's my home. I remained about a year with Mr. Inman, and received as wages ten dollars a month.

One day, when the family were visiting in Memphis, I chanced to pick up a newspaper, and read the advertisement of a Northern family for a cook to go to Boston. I went at once to the address given, and made agreement to take the place, but told the people that I could not leave my present position until Mr. Inman returned home. Mr. and Mrs. Inman did not want to let me go, but I made up my mind to go North. The Northern family whose service I was to enter had returned to Boston before I left, and had made arrangements with a friend, Mr. Bullock, to see me safely started North.

After deciding to go North, I went to Macon, to make arrangements with Mrs. Campbell for the care of my two sisters who lived with her. One sister was now about thirteen and the other fifteen, both old enough to do a little for themselves. My brother was dead. He went to Brunswick in 1875, and died there of the yellow fever in 1876. One sister I brought in later years to Boston. I stayed in Macon two weeks, and was in Atlanta three or four days before leaving for the North.

About the 15th of June, 1879, I arrived at the Old Colony Station in Boston, and had my first glimpse of the country I had heard so much about. From Boston I went to Newtonville, where I was to work. The gentleman whose service I was to enter, Mr. E. N. Kimball, was waiting at the station for me, and drove me to his home on Warner Street. For a few days, until I got somewhat adjusted to my new circumstances, I had no work to do. On June 17th the family took me with them to Auburndale. But in spite of the kindness of Mrs. Kimball and the colored nurse, I grew very homesick for the South, and would often look in the direction of my old home and cry.

The washing, a kind of work I knew nothing about,

was given to me; but I could not do it, and it was finally given over to a hired woman. I had to do the ironing of the fancy clothing for Mrs. Kimball and the children.

About five or six weeks after my arrival, Mrs. Kimball and the children went to the White Mountains for the summer, and I had more leisure. Mr. Kimball went up to the mountains every Saturday night, to stay with his family over Sunday; but he and his father-in-law were at home other nights, and I had to have dinner for them.

To keep away the homesickness and loneliness as much as possible, I made acquaintance with the hired girl across the street.

One morning I climbed up into the cherry tree that grew between Mr. Kimball's yard and the yard of his next-door neighbor, Mr. Roberts. I was thinking of the South, and as I picked the cherries, I sang a Southern song. Mr. Roberts heard me, and gave me a dollar for the song.

By agreement, Mrs. Kimball was to give me three dollars and a half a week, instead of four, until the difference amounted to my fare from the South; after that, I was to have four dollars. I had, however, received but little money. In the fall, after the family came home, we had a little difficulty about my

wages, and I left and came into Boston. One of my
Macon acquaintances had come North before me,
and now had a position as cook in a house on Colum-
bus Avenue. I looked this girl up. Then I went to
a lodging-house for colored people on Kendall
Street, and spent one night there. Mrs. Kimball had
refused to give me a recommendation, because she
wanted me to stay with her, and thought the lack of
a recommendation would be an inducement. In the
lodging-house I made acquaintance with a colored
girl, who took me to an intelligence office. The man
at the desk said he would give me a card to take to
24 Springfield Street, on receipt of fifty cents. I had
never heard of an office of this kind, and asked a
good many questions. After being assured that my
money would be returned in case I did not accept
the situation, I paid the fifty cents and started to find
the address on the card. Being ignorant of the
scheme of street numbering, I inquired of a woman
whom I met, where No. 24 was. This woman asked
me if I was looking for work, and when I told her I
was, she said a friend of hers on Springfield Street
wanted a servant immediately. Of course I went
with this lady, and after a conference with the
mistress of the house as to my ability, when I
could begin work, what wages I should want, etc.,

I was engaged as cook at three dollars and a half a week.

From this place I proceeded to 24 Springfield Street, as directed, hoping that I would be refused, so that I might go back to the intelligence office and get my fifty cents. The lady at No. 24 who wanted a servant, said she didn't think I was large and strong enough, and guessed I wouldn't do. Then I went and got my fifty cents.

Having now obtained a situation, I sent to Mr. Kimball's for my trunk. I remained in my new place a year and a half. At the end of that time the family moved to Dorchester, and because I did not care to go out there, I left their service.

From this place, I went to Narragansett Pier to work as a chambermaid for the summer. In the fall, I came back to Boston and obtained a situation with a family, in Berwick Park. This family afterward moved to Jamaica Plain, and I went with them. With this family I remained seven years. They were very kind to me, gave me two or three weeks' vacation, without loss of pay.

In June, 1884, I went with them to their summer home in the Isles of Shoals, as housekeeper for some guests who were coming from Paris. On the 6th of July I received word that my sister Caroline had died in June. This was a great blow to me. I remained with the Reeds until they closed their summer home, but I was not able to do much work after the news of my sister's death.

I wrote home to Georgia, to the white people who owned the house in which Caroline had lived, asking them to take care of her boy Lawrence until I should come in October. When we came back to Jamaica Plain in the fall, I was asked to decide what I should do in regard to this boy. Mrs. Reed wanted me to stay with her, and promised to help pay for the care of the boy in Georgia. Of course, she said, I could not expect to find positions if I had a child with me. As an inducement to remain in my present place and leave the boy in Georgia, I was promised provision for my future days, as long as I should live. It did not take me long to decide what I should do. The last time I had seen my sister, a little over a year before she died, she had said, when I was leaving, "I don't expect ever to see you again, but if I die I shall rest peacefully in my grave, because I know you will take care of my child."

I left Jamaica Plain and took a room on Village Street for the two or three weeks until my departure for the South. During this time, a lady came to the house to hire a girl for her home in Wellesley Hills.

The girl who was offered the place would not go. I volunteered to accept the position temporarily, and went at once to the beautiful farm. At the end of a week, a man and his wife had been engaged, and I was to leave the day after their arrival. These new servants, however, spoke very little English, and I had to stay through the next week until the new ones were broken in. After leaving there I started for Georgia, reaching there at the end of five days, at five o'clock.

I took a carriage and drove at once to the house where Lawrence was being taken care of. He was playing in the yard, and when he saw me leave the carriage he ran and threw his arms around my neck and cried for joy. I stayed a week in this house, looking after such things of my sister's as had not been already stored. One day I had a headache, and was lying down in the cook's room. Lawrence was in the dining-room with the cook's little girl, and the two got into a quarrel, in the course of which my nephew struck the cook's child. The cook, in her anger, chased the boy with a broom, and threatened to give him a good whipping at all costs. Hearing the noise, I came out into the yard, and when Lawrence saw me he ran to me for protection. I interceded for him, and promised he should get into no more trouble. We went at once to a neighbor's house for the night. The next day I got a room in the yard of a house belonging to some white people. Here we stayed two weeks. The only return I was asked to make for the room was to weed the garden. Lawrence and I dug out some weeds and burned them, but came so near setting fire to the place that we were told we need not dig any more weeds, but that we might have the use of the room so long as we cared to stay.

In about a week and a half more we got together such things as we wanted to keep and take away with us.

The last time I saw my sister, I had persuaded her to open a bank account, and she had done so, and had made small deposits from time to time. When I came to look for the bankbook, I discovered that her lodger, one Mayfield, had taken it at her death, and nobody knew where it might be now. I found out that Mayfield had drawn thirty dollars from the account for my sister's burial, and also an unknown amount for himself. He had done nothing for the boy. I went down to the bank, and was told that Mayfield claimed to look after my sister's burial and her affairs. He had made one Reuben Bennett, who was no relation and had no interest in the matter, administrator for Lawrence, until his coming of age. But Bennett had as yet done nothing for him. The book was in the bank, with some of the account still undrawn, how much I did not know. I next went to see a lawyer, to find out how much it would cost me to get this book. The lawyer said fifteen dollars. I said I would call again. In the meantime, I went to the court house, and when the case on trial was adjourned I went to the judge and stated my case. The judge, who was slightly acquainted with my sister and me, told me to have Reuben Bennett in court next morning at nine o'clock, and to bring Lawrence with me. When we had all assembled before the judge, he told Bennett to take Lawrence and go to the bank and get the money belonging to my sister. Bennett went and collected the money, some thirty-five dollars. The boy was then given into my care by the judge. For his kindness, the judge would accept no return. Happy at having obtained the money so easily, we went back to our room, and rested until our departure the next night for Jacksonville, Florida. I had decided to go to this place for the winter, on account of Lawrence, thinking the Northern winter would be too severe for him.

My youngest sister, who had come to Macon from

Atlanta a few days before my arrival, did not hear of Caroline's death until within a few days of our departure. This youngest sister decided to go to Florida with us for the winter.

Our trunks and baggage were taken to the station in a team. We had a goodly supply of food, given us by our friends and by the people whose hospitality we had shared during the latter part of our stay.

The next morning we got into Jacksonville. My idea was to get a place as chambermaid at Green Cove Springs, Florida, through the influence of the head waiter at a hotel there, whom I knew. After I got into Jacksonville I changed my plans. I did not see how I could move my things any farther, and we went to a hotel for colored people, hired a room for two dollars, and boarded ourselves on the food which had been given us in Macon. This food lasted about two weeks. Then I had to buy, and my money was going every day, and none coming in, I did not know what to do. One night the idea of keeping a restaurant came to me, and I decided to get a little home for the three of us, and then see what I could do in this line of business. After a long and hard search, I found a little house of two rooms where we could live, and the next day I found a place to start my restaurant. For house furnishings, we used at first, to the best advantage we could, the things we had brought from Macon. Caroline's cookstove had been left with my foster-mother in Macon. After hiring the room for the restaurant, I sent for this stove, and it arrived in a few days. Then I went to a dealer in second-hand furniture and got such things as were actually needed for the house and the restaurant, on the condition that he would take them back at a discount when I got through with them.

Trade at the restaurant was very good, and we got along nicely. My sister got a position as nurse for fifteen dollars a month. One day the cook from a shipwrecked vessel came to my restaurant, and in return for his board and a bed in the place, agreed to do my cooking. After trade became good, I changed my residence to a house of four rooms, and put three cheap cots in each of two of the rooms, and let the cots at a dollar a week apiece to colored men who worked nearby in hotels. Lawrence and I did the chamber work at night, after the day's work in the restaurant.

I introduced " Boston baked beans " into my restaurant, much to the amusement of the people at first; but after they had once eaten them it was hard to meet the demand for beans.

Lawrence, who was now about eleven years old,

was a great help to me. He took out dinners to the cigarmakers in a factory nearby.

At the end of the season, about four months, it had grown so hot that we could stay in Jacksonville no longer. From my restaurant and my lodgers I cleared one hundred and seventy-five dollars, which I put into the Jacksonville bank. Then I took the furniture back to the dealer, who fulfilled his agreement.

My sister decided to go back to Atlanta when she got through with her place as nurse, which would not be for some weeks.

I took seventy-five dollars out of my bank account, and with Lawrence went to Fernandina. There we took train to Port Royal, S. C., then steamer to New York. From New York we went to Brooklyn for a few days. Then we went to Newport and stayed with a woman who kept a lodging-house. I decided to see what I could do in Newport by keeping a boarding and lodging-house. I hired a little house and agreed to pay nine dollars a month for it. I left Lawrence with some neighbors while I came to Boston and took some things out of storage. These things I moved into the little house. But I found, after paying one month's rent, that the house was not properly located for the business I wanted. I left, and with Lawrence went to Narragansett Pier. I got a place there as

" runner " for a laundry; that is, I was to go to the hotels and leave cards and solicit trade. Then Lawrence thought he would like to help by doing a little work. One night when I came back from the laundry, I missed him. Nobody had seen him. All night I searched for him, but did not find him. In the early morning I met him coming home. He said a man who kept a bowling alley had hired him at fifty cents a week to set up the pins, and it was in the bowling alley he had been all night. He said the man let him take a nap on his coat when he got sleepy. I went at once to see this man, and told him not to hire my nephew again. A lady who kept a hotel offered me two dollars a week for Lawrence's services in helping the cook and serving in the help's dining-room. When the season closed, the lady who hired Lawrence was very reluctant to let him go.

We went back to Newport to see the landlady from whom I had hired the house, and I paid such part of the rent as I could. Then I packed my things and started for Boston. On reaching there, I kept such of my things as I needed, and stored the rest, and took a furnished room. In about a week's time I went to see the husband of the lady for whom I had worked at Wellesley Hills just previous to my departure for the South. He had told me to let him know when I returned to Boston. He said a man and his wife were at present employed at his farm, but he didn't know how long they would stay. Before another week had passed, this gentleman sent for me. He said his wife wanted me to go out to the farm, and that I could have Lawrence with me. The boy, he said, could help his wife with the poultry, and could have a chance to go to school. I was promised three dollars and a half a week, and no washing to do. I was told that the farm had been offered for sale, and of course it might change hands any day. I was promised, however, that I should lose nothing by the change.

Lawrence was very lonely at the farm, with no companions, and used to sit and cry.

The place was sold about ten weeks after I went there, and I came into Boston to look about for a restaurant, leaving Lawrence at the farm. When the home was broken up, the owners came to the Revere House, Boston. Barrels of apples, potatoes and other provisions were given to me.

I found a little restaurant near the Providence depot for sale. I made arrangements at once to buy the place for thirty-five dollars, and the next day I brought Lawrence and my things from Wellesley Hills. I paid two dollars a week rent for my little restaurant, and did very well. The next spring I sold the place for fifty dollars, in time to get a place at the beach for the summer.

Lawrence got a position in a drug store, and kept it four years. Then he went to Hampton College, Hampton, Va. After finishing there, he came back and then went to the World's Fair in Chicago. After that he took a position on one of the Fall River line boats. At the outbreak of the Spanish War, he enlisted in Brooklyn as powderman on the battleship Texas. He was on the Texas when the first shot was fired. He was present at the decoration of the graves of the American soldiers in Havana, and also at the decoration of the battleship Maine after she was raised. After the war, he came to Brooklyn and got an honorable discharge. Then he served as valet to a rich New York man, who travelled a good deal. About the middle of last November (1906) Lawrence came to Boston to see me. He is now in Atlantic City, a waiter in the Royal Hotel.

In 1888, I was married, at 27 Pemberton Street, to Samuel H. Burton, by Dr. O. P. Gifford. After my marriage, Mr. Burton got a place in Braintree as valet to an old gentleman who was slightly demented, and he could not be satisfied until I joined him. So I put our things into storage and went to Braintree. I remained there ten months, and then came back to Boston. Then I got a position as head matron in the help's dining-room in a hotel at Watch Hill, R. I. My husband was also there as waiter. At the end of the season we both came home, and rented a lodging-house, and lost money on it.

REMINISCENCES

The times changed from slavery days to freedom's days. As young as I was, my thoughts were mystified to see such wonderful changes; yet I did not know the meaning of these changing days. But days glided by, and in my mystified way I could see and hear many strange things. I would see my master and mistress in close conversation and they seemed anxious about something that I, a child, could not know the meaning of.

But as weeks went by, I began to understand. I saw all the slaves one by one disappearing from the plantation (for night and day they kept going) until there was not one to be seen.

All around the plantation was left barren. Day after day I could run down to the gate and see down the road troops and troops of Garrison's Brigade, and in the midst of them gangs and gangs of negro slaves who joined with the soldiers, shouting, dancing and clapping their hands. The war was ended, and from Mobile Bay to Clayton, Ala., all along the road, on all the plantations, the slaves thought that if they joined the Yankee soldiers they would be perfectly safe.

As I looked on these I did not know what it meant, for I had never seen such a circus. The Yankee soldiers found that they had such an army of men and women and children, that they had to build tents and feed them to keep them from starving. But from what I, a little child, saw and heard the older ones say, that must have been a terrible time of trouble. I heard my master and mistress talking. They said, " Well, I guess those Yankees had such a large family on their hands, we rather guessed those fanatics on freedom would be only too glad to send some back for their old masters to provide for them."

But they never came back to our plantation, and I could only speak of my own home, but I thought to myself, what would become of my good times all over the old plantation. Oh, the harvesting times, the great hog-killing times when several hundred hogs were killed, and we children watched and got our share of the slaughter in pig's liver roasted on a bed of coals, eaten ashes and all. Then came the great sugar-cane grinding time, when they were making the molasses, and we children would be hanging round, drinking the sugar-cane juice, and awaiting the moment to help ourselves to everything good. We did, too, making ourselves sticky and dirty with the sweet stuff being made. Not only were the slave children there, but the little white children from Massa's house would join us and have a jolly time. The negro child and the white child knew not the great chasm between their lives, only that they had dainties and we had crusts.

My sister, being the children's nurse, would take them and wash their hands and put them to bed in their luxurious bedrooms, while we little slaves would find what homes we could. My brother and I would go to sleep on some lumber under the house, where our sister Caroline would find us and put us to bed. She would wipe our hands and faces and make up our beds on the floor in Massa's house, for we had lived with him ever since our own mother had run away, after being whipped by her mistress. Later on, after the war, my mother returned and claimed us. I never knew my father, who was a white man.

During these changing times, just after the war, I was trying to find out what the change would bring about for us, as we were under the care of our mistress, living in the great house. I thought this: that Henry, Caroline and myself, Louise, would have to go as others had done, and where should we go and what should we do? But as time went on there were many changes. Our mistress and her two daughters, Martha and Mary, had to become their own servants, and do all the work of the house, going into the kitchen, cooking and washing, and feeling very angry that all their house servants had run away to the Yankees. The time had come when our good times were over, our many leisure hours spent among the cotton fields and woods and our half-holiday on Saturday. These were all gone. The boys had to leave school and take the runaway slaves' places to finish the planting and pick the cotton. I myself have worked in the cotton field, picking great baskets full, too heavy for me to carry. All was over! I now fully understood the change in our circumstances. Little Henry and I had no more time to sit basking ourselves in the sunshine of the sunny south. The land was empty and the servants all gone. I can see my dainty mistress coming down the steps saying, " Rit, you and Henry will have to go and pick up some chips, for Miss Mary and myself have to prepare the breakfast. You children will have to learn to work. Do you understand me, Rit and Henry?" " Yes, Missus, we understand." And away we flew, laughing, and thinking it a great joke that we, Massa's pets, must learn to work.

But it was a sad, sad change on the old plantation, and the beautiful, proud Sunny South, with its masters and mistresses, was bowed beneath the sin brought about by slavery. It was a terrible blow to the owners of plantations and slaves, and their children would feel it more than they, for they had been reared to be waited upon by willing or unwilling slaves.

In this place I will insert a poem my young mistress taught us, for she was always reading poems and good stories. But first I will record a talk I heard between my master and mistress. They were sitting in the dining-room, and we children were standing around the table. My mistress said, " I suppose, as Nancy has never returned, we had better keep Henry, Caroline and Louise until they are of age." " Yes, we will," said Massa, Miss Mary and Miss Martha, " but it is ' man proposes and God disposes.' "

So in the following pages you will read the sequel to my childhood life in the Sunny South.

Right after the war when my mother had got settled in her hut, with her little brood hovered around her, from which she had been so long absent, we had nothing to eat, and nothing to sleep on save some old pieces of horse-blankets and hay that the soldiers gave her. The first day in the hut was a rainy day; and as night drew near it grew more fierce, and we children had gathered some little fagots to make a fire by the time mother came home, with something for us to eat, such as she had gathered through the day. It was only corn meal and pease and ham-bone and skins which she had for our supper. She had started a little fire, and said, " Some of you close that door," for it was cold. She swung the pot over the fire and filled it with the pease and ham-bone and skins. Then she seated her little brood around the fire on the pieces of blanket, where we watched with all our eyes, our hearts filled with desire, looking to see what she would do next. She took down an old broken earthen bowl, and tossed into it the little meal she had brought, stirring it up with water, making a hoe cake. She said, " One of you draw that griddle out here," and she placed it on the few little coals. Perhaps this griddle you have never seen, or one like it. I will describe it to you. This griddle was a round piece of iron, quite thick, having three legs. It might have been made in a blacksmith's shop, for I have never seen one like it before or since. It was placed upon the coals, and with an old iron spoon she put on this griddle half of the corn meal she had mixed up. She said, " I will put

a tin plate over this, and put it away for your breakfast.'' We five children were eagerly watching the
pot boiling, with the pease and ham-bone. The rain
was pattering on the roof of the hut. All at once
there came a knock at the door. My mother answered
the knock. When she opened the door, there stood a
white woman and three little children, all dripping
with the rain. My mother said, '' In the name of the
Lord, where are you going on such a night, with
these children? '' The woman said, '' Auntie, I am
travelling. Will you please let me stop here to-night,
out of the rain, with my children? '' My mother
said, '' Yes, honey. I ain't got much, but what I
have got I will share with you.'' '' God bless you! ''
They all came in. We children looked in wonder at
what had come. But my mother scattered her own
little brood and made a place for the forlorn wanderers. She said, '' Wait, honey, let me turn over
that hoe cake.'' Then the two women fell to talking,
each telling a tale of woe. After a time, my mother
called out, '' Here, you, Louise, or some one of you,
put some fagots under the pot, so these pease can
get done.'' We couldn't put them under fast enough,
first one and then another of us children, the mothers
still talking. Soon my mother said, '' Draw that hoe
cake one side, I guess it is done.'' My mother said

to the woman, " Honey, ain't you got no husband? "
She said, " No, my husband got killed in the war."
My mother replied, " Well, my husband died right
after the war. I have been away from my little
brood for four years. With a hard struggle, I have
got them away from the Farrin plantation, for they
did not want to let them go. But I got them. I was
determined to have them. But they would not let
me have them if they could have kept them. With
God's help I will keep them from starving. The
white folks are good to me. They give me work, and
I know, with God's help, I can get along." The
white woman replied, " Yes, Auntie, my husband left
me on a rich man's plantation. This man promised
to look out for me until my husband came home; but
he got killed in the war, and the Yankees have set
his negroes free and he said he could not help me any
more, and we would have to do the best we could for
ourselves. I gave my things to a woman to keep
for me until I could find my kinsfolk. They live
about fifty miles from here, up in the country. I
am on my way there now." My mother said, " How
long will it take you to get there? " " About three
days, if it don't rain." My mother said, " Ain't
you got some way to ride there? " " No, Auntie,

42

there is no way of riding up where my folks live, the place where I am from."

We hoped the talk was most ended, for we were anxiously watching that pot. Pretty soon my mother seemed to realize our existence. She exclaimed, " My Lord! I suppose the little children are nearly starved. Are those pease done, young ones? " She turned and said to the white woman, " Have you-all had anything to eat? " " We stopped at a house about dinner time, but the woman didn't have anything but some bread and buttermilk." My mother said, " Well, honey, I ain't got but a little, but I will divide with you." The woman said, " Thank you, Auntie. You just give my children a little; I can do without it."

Then came the dividing. We all watched with all our eyes to see what the shares would be. My mother broke a mouthful of bread and put it on each of the tin plates. Then she took the old spoon and equally divided the pea soup. We children were seated around the fire, with some little wooden spoons. But the wooden spoons didn't quite go round, and some of us had to eat with our fingers. Our share of the meal, however, was so small that we were as hungry when we finished as when we began.

My mother said, " Take that rag and wipe your

face and hands, and give it to the others and let them use it, too. Put those plates upon the table.'' We immediately obeyed orders, and took our seats again around the fire. '' One of you go and pull that straw out of the corner and get ready to go to bed.'' We all lay down on the straw, the white children with us, and my mother covered us over with the blanket. We were soon in the '' Land of Nod,'' forgetting our empty stomachs. The two mothers still continued to talk, sitting down on the only seats, a couple of blocks. A little back against the wall my mother and the white woman slept.

Bright and early in the morning we were called up, and the rest of the hoe cake was eaten for breakfast, with a little meat, some coffee sweetened with molasses. The little wanderers and their mother shared our meal, and then they started again on their journey towards their home among their kinsfolk, and we never saw them again. My mother said, '' God bless you! I wish you all good luck. I hope you will reach your home safely.'' Then mother said to us, '' You young ones put away that straw and sweep up the place, because I have to go to my work.'' But she came at noon and brought us a nice dinner, more satisfactory than the supper and breakfast we had had. We children were delighted that there were no little white children to share our meal this time.

In time, my older sister, Caroline, and myself got work among good people, where we soon forgot all the hard times in the little log cabin by the roadside in Clayton, Alabama.

Up to my womanhood, even to this day, these memories fill my mind. Some kind friends' eyes may see these pages, and may they recall some fond memories of their happy childhood, as what I have written brings back my young life in the great Sunny South.

I am something of the type of Moses on this 49th birthday; not that I am wrapped in luxuries, but that my thoughts are wrapped in the luxuries of the heavenly life in store for me, when my life work is done, and my friends shall be blessed by the work I shall have done. For God has commanded me to write this book, that some one may read and receive comfort and courage to do what God commands them to do. God bless every soul who shall read this true life story of one born in slavery.

It is now six years since the inspiration to write this book came to me in the Franklin evening school. I have struggled on, helped by friends. God said, " Write the book and I will help you." And He has.

It was through a letter of my life that the principal

of the Franklin school said, " Write the book and I will help you." But he died before the next term, and I worked on. On this, my 49th birthday, I can say I believe that the book is close to the finish.

My life is like the summer rose
That opens to the morning sky,
But ere the shades of evening close
Is scattered on the ground to die.
Yet on the rose's humble bed
The sweetest dews of night are shed,
As if she wept a tear for me,
As if she wept the waste to see.

My life is like the autumn leaf
That trembles in the moon's pale ray.
Its hold is frail, its date is brief,
Restless, and soon to pass away.
Yet, ere that leaf shall fall and fade,
The parent tree will mourn its shade,
The winds bewail the leafless tree;
But none shall breathe a sigh for me.

My life is like the prints which feet
Have left on Tampa's desert strand.
Soon as the rising tide shall beat
All trace will vanish from the sand.
Yet, as if grieving to efface
All vestige of the human race,
On that lone shore loud moans the sea.
But none, alas, shall mourn for me.

A VISION

♪ ♪ ♪ A VISION ♪ ♪ ♪

There remains to be told the story of my conversion and how I came to write the foregoing history of my life.

In 1875 I was taken sick. I thought I was going to die, and I promised the Lord I would serve Him if he would only spare my life. When I got well again, however, I forgot all about my promise. Then I was taken sick again. It seemed I had to go through a dark desert place, where great demons stood on either side. In the distance I could just see a dim light, and I tried to get to this light, but could not reach it. Then I found myself in a great marsh, and was sinking. I threw up my hands and said, "Lord, if Thou wilt raise me from this pit, I will never fail to serve Thee." Then it seemed as if I mounted on wings into the air, and all the demons that stood about made a great roaring. My flight ended on the top of a hill. But I was troubled because I could not find the light. All at once, at the sound of a loud peal of thunder, the earth opened, and I fell down into the pits of hell. Again I prayed to God to save me from this, and again I promised to serve Him. My prayer was answered, and I was able to fly out of the pit, on to a bank. At the foot of the little hill on which I sat were some little children, and they called to me to come down. But I could not get down. Then the children raised a ladder for me, and I came down among them. A little cherub took me by the hand and led me in the River of Badjied of Jordan. I looked at my ankles and shoulders and discovered I had little wings. On the river was a ship. The children, the cherub and I got into the ship. When we reached a beautiful spot, the little cherub made the ship fast, and there opened before us pearly gates, and we all passed through into the golden street. The street led to the throne of God, about which we marched. Then the cherub conducted us to a table where a feast was spread. Then the children vanished. The cherub took me by the hand, and said, " Go back into the world, and tell the saints and sinners what a Savior you have found, and if you prove faithful I will take you to Heaven to live forever, when I come again."

When I recovered from my sickness, I was baptized by the Rev. Dr. Pope, and· joined the church in Macon. When I came North, I brought my letter. Not finding any church for colored people, I came among the white people, and was treated so kindly that I became very much attached to them. The first church I became connected with in the North, was in Newtonville. When I came to Boston, I went to the Warren Avenue Baptist Church. Before my marriage I joined Tremont Temple, when Dr. Lorimer was its pastor. When the church was burned, my letter was destroyed, but when I went South on a visit I had the letter duplicated, and took it to the new Temple. I am still a member of the Temple, and hope to remain there as long as God gives me life.

Five years ago, I began to go to the Franklin evening school. Mr. Guild was the master. At one time he requested all the pupils to write the story of their lives, and he considered my composition so interesting he said he thought if I could work it up and enlarge upon it, I could write a book. He promised to help me. My teacher was Miss Emerson, and she was interested in me. But the next year Miss Emerson gave up teaching, and Mr. Guild died.

In each of the terms that I have attended, I have received the certificates showing that I have been regular and punctual in attendance, have maintained good deportment, and shown general proficiency in the studies. I would have graduated in 1907, had it not been for sickness. The following was to have been my graduating composition.

ABRAHAM LINCOLN

BY

ANNIE L. BURTON

✎ ABRAHAM LINCOLN ✎

In a little clearing in the backwoods of Harding County, Kentucky, there stood years ago a rude cabin within whose walls Abraham Lincoln passed his childhood. An "unaccountable" man he has been called, and the adjective was well chosen, for who could account for a mind and nature like Lincoln's with the ancestry he owned? His father was a thriftless, idle carpenter, scarcely supporting his family, and with but the poorest living. His mother was an uneducated woman, but must have been of an entirely different nature, for she was able to impress upon her boy a love of learning. During her life, his chief, in fact his only book, was the Bible, and in this he learned to read. Just before he was nine years old, the father brought his family across the Ohio River into Illinois, and there in the unfloored log cabin, minus windows and doors, Abraham lived and grew. It was during this time that the mother died, and in a short time the shiftless father with his family drifted back to the old home, and here found another for his children in one who was a friend of earlier days. This woman was of a thrifty nature, and her energy made him floor the cabin, hang doors, and open up windows. She was fond of the children and cared for them tenderly, and to her the boy Abraham owed many pleasant hours.

As he grew older, his love for knowledge increased and he obtained whatever books he could, studying by the firelight, and once walking six miles for an English Grammar. After he read it, he walked the six miles to return it. He needed the book no longer, for with this as with his small collection of books, what he once read was his. He absorbed the books he read.

During these early years he did " odd jobs " for the neighbors. Even at this age, his gift of story telling was a notable one, as well as his sterling honesty. His first knowledge of slavery in all its horrors came to him when he was about twenty-one years old. He had made a trip to New Orleans, and there in the old slave market he saw an auction. His face paled, and his spirits rose in revolt at the coarse jest of the auctioneer, and there he registered a vow within himself, " If ever I have a chance to strike against slavery, I will strike and strike hard." To this end he worked and for this he paid " the last full measure of devotion."

His political life began with a defeat for the Illinois Legislature in 1830, but he was returned in 1834, 1836, 1838, and declined re-election in 1840, preferring to study law and prepare for his future. " Honest Abe " he has been called, and throughout Illinois that characteristic was the prominent one known of him. From this time his rise was rapid. Sent to the Congress of the nation, he seldom spoke, but when he did his terse though simple expression always won him a hearing. His simplicity and frankness was deceptive to the political leaders, and from its very fearlessness often defeated them.

His famous debates with Senator Douglas, the " Little Giant," spread his reputation from one end of the country to the other, and at their close there was no question as to Lincoln's position in the North, or on the vital question of the day.

The spirit of forbearance he carried with him to the White House, " with malice toward none, with charity for all." This was the spirit that carried him through the four awful years of the war. The martyr's crown hovered over him from the outset. The martyr's spirit was always his. The burden of the war always rested on his shoulders. The fathers, sons and brothers, the honored dead of Gettysburg, of Antietam, all lay upon his mighty heart.

He never forgot his home friends, and when occasionally one dropped in on him, the door was always open. They frequently had tea in the good old-fashioned way, and then Lincoln listened to the news of the village, old stories were retold, new ones told, and the old friendships cemented by new bonds.

Then came the end, swift and sudden, and gloom settled upon the country; for in spite of ancestry, self-education, ungainly figure, ill-fitting clothes, the soul of the man had conquered even the stubborn South, while the cold-blooded North was stricken to the heart. The noblest one of all had been taken.

THE RACE QUESTION IN AMERICA

BY

DR. P. THOMAS STANFORD

THE RACE QUESTION IN AMERICA

BY

DR. P. THOMAS STANFORD

AUTHOR OF THE "TRAGEDY OF THE NEGRO IN AMERICA"

As a member of the negro race, I myself have suffered as a child whose parents were born in slavery, deprived of all influences of the ennobling life, made obedient to the will of the white man by the lash and chain, and sold to the highest bidder when there was no more use for them.

The first negro fact for white thought is — that my clients, the colored people here in America, are not responsible for being here any more than they are responsible for their conditions of ignorance and poverty. They suddenly emerge from their prison house poor, without a home, without food or clothing, and ignorant. Now the enemies of God and of the progress of civilization in our country are to-day introducing a system of slavery with which they hope to again enslave the colored people. To carry out their evil designs they retain able politicians, lawyers and newspapers to represent them, such as Senator Tillman, the Hon. John Temple Graves of Georgia and the Baltimore Sun, and they are trying the negro on four counts which allege that the race is ignorant, cannot be taught, is lazy and immoral.

Now, are the negroes, as a whole, guilty of these charges? In the first place, the negro race of America is not ignorant. In the year 1833 John C. Calhoun, senator from South Carolina, is reported to have said that if he could find a single negro who understood the Greek syntax, he would believe the negro was human and would treat him as such. At that time it was a very safe test. God accepted the challenge in behalf of the negro race, and inspired his white sons and daughters both in the North and South to teach their brothers in black; and a few years afterward black men were examined and the world pronounced them scholars, while later still the schools were using a Greek grammar written by a black man, W. S. Scarborough of Wilberforce, O. In his class were Frederick Douglas, Henry Highland Garnett, Robert Elliot, the Rev. J. C. Price and John M. Langstone, as defenders of the race. Bishop Allen Payne, Bishop Hood and John B. Reaver will ever be remembered for their godly piety and Christian example, as we shall also remember Bishop, Sumner and Bubois for their great literary productions, William Washington Brown as the greatest organizer and financier of the century, Prof. Booker Washington as the greatest industrial educator of the world, and last, but not least, Thomas Condon, the greatest crank for the spiritual training and higher education of the negro race.

Under the leadership of such men, assisted by our white friends and backed up by our colored race journals — the Christian Banner of Philadelphia, the Christian Recorder, the Star of Zion and the Afro-American Ledger of Baltimore,

Ind., the National Baptist Union of Pennsylvania, the Age of New York, the Christian Organizer of Virginia and the Guardian of Boston — our onward march to civilization is phenomenal and by these means we have reduced illiteracy 50 per cent.

" In the South we have over $12,000,000 worth of school property, 3,000 teachers, 50 high schools, 17 academies, 125 colleges, 10 law and medical schools, 25 theological seminaries, all doing a mighty work for God and humanity.

Now as to laziness. We have now in practice 14,000 lawyers and doctors, and have accumulated over $150,000,000 worth of church property. In the South we have over 150,000 farms and houses, valued at $900,000,000, and personal property at $170,000,000. We have raised over $11,000,000 for educational purposes. The property per capita for every colored man, woman and child in the United States is estimated at $75, and we are operating successfully several banks and factories; we have 7,500,000 acres of land, and the business activity of the colored people was never as thoroughly aroused as it is to-day.

When I come to deal with the charge of immorality I bow my head and blush for shame, first because if the charge be true, I see they are getting like the white man every day. I know that at the close of the American civil war the 4,000,-000 negroes had more than 25 per cent. of white blood coursing through their veins.

What about this new educated negro? Just ask the Pullman Car Company, which employs hundreds of negroes, into whose care thousands of women and children of our best American families are entrusted every day.

Now, you cannot do without the negro, because if you send him away, you will run after him. He is here to stay. The only way to deal successfully with the colored race is God's way. First, recognize that he is your guest; second, recognize that you have robbed him of his birthplace, home, family and savings. It is these facts that are causing so much unrest on the part of the whites in this country. The negro loves his country, which he has proved beyond a doubt in every American battle, in every act of loyalty to his country, and in his long and patient suffering. Pay him what you owe him by educating him. Give him an opportunity to live. Allow him to live in decent parts of your city. Pay wages sufficient to support his children. Do this and God will remove the objectionable negro from the land.

The Negro stands to-day upon an eminence that overlooks more than two decades spent in efforts to ameliorate the condition of seven million immortal souls by opening before their hitherto dark and cheerless lives possibilities of development into a perfect and symmetrical manhood and womanhood.

The retrospect presents to us a picture of a people's moral degradation and mental gloom caused by slavery. A people absolutely sunk in the lowest depth of a poverty which reduced them to objects of charity and surrounded them with difficulties which have ever stood as impregnable barriers in their way to speedy advancement in all those qualities that make the useful citizen. Every influence of state and society life seems to be against their progress and like some evil genius, these Negro hating ghosts are forever hunting them with the idea that their future must be one of subserviency to the white race.

Hated and oppressed by the combined wisdom, wealth and statesmanship of a mighty confederacy who watched and criticised their mistakes which were strongly magnified by those who fain would write destruction upon the Emancipation; they are expected to rise from this condition.

The idea of giving to the newly enfranchised a sound, practical education was considered at the dawn of freedom, an easy solution of what as an unsolved problem threatened the perpetuity of republican institutions. Within a year from the firing on Sumter, benevolent and farsighted Northern friends had established schools from Washington to the Gulf of Mexico, which became centers of light penetrating the darkness and scattering the blessings of an enlightened manhood far and wide.

The history of the world cannot produce a more affecting spectacle than the growth of this mighty Christian philanthropy which, in beginning amid the din of battle, has steadily marched on through every opposing influence, and lifted a race from weakness to strength, from poverty to wealth, from moral and intellectual nonentity to place and power among the nations of the earth.

We have ten millions of colored people in the United States

whose condition is much better to-day than it was fifty years ago. Then he had nothing, not even a name. To-day he has 160,000 farms under good cultivation and valued at $4,000,000 and has personal property valued at $200,000,000. In the Southland the negroes own 160 first-class drug stores, nine banks, 13 building associations, and 100 insurance and benefit companies, two street railways and an electric at Jacksonville, Fla., which they started some few years ago when the white people passed the Jim Crow law for that state.

Now it is reckoned that the negroes in the United States are paying about $700,000,000 property taxes and this is only one-fifth of all they have accumulated, for the negro is getting more like the white people every day and has learned from him that it is not a sign of loyalty and patriotism to publish his property at its full taxable value.

In education and morals the progress is still greater. As you all know, at the close of the war the whole race was practically illiterate. It was a rare thing, indeed, to find a man of the race who even knew his letters. In 1880 the illiteracy had fallen to 70 per cent. and rapid strides along that line have been made ever since.

To-day there are 37,000 negro teachers in America, of which number 23,000 are regular graduates of high and normal schools and colleges, 23 are college presidents, 169 are principals of seminaries and many are principals of higher institutions. At present there are 369 negro men and women taking courses in the universities of Europe. The negro ministry, together with these teachers have been prepared for their work by our schools and are the greatest factors the North has produced for the uplift of the colored man.

To-day there are those who wish to impede the negro's progress and lessen his educational advantages by industrializing such colleges as Howard University of Washington by placing on their Boards of Trustees and Managers the pronounced leaders of industrialism, giving as a reason that the better he is educated the worse he is; in other words, they say crime has increased among educated negroes. While stern facts show the opposite, the exact figures from the last census show that the greater proportion of the negro criminals are from the illiterate class. To-day the marriage vow, which by the teaching of the whites the negro held to be of so little importance before the war, is guarded more sacredly. The one room cabin, with its attendant evils, is passing away, and the negro woman, the mightiest moral factor in the life of her people, is beginning to be more careful in her deportment and is no longer the easy victim of the unlicensed passion of certain white men. This is a great gain and is a sign of real progress, for no race can rise higher than its women.

Let me plead with the friends of the negro. Please continue to give him higher ideals of a better life and stand by him in the struggle. He has done well with the opportunities given him and is doing something along all the walks of life to help himself, which is gratitude of the best sort. What he needs to-day is moral sympathy, which in his condition years ago he could hardly appreciate. The sympathy must be moral, not necessarily social. It must be the sympathy of a soul set on fire for righteousness and fair play in a republic like ours. A sympathy which will see to it that every man shall have a man's chance in all the affairs of this great nation which boasts of being the land of the free and the home of the brave for which the black man has suffered and done so much in every sense of the word.

Let this great Christian nation of eighty millions of people do justice to the Black Battalion, and seeing President Roosevelt acknowledges that he overstepped the bounds of his power in discharging and renouncing them before they had a fair trial, and now that they are vindicated before the world, to take back what he called them, Cutthroats, Brutal Murderers, Black Midnight Assassins, and Cowards. This and this alone will to some extent atone for the wrong he has done and help him to regain the respect and confidence of the world.

Now in order to change the condition of things, I would suggest: First, that an international, industrial association be formed to help Afro-Americans to engage in manufacturing and commercial pursuits, assist them to buy farms, erect factories, open shops in which their young men and women can enter and produce what the world requires every day for its inhabitants.

If they were able to-day to produce the articles in common use as boots, shoes, hats, cotton and woolen goods, made-up clothing and enterprises such as farming, mining, forging, carpentering, etc., negroes would find a ready sale in preference to all others, because of its being a race enterprise, doing what no other corporation does, giving employment to members of the race as tradesmen, and teaching others to become skilled workers. These enterprises should be started in the southern, northern and western states, where the negro population will warrant such an undertaking.

I would suggest " A School History of the Negro Race " to be placed in our public schools as a text book. The general tone of all the histories taught in our public schools points to the inferiority of the negro and the superiority of the white. It must be indeed a stimulus to any people to be able to refer to their ancestry as distinguished in deeds of valor, and particularly so to the colored people. With what eyes can the white child look upon the colored child and the colored child look upon himself, when they have completed the assigned course of United States history, and in it found not one word of credit, not one word of favorable comment for even one among the millions of his fore-parents who have lived through nearly three centuries of his country's history. In them he is credited with no heritage of valor, he is mentioned only as a slave, while true historical records prove him to have been among the bravest of soldiers and a faithful producer of the nation's wealth. Though then a slave to the government, the negro's was the first blood shed in its defence in those days when a foreign foe threatened its destruction. In each and all of the American wars the negro was faithful, yes, faithful in battle while members of his race were being lynched to death; faithful to a land not his own in points of rights and freedom, all and that after he had enriched with his own life's blood, shouldered his musket to defend, when all this was done, regarded him with renewed terms, Black, Negro.

Last but not least the negro needs a daily newspaper in every large city, managed and edited by members of the race.

Such papers are needed to deal with questions of state and reflect the thoughts of the social world, to enter the province of ethics and tread the domain of morals and to give their opinion on the varying phases of religious truths and pass judgment on matters of a political nature.

There are hidden wrongs perpetrated by the whites against the negro race that will never be brought to light until the race owns and controls its own daily newspapers which alone have the power to discover and enthrone truth, thus becoming a safe guide to all honest seekers of facts respecting the race whether from a moral, educational, political or religious field. To carry out the plans suggested, whether viewed from an intellectual, industrial, commercial, or editorial standpoint, the world must acknowledge that to-day the negro race has the men and women, who are true to their race and all that stands for negro progress.

HISTORICAL COMPOSITION

BY

ANNIE L. BURTON

HISTORICAL COMPOSITION

It is only 132 years ago to-day that the British troops, who had occupied Boston, made a riding school of the Old South church, and otherwise sacrilegiously disported themselves, were persuaded to get out under the compulsion of the batteries set up on Dorchester Heights. But when the last company embarked for Halifax, it carried the last British flag ever unfurled by a military organization on Massachusetts soil. That was the end of foreign domination in Massachusetts. And by a happy coincidence this is the legendary anniversary of the birth of St. Patrick, the patron saint of Ireland, whose memory has been an inspiration in the struggle of another race for Liberty.

A QUESTION OF ETHICS

New York, Dec. 17. — Andrew Carnegie declared yesterday in a speech on the negro question that the negroes are a blessing to America, and that their presence in the South makes this country impregnable and without need of a navy to defend itself.

"Suppose," said Mr. Carnegie, "Great Britain were to send her war fleets to America. It would amount to nothing. All that the President of the United States would have to do would be to say, 'Stop exporting cotton.' The war would be ended in four days, for England cannot do without our cotton.

"We don't need a navy; we are impregnable. Because we have 9,000,000 colored men anxious and willing to work we hold this strong position, and I am interested in the negro from this material standpoint, as well as from the more humane point of view."

MY FAVORITE POEMS

❧ ❧ MY FAVORITE POEMS ❧ ❧

Verses

On a green slope, most fragrant with the Spring,
   One sweet, fair day I planted a red rose,
That grew, beneath my tender nourishing,
   So tall, so riotous of bloom, that those
Who passed the little valley where it grew
   Smiled at its beauty. All the air was sweet
About it! Still I tended it, and knew
   That he would come, e'en as it grew complete.

And a day brought him! Up I led him, where
   In the warm sun my rose bloomed gloriously —
Smiling and saying, Lo, is it not fair?
   And all for thee — all thine! But he passed by
Coldly, and answered, Rose? I see no rose, —
   Leaving me standing in the barren vale
Alone! alone! feeling the darkness close
   Deep o'er my heart, and all my being fail.

Then came one, gently, yet with eager tread,
Begging one rose-bud — but my rose was dead.

Verses

The old, old Wind that whispers to old trees,
   Round the dark country when the sun has set,
Goes murmuring still of unremembered seas
   And cities of the dead that men forget —
An old blind beggar-man, distained and gray,
   With ancient tales to tell,
Mumbling of this and that upon his way,
   Strange song and muttered spell —
Neither to East or West, or South or North,
   His habitation lies,
This roofless vagabond who wanders forth
   Aye under alien skies —
A gypsy of the air, he comes and goes
   Between the tall trees and the shadowed grass,
And what he tells only the twilight knows . . .
   The tall trees and the twilight hear him pass.

To him the Dead stretch forth their strengthless hands,
   He who campaigns in other climes than this,
He who is free of the Unshapen Lands,
   The empty homes of Dis.

Verses

Out of the scattered fragments
   Of castles I built in the air
I gathered enough together
   To fashion a cottage with care;
Thoughtfully, slowly, I planned it,
   And little by little it grew —
Perfect in form and in substance,
   Because I designed it for you.

The castles that time has shattered
  Gleamed spotless and pearly white
As they stood in the misty distance
  That borders the Land of Delight;
Sleeping and waking I saw them
  Grow brighter and fairer each day;
But, alas! at the touch of a finger
  They trembled and crumbled away!

Then out of the dust I gathered
  A bit of untarnished gold,
And a gem unharmed by contact
  With stones of a baser mold;
For sometimes a priceless jewel
  Gleams wondrously pure and fair
From glittering paste foundations
  Of castles we see in the air.

So, I turned from the realms of fancy,
  As remote as the stars above,
And into the land of the living
  I carried the jewel of love;
The mansions of dazzling brightness
  Have crumbled away, it is true;
But firm upon gold foundations
  Stands the cottage I built for you!

Verses

You do but jest, sir, and you jest not well.
How could the hand be enemy of the arm,
Or seed and sod be rivals? How could light
Feel jealousy of heat, plant of the leaf,
Or competition dwell 'twixt lip and smile?
Are we not part and parcel of yourselves?
Like strands in one great braid we intertwine
And make the perfect whole. You could not be
Unless we gave you birth: we are the soil
From which you sprang, yet sterile were that soil
Save as you planted. (Though in the Book we read
One woman bore a child with no man's aid, ?
We find no record of a man-child born
Without the aid of woman! Fatherhood
Is but a small achievement at the best,
While motherhood is heaven and hell.)
This ever-growing argument of sex
Is most unseemly, and devoid of sense.
Why waste more time in controversy, when
There is not time enough for all of love,
Our rightful occupation in this life?
Why prate of our defects — of where we fail,
When just the story of our worth would need
Eternity for telling; and our best
Development comes ever through your praise,
As through our praise you reach your highest self?
Oh! had you not been miser of your praise
And let our virtues be their own reward,

The old established order of the world
Would never have been changed. Small blame is ours
For this unsexing of ourselves, and worse
Effeminizing of the male. We were
Content, sir, till you starved us, heart and brain.
All we have done, or wise or otherwise,
Traced to the root, was done for love of you.
Let us taboo all vain comparisons,
And go forth as God meant us, hand in hand,
Companions, mates and comrades evermore;
Two parts of one divinely ordained whole.

Verses

A widow had two sons,
　　And one knelt at her knees,
And sought to give her joy
　　And toiled to give her ease;
He heard his country's call
　　And longed to go, to die
If God so willed, but saw
Her tears and heard her sigh.

A widow had two sons,
　　One filled her days with care
And creased her brow and brought
　　Her many a whitened hair
His country called — he went.
　　Nor thought to say good-by,
And recklessly he fought,
　　And died as heroes die.

A widow had two sons,
    One fell as heroes fall,
And one remained and toiled,
    And gave to her his all.
She watched " her hero's " grave
    In dismal days and fair,
And told the world her love,
    Her heart was buried there.

Our Mission

In the legends of the Norsemen,
    Stories quaint and weird and wild,
There's a strange and thrilling story,
    Of a mother and her child.
And that child, so runs the story,
    In those quaint old Norsemen books,
Fell one day from dangerous play ground,
    Dashed in pieces on the rocks;
But with gentle hand that mother
    Gathered every tender part,
Bore them gently, torn and bleeding,
    On her loving mother heart.
And within her humble dwelling,
    Strong in faith and brave of soul,
With her love-song low and tender
    Rocked and sang the fragments whole.
Such the mission of the Christian,
    Taught by Christ so long ago;
This the mark that bids us stay not,
    This the spirit each should know:
Rent and torn by sin the race is,
    Heart from heart, and soul from soul;
This our task with Christ's sweet love-song,
    Join, and heal, and make them whole.

                    —Rev. E. M. Bartlett

Verses

Lord over all! Whose power the sceptre swayed,
   Ere first Creation's wondrous form was framed,
When by His will Divine all things were made;
   Then, King, Almighty was His name proclaimed.

When all shall cease — the universe be o'er,
   In awful greatness He alone will reign,
Who was, Who is, and Who will evermore
   In glory most refulgent still remain.

Sole God! unequalled and beyond compare,
   Without division or associate;
Without commencing date, or final year,
   Omnipotent He reigns in awful state.

He is my God! my living Savior He!
   My sheltering Rock in sad misfortune's hour!
My standard, refuge, portion, still shall be,
   My lot's disposer when I seek His power.

Into His hands my spirit I consign
   Whilst wrapped in sleep, that I again may wake,
And with my soul, my body I resign;
   The Lord's with me — no fears my soul can shake.

THE CREATION

BY

ANNIE L. BURTON

The earth, the firmament on high,
With all the blue ethereal sky,
Were made by God's creative power
Six thousand years ago or more.
Man, too, was formed to till the ground;
Birds, beasts, and fish to move around;
The fish to swim, the birds to fly,
And all to praise the Love most high.
This world is round, wise men declare,
And hung on nothing in the air.
The moon around the earth doth run;
 The earth moves on its center, too;
The earth and moon around the sun
 As wheels and tops and pulleys do.
Water and land make up the whole,
 From East to West, from pole to pole.
Vast mountains rear their lofty heads,
 Rivers roll down their sandy beds;
And all join in one grand acclaim
 To praise the Lord's almighty name.

MY FAVORITE HYMNS

The Ninety and Nine

There were ninety and nine that safely lay
   In the shelter of the fold,
But one was out on the hills away,
   Far-off from the gates of gold —
Away on the mountains lone and bare,
Away from the tender Shepherd's care.

"Lord, Thou hast here Thy ninety and nine:
   Are they not enough for Thee?"
But the Shepherd made answer: "This of mine
   Has wandered away from me,
And, although the road be rough and steep,
I go to the desert to find my sheep."

But none of the ransomed ever knew
   How deep were the waters crossed;
Nor how dark was the night that the Lord passed through
   Ere he found His sheep that was lost.
Out in the desert he heard the cry —
Sick and helpless, and ready to die.

"Lord, whence are those blood-drops all the way
   That mark out the mountain's track?"

"They were shed for one who had gone astray
  Ere the Shepherd could bring him back."
"Lord, whence are Thy hands so rent and torn?"
"They are pierced tonight by many a thorn."

But all through the mountains, thunder-riven,
  And up from the rocky steep,
There arose a glad cry to the height of heaven,
  "Rejoice! I have found my sheep!"
And the angels echoed around the throne:
"Rejoice, for the Lord brings back His own!"

My Faith looks up to Thee

My faith looks up to Thee,
Thou Lamb of Calvary,
    Saviour divine!
Now hear me while I pray,
Take all my guilt away,
O, let me from this day
    Be wholly Thine.

May Thy rich grace impart
Strength to my fainting heart,
    My zeal inspire;
As Thou hast died for me,
O, may my love to Thee
Pure, warm, and changeless be,
    A living fire.

When ends life's transient dream,
When death's cold, sullen stream
    Shall o'er me roll,
Blest Saviour, then, in love,
Fear and distrust remove;
O, bear me safe above,
    A ransomed soul.

Jordan's Strand

My days are gliding swiftly by,
    And I, a pilgrim stranger,
Would not detain them as they fly,
    Those hours of toil and danger.

Chorus

For, O we stand on Jordan's strand,
    Our friends are passing over;
And, just before, the shining shore
    We may almost discover!

We'll gird our loins, my brethren dear,
    Our heavenly home discerning;
Our absent Lord has left us word,
    "Let every lamp be burning."

Should coming days be cold and dark,
    We need not cease our singing;
That perfect rest nought can molest,
    Where golden harps are ringing.

Let sorrow's rudest tempest blow,
　　Each cord on earth to sever;
Our King says, " Come!" and there's our home,
　　Forever, O forever.

Over the Line

O tender and sweet was the Master's voice
　　As he lovingly call'd to me,
" Come over the line, it is only a step —
　　I am waiting my child, for thee.

Refrain

" Over the line," hear the sweet refrain,
　　Angels are chanting the heavenly strain:
" Over the line," — Why should I remain
　　With a step between me and Jesus?

But my sins are many, my faith is small,
　　Lo! the answer came quick and clear;
" Thou needest not trust in thyself at all,
　　Step over the line, I am here."

But my flesh is weak, I tearfully said,
　　And the way I cannot see;
I fear if I try I may sadly fail,
　　And thus may dishonor Thee.

Ah, the world is cold, and I cannot go back
   Press forward I surely must;
I will place my hand in his wounded palm
   Step over the line, and trust.

O could I speak the Matchless Worth

O could I speak the matchless worth,
O could I sound the glories forth,
   Which in my Saviour shine,
I'd soar, and touch the heav'nly strings,
And vie with Gabriel while he sings,
   In notes almost divine.

I'd sing the precious blood He spilt,
My ransom from the dreadful guilt
   Of sin and wrath divine;
I'd sing His glorious righteousness,
In which all-perfect, heavenly dress
   My soul shall ever shine.

I'd sing the characters He bears,
And all the forms of love He wears,
   Exalted on His throne;
In loftiest songs of sweetest praise,
I would to everlasting days
   Make all His glories known.

Well, the delightful day will come
When my dear Lord will bring me home,
   And I shall see His face;
Then with my Saviour, Brother, Friend,
A blest eternity I'll spend,
   Triumphant in His grace.

O God, beneath Thy Guiding Hand

O God, beneath Thy guiding hand,
   Our exiled fathers cross'd the sea;
And when they trod the wintry strand,
   With pray'r and psalm they worshipp'd Thee.

Thou heard'st, well pleased, the song, the prayer:
   Thy blessing came and still its power
Shall onward through all ages bear
   The memory of that holy hour.

Laws, freedom, truth, and faith in God
   Came with those exiles o'er the waves;
And where their pilgrim feet have trod,
   The God they trusted guards their graves.

And here Thy name, O God of love,
   Their children's children shall adore
Till these eternal hills remove
And spring adorns the earth no more.

America

My country, 'tis of thee,
Sweet land of liberty,
  Of thee I sing;
Land where my fathers died,
Land of the pilgrim's pride,
From every mountain side
  Let freedom ring.

My native country, thee,
Land of the noble free,
  Thy name I love;
I love thy rocks and rills,
Thy woods and templed hills;
My heart with rapture thrills
  Like that above.

Let music swell the breeze,
And ring from all the trees
  Sweet freedom's song;
Let mortal tongues awake,
Let all that breathe partake,
Let rocks their silence break,
  The sound prolong.

Our fathers' God to Thee,
Author of liberty,
  To Thee we sing;
Long may our land be bright
With freedom's holy light;
Protect us with Thy might,
  Great God our King.

In the Cross of Christ I Glory

In the cross of Christ I glory,
　Towering o'er the wrecks of time;
All the light of sacred story
　Gathers round its head sublime.

When the woes of life o'ertake me,
　Hopes deceive and fears annoy,
Never shall the cross forsake me:
　Lo! it glows with peace and joy.

When the sun of bliss is beaming
　Light and love upon my way,
From the cross the radiance streaming,
　Add more luster to the day.

Bane and blessing, pain and pleasure,
　By the cross are sanctified;
Peace is there that knows no measure,
　Joys that through all time abide.

Guide Me, O Thou Great Jehovah

Guide me, O Thou great Jehovah,
　Pilgrim thro' this barren land;
I am weak, but Thou art mighty;
　Hold me with Thy pow'rful hand;
　　Bread of heaven,
　Feed me till I want no more.

Open now the crystal fountain
　Whence the healing waters flow;
Let the fiery, cloudy pillar
　Lead me all my journey through;
　　Strong Deliverer,
　Be Thou still my strength and shield.

When I tread the verge of Jordan,
　Bid my anxious fears subside;
Bear me through the swelling current,
　Land me safe on Canaan's side;
　　Songs of praises
　I will ever give to Thee.

Christ receiveth Sinful Men

Sinners Jesus will receive;
　Sound this word of grace to all
Who the heav'nly pathway leave,
　All who linger, all who fall.

Chorus
Sing it o'er and o'er again:
　Christ receiveth sinful men;
Make the message clear and plain:
　Christ receiveth sinful men.

Come, and He will give you rest;
　Trust Him, for His word is plain;
He will take the sinfulest;
　Christ receiveth sinful men.

Christ receiveth sinful men,
　Even me with all my sin;
Purged from ev'ry spot and stain,
　Heav'n with Him I enter in.

Some Day the Silver Cord will break

Some day the silver cord will break,
　And I no more as now shall sing;
But, O, the joy when I shall wake
　Within the palace of the King!

And I shall see Him face to face,
And tell the story — Saved by grace.

Some day my earthly house will fall,
　I cannot tell how soon 'twill be,
But this I know — my All in All
　Has now a place in heaven for me.

Some day; till then I'll watch and wait,
　My lamp all trimmed and burning bright,
That when my Saviour ope's the gate.
　My soul to Him may take its flight.

Battle Hymn of the Republic

Mine eyes have seen the glory of the coming of the Lord;
He is trampling out the vintage where the grapes of wrath are
      stored;
He hath loos'd the fateful lightning of His terrible swift sword;
      His truth is marching on.

I have seen Him in the watch-fires of a hundred circling camps;
They have builded Him an altar in the evening dews and damps;
I can read His righteous sentence in the dim and flaring lamps;
      His day is marching on.

I have read a fiery gospel writ in burnished rows of steel,
" As ye deal with my contemners, so with you My grace shall
      deal;
Let the hero born of woman crush the serpent with his hee,l
      Since God is marching on.

He has sounded forth the trumpet that shall never sound retreat,
He is sifting out the hearts of men before His judgment seat;
O, be swift, my soul, to answer Him, be jubilant, my feet!
      Our God is marching on.

In the beauty of the lilies Christ was born across the sea,
With a glory in His bosom that transfigures you and me;
As He died to make men holy, let us die to make men free,
      While God is marching on.